HUMAN RIGHTS

HUMAN RIGHTS

By

Prakash Talwar

ISHA

Human Rights

ISBN : 978-81-820-5351-9

First Published 2006, reprint 2014 in India by
Isha Books
B-69, New Gupta Colony,
New DDA Market, New Delhi - 110009
Printed at : Sagar Color Scan, New Delhi.

Preface

Human rights are the natural-born rights for every human being, universally. These are those basic standards without which people cannot live in dignity. To violate someone's human rights is to treat that person as though she or he were not a human being. To advocate human rights is to demand that the human dignity of all people be respected.

Everyone is entitled to human rights without discrimination of any kind. The non-discrimination principle is a fundamental rule of international law. This means that human rights are for all human beings, regardless of race, colour, sex, language, religion, political or other opinion, national or social origin, property, birth or other status. Non-discrimination protects individuals and groups against the denial and violation of their human rights. To deny human rights on the grounds of cultural distinction is discriminatory. Human rights are intended for everyone, in every culture.

Largely through the ongoing work of the United Nations, the universality of human rights has been clearly established and recognised in international law. Human rights are emphasised among the purposes of the United Nations as proclaimed in its Charter, which states that human rights are for all without distinction. Universal human rights are further established by the two international covenants on human rights (International

Covenant on Economic, Social and Cultural Rights, and International Covenant on Civil and Political Rights), and the other international standard-setting instruments which address numerous concerns, including genocide, slavery, torture, racial discrimination, discrimination against women, rights of the child, minorities and religious tolerance.

This book gives an introduction to the concept of human rights—its meaning; rights and duties; general conditions underlying the idea of human rights; theories of human rights and issues of human rights. It will be a useful reference tool for students and teachers of human rights courses, administrators, lawyers, human rights activists, and all others who are concerned with human rights.

Editor

Contents

1

Meaning, Nature and Scope of Human Rights

Human rights refers to the concept of human beings as having universal rights, or status, regardless of legal jurisdiction, and likewise other localizing factors, such as ethnicity and nationality. For many, the concept of "human rights" is based in religious principles, or else is otherwise directly related to them. However, because a formal concept of human rights has not been universally accepted, the term has some degree of variance between its use in different local jurisdictions -difference in both meaningful substance as well as in protocols for and styles of application.

All humans hold all human rights; after all, human rights are said to be those benefits to which we are entitled simply by being human. But what is meant by being 'human' is vague since the life cycle of homo sapiens ranges from conception to death and decay. There is profound controversy over how and when a human acquires and then loses human rights between those two periods. Even before conception, sperm and eggs exist that contain human genetic material. One may decide easily that these are human cells but not 'human beings', because they contain incomplete sets of human genes.

After conception, however, controversies arise about the status of the developing foetus. From a mass of undifferentiated cells, the embryo quickly grows into a recognizably human entity. Many distinguish foetuses from babies that have emerged from their mothers and say that separate human life only begins with 'birth'. This can be an arbitrary distinction since a very premature baby is at much the same stage of development whether inside or outside the womb; the differences centre on how a baby receives nutrition and oxygen. One can specify an arbitrary point for the acquisition of rights, such as conception, neural development, viability, or emergence from the womb. But this approach is bound to erupt in controversy, because not everyone will agree on a given point.

Abortion is such a divisive issue precisely because various groups hold different beliefs about when human life starts. Alternatively, one can argue that there is some special quality of human life that provides a basis for possessing rights; when that quality is acquired, so are rights. This approach is favoured by many, since it allows for the distinction between humans and other animals. Human rights are rights particular to human beings, thus the basis of the claim to rights should be something that differentiates humans from other animals. With a sharing of an enormous proportion of genetic material between humans and primates, the distinction is usually drawn on the basis of some quality of human life not shared by other animals rather than physiological characteristics.

Specifically human qualities are usually identified from our capacity for intellectual, moral, or spiritual development. The difficulty with trying to assign rights on the basis of some quality of human life is that not all human beings may possess such an attribute. Douglas Husak has written a poignant critique of the notion of human rights based on his objection that some human beings merely exist. Some mentally-ill patients lack any basis for purposive agency; they are seemingly unaware of their surroundings, incapable of rationale thought, or unable to distinguish right from wrong. But, his most telling arguments arise from comatose patients, notably those with no known chance for recovery.

Husak distinguishes between humans and persons, and he points out that some humans, such as the comatose, are non-persons: Persons are human beings with capacities beyond mere existence that produce a quality of life. Non-persons simply lack the qualities of life that one wishes either to protect or use as the key to acquiring rights. The distinction between humans and persons is often used to justify aborting foetuses, because the human foetus is not considered by many to be a person. In the end, Husak argues that the phenomena called human rights are really rights of persons: "There are no human rights".

The rights of children and the mentally ill may depend greatly upon what foundation one adopts for the possession of rights. Similarly, the existence of rights to life in abortion, infanticide, and euthanasia are directly related to what status one accords to undeveloped foetuses, mutant newborns, or terminally-comatose adults. If human rights are justified on some characteristics of the human species, can those rights be held by individual humans who lack these species traits? Some answer this question by distinguishing between possessing rights and exercising them. Thus a healthy child may possess the full range of human rights, but be unable to exercise them, particularly rights of an intellectual nature.

Another controversy over the possession of human rights relates to whether they are benefits intended for individual humans, or whether they can also be collective benefits for groups of humans. Some, such as Donnelly, argue that human rights are properly held by only individuals. Others contend that human lives are lived within group settings and the full enjoyment of human life can only be realized when those groups are able to flourish. Whether human rights can include collective rights Is a particularly crucial issue in analyzing whether the human rights regime protects a group's culture and language, or a group's right to self-determination.

The nature of human rights is complicated even beyond the controversy over their source or who may hold them. A critical debate continues over what is meant by human rights. The universality and inalienability of a human right depends to a large extent on the character of the 'right' involved. It is necessary first of all to distinguish between the adjectival use of the word 'right', which means good or proper, from the substantive 'a right', which is a special, possessable benefit.

Not everything which is right (good) is a right, although many people mistakenly inflate the concept of a right by asserting benefits they believe are 'right' to be 'rights'. This confusion has become evident in the assertion of what are known as 'second-generation human rights' - such as the right to economic development and prosperity - and 'third generation human rights' - which cover the rights to world peace and a clean environment. While some human rights advocates accept the inclusion of these benefits as rights, others argue that prosperity and peace are 'right' but not substantive rights. Even with the substantive term 'a right', however, there are several different meanings.

In 1919, Wesley Hohfeld laid down a useful set of four distinctive connotations that can be given to the phrase "A has a right to X". Perhaps the most common meaning given to this phrase conveys the notion of a claim-right. It is a claim that A has against a correlative duty of another, B; A has a right to X, and B has a duty to let A have or do X. The duty B has may be positive, in the sense that action is required on B's part to allow A to enjoy X; if A has a right to health care, B has a duty to provide it. There may also be a negative duty, in the sense of B having to refrain from interfering in A's possession of benefit X; if A has a right to privacy, B must refrain from prying in A's affairs. It is important to note that the duty may be owed by a particular person or official, or the duty may generally lie in the whole community.

The essential characteristic of a claim-right is the inherent connection between A's claim to a benefit and B's duty - A can make a claim that B must perform the duty. However, there are other connotations of the phrase 'A has a right to X' that do not involve a corresponding duty on another's part. The term may mean that A has a liberty with respect to X. In this view, A has no obligation not to do or have X, which may be different from the status of other people. Also, A can make no claim against another, because no-one else as a duty with respect to A's enjoyment of X. A liberty may be enjoyed by all, such as the right to wear what one pleases while doing household chores.

A subset of liberty is privilege, because A may have no duty not to do X but others do. For instance, in some English colleges the dons have a right to walk across the grass in the quadrangle, although others must use the pathways instead. In any liberty there is no duty on anyone to provide the X involved; i.e., no-one has a duty to provide the lawns simply for the dons to walk upon. To say that 'A has a right to X' may also indicate that A has a power to effect changes in X. Thus an owner of a bicycle has the right to sell it, and a customs officer has the right to confiscate property or detain people at the border.

Hohfeld's fourth interpretation of 'A has a right to X' conveys the notion that A has an immunity that B is unable to change. Thus, MP's have a right to free speech that protects them from prosecution for speeches given in the House of Commons, and it is a right which cannot be changed by the executive, police, or courts. There are other uses of 'having a right' that should be added to those identified by Hohfeld, because these other uses refer to ideals, needs, or wants that are simply expressed as rights. The confusion between adjectival and substantive right has led to the frequent use of rights to describe ideals. Thus, the rights to prosperity and peace are ideals or goals to strive for that some express as rights.

Another confusion arises when people assert a right to a benefit because it fills a need. One does not hold a right simply because one claims so, neither is it necessary to make claims in order to possess rights. It is not the act of claiming that creates rights. Thus, the claim to a right to prosperity or world peace does not establish that those benefits exist as rights. Neither does the fact that someone satisfies another's claim confirm a right's existence; a beggar may claim a right to $5 from a businessman, who may give the money, but that does not establish the beggar's right to it. It is important also to note that one may benefit from another's duty, without having a right to that benefit. Christians may believe that they have a duty to give money to charity, but that does not mean that charities have a right to Christians' money.

These different notions of 'right' are important to bear in mind when discussing human rights. The most common interpretation given to the 'right' in human rights is that of claim-rights. There is a defined benefit to which individuals are entitled, and there is a correlative duty on others in relation to that benefit. This tendency may be partly due to the increasing codification of human rights into legal documents. It is far more efficacious if human rights are conceived of as claim-rights, because those who are deprived of their rights may argue that others (usually their government) must be compelled to fulfill a duty to provide the benefit.

Since much human rights activism centres on the respect for rights contained in international agreements, it is natural for attention to centre on governments as duty-holders since they are the entities directly bound by the human rights documents. If human rights are claim-rights with a correlative duty on some body to provide or safeguard the benefit, however, a major problem arises in identifying that duty-holder. Most often it is assumed that if an individual is being denied some human right, the duty falls on their government to rectify the situation.

A serious difficulty emerges if the correlative duty lies only with an individual's government, however, because the abuse of human rights may occur by private individuals or corporations. For example, tremendous injustices result from the caste system in India because of the way people treat others who belong to a lower caste. In this instance, the actual infringement of human rights is largely perpetrated by individuals rather than the government. While the government has accepted a responsibility to try and end the practise, caste is so deeply entrenched in Indian society that it has so far proved impossible to stamp out.

A further complication arises when a government either is incapable of providing a benefit protected by human rights - such as the Ethiopian government's inability to provide food during the worst of the famines - or when a government simply fails to respect human rights. If an individual's government is the central duty-holder, then the rest of the world can shake their heads saying 'tut-tut' without feeling any sense of duty to intervene. Other governments may feel bound to act, but that feeling of obligation may simply come from their own sense of altruism rather than a belief that human rights bind all governments to help if the government most directly responsible fails to fulfill its duties. Another scenario may arise when government leaders believe that a duty to help lies directly with its citizens rather than the government.

If human rights set moral standards for the treatment of all humans, those standards should bind anyone who is capable of infringing those rights - be they corporations, governments, or other human beings. Thus, the correlative duties involved in human rights as claim-rights are duties that do not necessarily reside solely with an individual's government. The violation of some human right may be perpetrated by one individual against others, such as an employer who discriminates against a racial group in hiring. Or, a duty to respect human rights may be held by a group within society, such as a religious majority's obligation to tolerate other religious practices. There may be a general duty on the community to act collectively, as with the example of community efforts to run food banks.

An individual's own government often has a direct duty, for example, to refrain from arbitrary detention and torture. On some occasions, many will argue that foreign governments have a duty to intervene; for instance, the Front Line States in southern Africa believed they had some duty to help liberate the black majority from apartheid in South Africa. Finally, there may be a duty that lies with all humanity; such an obligation is often expressed in private, international relief movements to alleviate suffering among famine victims. Governments may only be intermediary duty-holders who should try and intervene to safeguard human rights from actions by their citizens, but those citizens bear the direct duty to respect the human rights of others.

With any form of rights, but particularly with claim-rights, there are problems that arise with their definition, exercise, and enforcement. There may be conflicting views even on the existence of a particular right. For example, some islamic governments have denied that there can be freedom of religion because the Koran proclaims that one of the greatest sins for a muslim is to forsake Islam for another religion. Even if there is agreement in principle on the existence of a particular right, there may be conflicts over what activities or goods are specifically protected by that right. In Canada, for instance, judges have been divided over whether the freedom of expression includes communications between prostitutes and their clients.

There can also be profound debate when two or more rights conflict in a given situation. A continuing problem is posed for women's rights by several religions that stipulate particular roles for women that are subservient to men; in these instances the right to equality conflicts with the freedom of religion. Another difficulty may arise over whether a benefit is really a claim-right, with correlative duties, or some other type of right or claim without corresponding obligations. For instance, academic freedom may be viewed as either a privilege or a claim-right. If a claim-right is involved, there may still be many questions about who in particular holds a correlative duty, and what type of action is required to satisfy that duty.

A central dilemma revolves around how to settle these questions of enforcement. If human rights operate uniquely in a moral plane, then the definition, acceptance, and respect for rights can involve a controversial, tortuous route. In the end, fulfillment of human rights will depend upon a spirit of consensus and the effect of community opprobrium. Disputes that involve profoundly different value systems, however, may go unresolved. With the codification of human rights into legal documents, one may limit some of the range of debate, but only with institutional structures for adjudicating can there be authoritative resolutions. Controversial interpretations of human rights are not eliminated with the creation of agencies to enforce human rights.

Types of Human Rights

Human rights are typically divided into two categories: negative human rights (rights to be free from) and positive human rights (rights to), although other categorizations exist. Negative human rights, which follow mainly from the Anglo-American legal tradition, denote actions that a government should not take. These are codified in the United States Bill of Rights, the English Bill of Rights and the Canadian Charter of Rights and Freedoms and include freedoms of speech, religion and assembly. Positive human rights follow mainly from the Rousseauian Continental European legal tradition, denote rights that the state is obligated to protect and provide. Examples of such rights include: the rights to education, to a livelihood, and to legal equality. Positive rights have been codified in the Universal Declaration of Human Rights and in many 20th-century constitutions.

A categorization offered by Karel Vasak is the three generations of human rights: first-generation civil and political rights (right to life and political participation), second-generation economic, social and cultural rights (right to subsistence) and third-generation solidarity rights (right to peace, right to clean environment). Out of these generations, the third generation is the most debated and lacks both legal and political recognition. Some theorists discredit these divisions by claiming that rights are interconnected. Arguably, for example, basic education is necessary for the right to political participation.

Theoretical Foundation

Numerous theoretical approaches have been advanced to explain how human rights become part of social expectations. The biological theory considers the comparative reproductive advantage of human social behavior based on empathy and altruism in the context of natural selection. Other theories hold that human rights codify moral behavior, which is a human, social product developed by a process of biological and social evolution (associated with Hume) or as a sociological pattern of rule setting. This approach includes the notion that individuals in a society accept rules from legitimate authority in exchange for security and economic advantage. Natural law theories base human rights on the "natural" moral order based on religious precepts, the assumed common understandings of justice, or the belief that moral behavior is a set of objectively valid prescriptions.

In legend, literature, religion and political thought, justice (and eventually the concept of human rights) became socially constructed over time into complex webs of social interaction striving toward a social order in which human beings are treated fairly. Religious societies tend to try to justify human rights through religious arguments. For example, liberal movements within Islam have tried to use the story of Adam in the Qur'an to support human rights in a Muslim context. Other theories are based on human agency, positing such constructs for agreement to rules on the utilitarian principles mediated by public reasoning. The social evolution model is based on human needs and struggle that incorporates an analysis of the norm-creating process.

Values become norms through the constitutive process of authoritative decision-making. Such norms may take the form of law through a particular form of authoritative decision making of institutions associated with a legal system. It is the process of public reasoning through human rights norm-creating that progressively weeds out the culturally bound behaviors that are inconsistent with contemporary human rights. In this sense, culturally particular norms adapt to evolving human rights standards as defined in national constitutions and international human rights instruments.

Several competing bases have been asserted for universal human rights. It is essential to understand these various foundations, since they can result in quite different understandings of the specific benefits protected by human rights. As well, each approach to human rights has different strengths and vulnerabilities in facing the challenges posed by relativism and utilitarianism. Many have argued that human rights exist in order to protect the basic dignity of human life. Indeed, the United Nations Declaration on Human Rights embodies this goal by declaring that human rights flow from "the inherent dignity of the human person".

Strong arguments have been made, especially by western liberals, that human rights must be directed to protecting and promoting human dignity. As Jack Donnelly has written, "We have human rights not to the requisites for health but to those things 'needed' for a life of dignity, for a life worthy of a human being, a life that cannot be enjoyed without these rights" (original emphasis). This view is perhaps the most pervasively held, especially among human rights activists; the rhetoric of human-rights disputes most frequently invokes this notion of striving for the dignity that makes human life worth living.

The idea of promoting human dignity has considerable appeal, since human life is given a distinctive weight over other animals in most societies precisely because we are capable of cultivating the quality of our lives. Unfortunately, the promotion of dignity may well provide an unstable foundation for the construction of universal moral standards. The inherent weakness of this approach lies in trying to identify the nature of this dignity. Donnelly unwittingly reveals this shortcoming in expanding upon the deliberate human action that creates human rights.

"Human rights represent a social choice of a particular moral vision of human potentiality, which rests on a particular substantive account of the minimum requirements of a life of dignity". Dignity is a very elastic concept and the substance given to it is very much a moral choice, and a particular conception of dignity becomes paramount. Even general rejection of outlandish assertions of dignity may not indicate agreement on a core substance.

One of the most basic liberal beliefs about human dignity is that all humans are equal, social division and hierarchy play important roles in aspects of Hindu, Confucian, Muslim, and Roman Catholic views of human life. Indeed, 'dignity' is often achieved in these views by striving to fulfill one's particular vocation within an ordered set of roles. But, if human rights are meant to be universal standards, the inherent dignity that is supposed to be protected should be a common vision. Without sufficient commonality, dignity cannot suffice as the ultimate goal of human rights.

An alternative basis for human rights draws from the requisites for human well-being. One advocate of this approach, Allan Gewirth, would agree with Donnelly that human rights are drawn in essence from humankind's moral nature, but Gewirth does not follow Donnelly's conclusion that human rights are a moral vision of human dignity. Rather, Gewirth argues that "agency or action is the common subject of all morality and practice". Human rights are not just a product of morality but protect the basic freedom and well-being necessary for human agency. Gewirth distinguished between three types of rights that address different levels of well-being. Basic rights safeguard one's subsistence or basic well-being. Nonsubtractive rights maintain the capacity for fulfilling purposive agency, while additive rights provide the requisites for developing one's capabilities - such as education.

Gewirth differentiates between these rights because he accepts that humans vary tremendously in their capacity for purposive agency. Through what he calls the principle of proportionality, humans are entitled to those rights that are proportionate to their capacity for agency. Thus, individuals who are comatose only have basic rights to subsistence, since they are incapable of any purposive action. Gewirth's approach, however, has been strongly criticized by those who argue that human rights cannot be universal if they are derived from one's capacity for agency. Indeed Douglas Husak has used Gewirth's theories to argue that there can be no rights that extend to all human beings.

Husak makes the crucial distinction between humans and persons, and he points out that some humans may be considered non-persons because they are incapable of ever performing any purposive agency. Even if one accepts Gewirth's rebuttal that all humans are entitled to at least basic rights because they are either prospective or former purposive agents, there still remains in his theory the notion some will find unsettling: not all humans possess all human rights to the same degree (or at all). Another basis for human rights has been put forward by John O'Manique that is based on evolution and human development.

O'Manique was motivated by the desire to find a truly universal basis for human rights theories that are not as susceptible, as is dignity, to controversial interpretations or denial by others. Thus, human rights should be founded upon something inherent to humans rather than some moral vision that is created by human action. O'Manique argues that a satisfactory basis may lie in the following set of propositions:

— P1 I ought to survive

— P2 X is necessary for my survival

— P3 Therefore, I ought to do/have X.

The real hurdle in this set of propositions lies in finding agreement in P1. The requisites for survival are fairly easily ascertained by scientific inquiry. O'Manique is on fairly firm ground when he asserts that, "The belief that survival is good is virtually universal". He does concede that there are religious beliefs that hold that a person's life can be sacrificed, but usually this sacrifice is done to further the survival of others. So O'Manique determines, "The exceptions do not 'prove' the rule, but they do point to the strong probability that the belief that survival is good is found, explicitly or implicitly, in almost all human beings".

One might add that some value in human survival may be found in any society, since no culture comes to mind that has tolerated unrestricted, recreational homicide. O'Manique also draws from theories of evolution to establish that the goal of humans has to be the survival of the species. So, there would be universal agreement with the statement, "Humans ought to survive". But survival of the group, community, or human species is very different from the survival of each and every particular individual. O'Manique develops his theory much beyond the notion of survival. Indeed, he explicitly dismisses the idea that the source of human rights lies in the needs for human subsistence.

O'Manique wishes to propel human rights into a further plane, by basing human survival upon the full development of human potential. The initial proposition P1 in the model above really becomes "I ought to develop". As O'Manique says, "Human aspirations are not to the maintenance of existence but to the fulfilment of life... If we believe that one ought to survive, it is because we believe that one ought to develop". In O'Manique's vision, human rights would include rights to things needed for subsistence but also go on to cover all aspects of intellectual and emotional development. He tries to limit in some way the range by insisting that the needs for development can be ascertained through research.

However, he also reveals the broad sweep of matters that could be included when he addresses this issue: "The existence of such needs for human development - the need for association with other human beings, for self expression, for some control over one's destiny, and even the need for love and for beauty - can be observed and even empirically confirmed within the social sciences and psychology". O'Manique may well lose some support with this incredibly vast range of issues that he would include within the human rights rubric.

A fundamental difficulty with using the fulfillment of human development as a basis for human rights is that it can have a meaning that is relative to each culture and individual. This relativism even creeps into O'Manique's discussion when he concludes, "A community and its members will develop to the extent that the members of the community support the development needs of others in the community, in ways that are appropriate to that community" (emphasis added). Just what is needed for fulfillment in expression, love, or autonomy will be given profoundly different interpretations in Bedouin, German, or Japanese societies. O'Manique tries to address this aspect of his theory by conceding that the specific entitlements necessary to human development may vary over space and time, but the general grounds for those claims will remain constant.

The final alternative basis for human rights would provide the needs for human existence. Human rights may be limited to providing all humans with the needs for their physical subsistence. But, this subsistence would involve a certain degree of minimal comfort beyond merely keeping one's organs working, because human subsistence also consists of being able to function. Advocates of the other approaches to human rights have dismissed needs to subsistence as too narrow a foundation, but this criticism may not account for the ramifications that flow from the range of human needs.

Human rights would guarantee the provision of the food, clothing, and shelter without which anyone would perish. In a broad socialist view, work should be guaranteed to all that are capable. In a more restricted view, the education necessary to obtaining the work needed to sustain oneself is a human right. Thus, human rights can cover a large, and very expensive, array of social-welfare programs. Quite a fundamental reformation of most political systems would occur if governments seriously addressed welfare programs as essential human rights. There are some distinct advantages in basing human rights on the needs of subsistence. The prime benefit lies in a universality possible with this foundation that eludes the other approaches to human rights that have been outlined above.

One might possibly find a similar consensus on the propositions "Humans should survive", "Humans should develop", "Humans should lead a life of dignity (or well being)". However, there will be much less disagreement over what is meant by, or needed for, 'survival' than one will find for 'dignity', 'well-being', or 'development'. Human rights based on subsistence can be much more readily applied as global standards. Nevertheless, there is still some concern with variations that will result from different societies' views of the specific ways in which needs should be satisfied. As noted earlier, different cultures have quite diverse notions of what food, dress, or shelter are acceptable. There are even profound differences in approaches to health care, with some societies rejecting 'western' medicine in favour of spiritually-based theories of ailments and therapies.

There is also a concern that it is just not practical to translate the proposition that humans in general should survive into concrete action to ensure that each and every human being survives. There is a point at which no society can afford to devote the resources needed to keep every individual alive as long as possible. These four approaches to human rights reflect quite different inspirations and ultimate goals, but there is common ground among them. Theories of human rights based on dignity, well-being, or development all are motivated by a desire to protect and cultivate some quality of life; because one is alive, one should lead a life filled with dignity, well-being, or continuing development.

A view of human rights based on subsistence is ultimately concerned with simply preserving life itself. But this distinction should not ignore an overlap, as a common ground among all theories of human rights is the assumption that human rights include subsistence rights. Approaches based on dignity, well-being, and development add protections for these qualities of life onto the right to existence, although subsistence rights often seem to be forgotten. However, the recognition of these common aspects of the four theories of human rights should not lead one to conclude that their differences are simply ones of emphasis.

The distinctive focus of each theory results in significant variations in their lists of specific human rights or the kind of activities humans may indulge in. Human rights based on subsistence would not include the range of democratic rights that most liberals argue are an essential element of human rights based on dignity. Some liberals would argue that a life without dignity may not be a life worth living; so disenfranchised, repressed people - such as Iraqi Kurds - may be justified in an armed rebellion involving deaths but which ultimately brought liberty to the whole population. However, a human rights approach based on subsistence may require on a non-violent strategy for political change since the preservation of life is the ultimate goal.

In the end, the choice of foundation for human rights may depend upon what one wishes to protect. One may be alarmed that democratic rights or equality may not be included in a human rights approach based on subsistence, in which case a theory based on liberal dignity would be adopted. But consequentialist motivations will not serve as a firm basis upon which to promote human rights among those who do not share one's concerns. These discussions illustrate that the foundation for human rights may be neither self-evident nor universally accepted. One chooses, explicitly or implicitly a particular justification or basis for human rights, and that choice will have important consequences upon the range of benefits that fall within human rights. Choice pervades human rights from their conception to their delivery, and those choices may well undermine the very foundation of human rights' moral authority.

Historical Development

The world's oldest recorded charter of human rights was engraved on the famous Cyrus Cylinder, written and confirmed by the Persian emperor Cyrus the Great at around 538 BCE. Cyrus' charter, adopted by the first Persian Empire (Iranian Empire of the Achaemenids), is thought to be very advanced for the age, even comparing favorably with modern declarations of human rights, against which it is also contrasted as being much more spiritual.

The best-known histories of the human rights movement tend to begin with the ancient religions and societies and show the evolution of concepts and institutions of human rights across civilizations. The roots of the notion of Human Rights can be drawn as far back as the Ancients (the role of the individual in the state) but the idea of civil and political rights stems from liberal freedoms advocated by John Stuart Mill in On Liberty. The concepts of economic, social and cultural Rights can be traced back to Hegel's Elements of the Philosophy of Right. The origin of modern positive rights in international law may be traced to the creation of the International Labour Organization in 1919 as a Western response to the andsocialist ideology of the Russian Revolution of 1917.

Human rights are a product of a philosophical debate that has raged for over two thousand years within the European societies and their colonial descendants. This argument has focused on a search for moral standards of political organization and behaviour that is independent of the contemporary society. In other words, many people have been unsatisfied with the notion that what is right or good is simply what a particular society or ruling elite feels is right or good at any given time. This unease has led to a quest for enduring moral imperatives that bind societies and their rulers over time and from place to place. Fierce debates raged among political philosophers as these issue were argued through. While a path was paved by successive thinkers that lead to contemporary human rights, a second lane was laid down at the same time by those who resisted this direction.

The emergence of human rights from the natural rights tradition did not come without opposition, as some argued that rights could only from the law of a particular society and could not come from any natural or inherent source. The earliest direct precursor to human rights might be found in the notions of 'natural right' developed by classical Greek philosophers, such as Aristotle, but this concept was more fully developed by Thomas Aquinas in his Summa Theologica. For several centuries Aquinas' conception held sway: there were goods or behaviours that were naturally right (or wrong) because God ordained it so.

What was naturally right could be ascertained by humans by 'right reason' - thinking properly. Hugo Grotius further expanded on this notion in De jure belli et paci, where he propounded the immutability of what is naturally right and wrong: Now the Law of Nature is so unalterable, that it cannot be changed even by God himself. For although the power of God is infinite, yet there are some things, to which it does not extend....Thus two and two must make four, nor is it possible otherwise; nor, again, can what is really evil not be evil.

The moral authority of natural right was assured because it had divine authorship. In effect, God decided what limits should be placed on the human political activity. But the long-term difficulty for this train of political thought lay precisely in its religious foundations. As the reformation caught on and ecclesiastical authority was shaken and challenged by rationalism, political philosophers argued for new bases of natural right. Thomas Hobbes posed the first major assault in 1651 on the divine basis of natural right by describing a State of Nature in which God did not seem to play any role. Perhaps more importantly, however, Hobbes also made a crucial leap from 'natural right' to 'a natural right'.

In other words, there was no longer just a list of behaviour that was naturally right or wrong; Hobbes added that there could be some claim or entitlement which was derived from nature. In Hobbes' view, this natural right was one of self-preservation. Further reinforcement of natural rights came with Immanuel Kant's writings later in the 17th century that reacted to Hobbes' work. In his view, the congregation of humans into a state-structured society resulted from a rational need for protection from each other's violence that would be found in a state of nature. However, the fundamental requirements of morality required that each treat another according to universal principles.

Kant's political doctrine was derived from his moral philosophy, and as such he argued that a state had to be organized through the imposition of, and obedience to, laws that applied universally; nevertheless, these laws should respect the equality, freedom, and autonomy of the citizens. In this way Kant, prescribed that basic rights were necessary for civil society: A true system of politics cannot therefore take a single step without first paying tribute to morality....The rights of man must be held sacred, however great a sacrifice the ruling power must make.

However, the divine basis of natural right was still pursued for more than a century after Hobbes published his Leviathan. John Locke wrote a strong defence of natural rights in the late 17th century with the publication of his Two Treatises on Government, but his arguments were filled with references to what God had ordained or given to mankind. Locke had a lasting influence on political discourse that was reflected in both the American Declaration of Independence and France's Declaration of the Rights of Man and the Citizen, passed by the Republican Assembly after the revolution in 1789. The French declaration proclaimed 17 rights as "the natural, inalienable and sacred rights of man".

The French Declaration of Rights immediately galvanized political writers in England and provoked two scathing attacks on its notion of natural rights. Jeremy Bentham's clause-by-clause critique of the Declaration, entitled Anarchical Fallacies, argued vehemently that there can be no natural rights, since rights are created by the law of a society: Right, the substantive right, is the child of law: from real laws come real rights; but from laws of nature, fancied and invented by poets, rhetoriticians, and dealers in moral and intellectual poisons come imaginary rights, a bastard brood of monsters, 'gorgons and chimeras dire'.

Natural rights is simple nonsense: natural and imprescriptible rights, rhetorical nonsense, - nonsense upon stilts. Edmund Burke also wrote a stinging attack on the French Declaration's assertion of natural rights, in which he argued that rights were those benefits won within each society. The rights held by the English and French were different, since they were the product of different political struggles through history. Soon after the attacks on the French Declaration, Thomas Paine wrote a defence of the conception of natural rights and their connection to the rights of a particular society.

In The Rights of Man, published in two parts in 1791 and 1792, Paine made a distinction between natural rights and civil rights, but he continued to see a necessary connection: Natural rights are those which appertain to man in right of his existence. Of this kind are all the intellectual rights, or rights of the mind, and also all those rights of acting as an individual for his own comfort and happiness, which are not injurious to the natural rights of others. Civil rights are those which appertain to man in right of being a member of society. Every civil right has for its foundation, some natural right pre-existing in the individual, but to the enjoyment of which his individual power is not, in all cases, sufficiently competent. Of this kind are all those which relate to security and protection.

Earlier inspiration for human rights from the social contract views of writers such as Jean-Jacques Rousseau, who argued that people agree to live in common if society protects them. Indeed, the purpose of the state is to protect those rights that individuals cannot defend on their own. Rousseau had set the ground for Paine decades earlier with his Social Contract, in which he not only lambasted attempts to tie religion to the foundations of political order but disentangled the rights of a society from natural rights.

In Rousseau's view, the rights in a civil society are hallowed: "But the social order is a scared right which serves as a basis for other rights. And as it is not a natural right, it must be one founded on covenants."

Rousseau then eleaborated a number of rights of citizens and limits on the sovereign's power. The debate in the late eighteenth century has left telling traces. Controversy continues to swirl over the question whether rights are creations of particular societies or independent of them. Modern theorists have developed a notion of natural rights that does not draw its source or inspiration from a divine ordering. The ground work for this secular natural rights trend was laid by Paine and even Rousseau. In its place has arisen a variety of theories that are humanist and rationalist; the 'natural' element is determined from the prerequisites of human society which are said to be rationally ascertainable. Thus there are constant criteria which can be identified for peaceful governance and the development of human society. But problems can develop for this school of thought when notions of a social contract are said to underlie the society from which rights are deduced.

Contemporary notions of human rights draw very deeply from this natural rights tradition. In a further extension of the natural rights tradition, human rights are now often viewed as arising essentially from the nature of humankind itself. The idea that all humans possess human rights simply by existing and that these rights cannot be taken away from them are direct descendants of natural rights. However, a persistent opposition to this view builds on the criticisms of Burke and Bentham, and even from the contractarian views of Rousseau's image of civil society. In this perspective rights do not exist independently of human endeavour; they can only be created by human action. Rights are viewed as the product a particular society and its legal system.

In this vein, Karl Marx also left a legacy of opposition to rights that hindered socialist thinkers from accommodating rights within their theories of society. Marx denounced rights as a fabrication of bourgeois society, in which the individual was divorced from his or her society; rights were needed in capitalist states in order to provide protection from the state. In the marxist view of society, an individual is essentially a product of society and, ideally, should not be seen in an antagonistic relationship where rights are needed. However, many socialists have come to accept certain conceptions of rights in the late twentieth century. Thus, the history of political philosophy has been one of several centuries of debate.

The child of natural rights philosophers, human rights, has come to hold a powerful place in contemporary political consciousness. However, neither preponderant belief in, nor even a consensus of support for human rights do not answer the concerns raised by the earlier thinkers - are rights truly the product of a particular vision and laws of a society? Or, are human rights so inherent in humanness that their origins and foundations are incontestable? A further difficulty, with profound implications, that human rights theories have to overcome is their emergence from these Western political traditions. Not only are they a product of European natural rights, but the particular rights that are viewed as 'natural' have been profoundly shaped by the liberalism that emerged in the 19th and 20th centuries.

With human rights, the rhetorical framework of the natural rights tradition has come to serve as a vehicle for the values of Western liberalism. An easy and powerful criticism is that human rights cannot be universal. In their basic concept they are a Western creation, based on the European tradition that individuals are separable from their society. But one may question whether these rights can apply to collectivist or communitarian societies that view the individual as an indivisible element of the whole society. Westerners, and many others, have come to place a high value on each individual human, but this is not a value judgment that is universal. There is substantive disagreement on the extent of, or even the need for, any protection of individuals against their society.

In addition to this problem with the concept itself, there are strong objections to the manner in which human rights have been conceptualized. Many lists of human rights read like specifications for liberal democracy. A variety of traditional societies can be found in the world that operate harmoniously, but are not based on equality let alone universal suffrage. A question that will recur in later discussions is whether the 'human rights' advocated today are really civil rights that pertain to a particular - liberal - conception of society.

To a large extent, the resolution of this issue depends upon the ultimate goal of human rights. If human rights are really surrogate liberalism, then it will be next to impossible to argue their inherent authority over competing political values. In order for human rights to enjoy universal legitimacy they must have a basis that survives charges of ideological imperialism. Human rights must have a universally acceptable basis in order for there to be any substantial measure of compliance.

Motivation for Human Rights

Some understanding about the nature of human rights can be gleaned from the various reasons that can be advanced for holding them. A prime concern is to offer protection from tyrannical and authoritarian calculations. Capricious or repressive measures of an autocratic government may be constrained with the recognition of supreme moral limits on any government's freedom of action. But even among governments that are genuinely limited by moral considerations, there may still be a need to shield the populace from utilitarian decision-making.

The greater good of the whole society may lead to sacrifice or exploitation of minority interests. Or, the provision of important benefits within the society may be limited by calculations that public resources should be spent on other enterprises. The attraction of human rights is that they are often thought to exist beyond the determination of specific societies. Thus, they set a universal standard that can be used to judge any society. Human rights provide an acceptable bench mark with which individuals or governments from one part of the world may criticize the norms followed by other governments or cultures. With an acceptance of human rights, Moslems, Hindus, Christians, capitalists, socialists, democracies, or tribal oligarchies may all legitimately censure each other. This criticism across religious, political, and economic divides gains its legitimacy because human rights are said to enshrine universal moral standards.

Without fully universal human rights, one is left simply trying to assert that one's own way of thinking is better than somebody else's. The prime rhetorical benefit of human rights is that they are viewed as being so basic and so fundamental to human existence that they should trump any other consideration. Just as Dworkin has argued that any conception of 'rights' trumps other claims within a society, human rights may be of a higher order that supersedes even other rights claims within a society. Other motivations for human rights may stem from a fear of the consequences of denying their existence. Because of the currency given human rights in contemporary political debate, there is a danger that such a denial will provide support for brutal regimes who defend their repression on the grounds that international human rights norms are simply a fanciful creation that has no universal authority.

Challenges to the Universality and Inalienability

Unfortunately, the very motivations and benefits of human rights pose direct challenges to their existence. Human rights are universal since they are said to belong to all humans in every society. Human rights are also supposed to be inalienable; because they flow from and protect human existence, they cannot be taken away without endangering the value of that existence. However, these universal and inalienable qualities of human rights are disputable in both their conception and operation. To some extent, the universality of human rights depends upon their genesis.

Moral standards, such as human rights, can come into being in two manners. They may simply be invented by people, or they may only need to be revealed to, or discovered by, humans. If human rights are simply an invention; then it is rather difficult to argue that every society and government should be bound by something they disagree with. If human rights have some existence independent of human creation, however, then it is easier to assert their universality. But such independent moral standards may arise in only two ways: if they are created by God, or if they are inherent in the nature of humankind or human society.

Unfortunately, both these routes pose substantive pitfalls. No divine origin for universal human rights would be acceptable, nor is it often advanced, since there is no one God that is recognized universally; just because Christians or Moslems claim that their divinity has ordained and proscribed certain treatment of humans does not provide the legitimacy needed for that moral code to bind devotees of another religion. The alternative origin that could justify universality would be the acceptance of human rights as natural rights that anyone could deduce from the nature of humankind or human society.

However, an atheistic critique of divine moral standards is just as telling when applied to rights derived from human nature.

The God or human nature that is said to be the source of human rights may be nothing more than an invention of the human mind, an invention that may vary according to whoever is reflecting on the issue. A less astringent argument is still just as damning. Even if one accepts that there is a God or a core human nature, there is no definitive way to sort out differing visions that people have of God or human nature. The universal authority of any particular view is initially endorsed only by the adherents of that view. Nevertheless it is possible for human rights to have their genesis in religion or the prerequisites of human society.

Even if human rights start within a specific religious or societal tradition, they could acquire universality as other people come to agree. It is also possible for human rights to become globally recognized because several different approaches may reach the same conclusion. For instance, atheistic natural rights theorists, Christians, and Muslims, may all eventually agree for quite different reasons on a number of ways in which people should be treated; these then can form the basis of human rights standards. However, the different paths to that agreement only lead to an agreement on the benefits, not necessarily on their origin, justification, or application.

The differences become important when one moves from a focus on the benefits identified as "human rights" to their practical operation; there is, as will be discussed below, a great difference between a duty-based and claim-based fulfillment of the benefits. Another set of problems arise if human rights are creations, pure and simple, of the human intellect. Human rights standards could be created in a variety of ways. In one method, a gradual growth of consensus builds around norms of behaviour that eventually acquire an obligatory character. It may be difficult to trace the epistemological origins of this consensus, but the end result is a broad base of agreement that human beings should be treated in certain ways.

In another method, there may be a conscious attempt to create binding rules of behaviour in a more contractarian manner. A certain group of individuals or state governments may lead the development of international agreements on human rights. And, as more states join in these agreements, the moral and legal force of the international accords become stronger and stronger. Essentially this is the course that has been followed in the development of the human rights documents created by the United Nations and other regional international organizations. In both these approaches to the creation of human rights, the motivation may be principled or consequentialist.

If principled, human rights are necessary because they reflect certain moral standards of how humans should be treated. If consequentialist, human rights are needed because they standards may prevent the awful repercussions of having no limits on the manner in which governments or groups may treat other human beings. Beyond the genesis of human rights, wherever they come from, lies a fundamental challenge to their universality, regardless of their origin. With any inception of human rights, one is faced with having to acquire acceptance of their authority. There is a problem in that not everyone will share the same motivation or inspiration for human rights.

Not everyone will agree that everything asserted as a human right is indeed one. At a very basic level, the proclamation and acceptance of human rights norms inherently involves majoritarian morality. Human rights are agreed to exist because a majority says they do. Specific goods and benefits are treated as human rights because a majority says they do. With either an invented or natural genesis, human rights are meant to protect some aspect of humanity. Human rights may be those entitlements that we have by virtue of being human, but there are real difficulties in determining which attributes of human life require protection under human rights standards.

Basic human traits are determined by both physical attributes and the activities undertaken by a human. The most obvious physical qualities encompass gender, race, size, shape, and health - including disabilities. Among human activities, one can distinguish between those necessary for sustaining life and those which fill that life. The requirements for sustaining life include nourishment, shelter, clothing, and sleep. Proper health care is needed for human life to be sustained in the long term. And the human species can only survive with procreation. But most humans do not merely exist, they fill their lives with myriad activities.

Perhaps the most important activity is that which is usually referred to in order to distinguish humans from all other animals: humans have a creative imagination that provides higher forms of thought that lead to intellectual inquiry and spirituality. Humans also communicate constantly the results of their thinking. Physical movement from one place to another is another continuous activity of all but the most disabled humans. Human beings are in essence very social animals and much of our activities take place through associating with other humans. In some instances this association is the special intimacy of kinship or close friendships. In others, humans act gregariously with acquaintances and many perfect strangers.

The consequences of this gregariousness furnish the underlying problems of establishing universality in the human attributes described above. Most humans live within readily identifiable social units, such as family, tribal, or national groups, that fundamentally shape the manner in which an individual's most basic characteristics are manifested. These social groupings determine what languages one learns to speak, the style of dress, acceptable foods, religion, form of communication and etiquette, sense of physical beauty and ugliness, the kind of shelter, and the notion of division of roles within one's social groupings. These are not simply superficial differences.

While some individuals willingly adopt new life styles, many believe that their lives can only be satisfying by maintaining their traditional ways. For some, indeed, styles of dress, food, and behaviour are inextricably linked to deep religious beliefs. One group's delicacies or even staples may be quite unacceptable to others. There may be just disdain or revulsion, such as the reaction of many people to eating raw fish, or there may be a strong, religious offence taken to certain foods, such as offering pork to Moslems or beef to Hindus. Thus, many profound differences emerge among human beings that are the product of where they were born and with whom they grew up.

While one could identify various qualities of human life that are universal, there is tremendous variation in the manner in which those qualities are realized. These acquired societal values pose difficulties when they define, or even conflict with, the basic attributes of human life listed earlier. Individual societies develop particular conceptions of what constitutes a dignified life, the essential needs of humans, as well as the relationship between individuals and their community. Particularly complex issues arise when there is a clash between conflicting spiritual and temporal values within or between societies. These difficulties come to the forefront when one tries to ascertain whether global standards can be set by human rights on the treatment that must be given to all human beings.

2

Universal Declaration of Human Rights

(Published by the United Nations, 1948-12-10)

Preamble

Whereas recognition of the inherent dignity and of the equal and inalienable rights of all members of the human family is the foundation of freedom, justice and peace in the world,

Whereas disregard and contempt for human rights have resulted in barbarous acts which have outraged the conscience of mankind, and the advent of a world in which human beings shall enjoy freedom of speech and belief and freedom from fear and want has been proclaimed as the highest aspiration of the common people,

Whereas it is essential, if man is not to be compelled to have recourse, as a last resort, to rebellion against tyranny and oppression, that human rights should be potected by the rule of law,

Whereas it is essential to promote the development of friendly relations between nations,

Whereas the peoples of the United Nations have in the Charter reaffirmed their faith in fundamental human rights, in the dignity and worth of the human person and in the equal rights of men and women and have determined to pomote social progress and better standards of life in larger freedom,

Whereas Member States have pledged themselves to achieve, in co-operation with the United Nations, the promotion of universal respect for and observance of human rights and fundamental freedoms,

Whereas common understanding of these rights and freedoms is of the greatest importance for the full realization of this pledge,

Now, therefore,

The General Assembly Proclaims this Universal Declaration of Human Rights as a common standard of achievement for all peoples and all nations, to the end that every individual and every organ of society, keeping this Declaration constantly in mind, shall strive by teaching and education to promote respect for these rights and freedoms and by pogressive measures, national and international, to secure their universal and effective recognition and observance, both among the peoples of Member States themselves and among the peoples of territories under their jurisdiction.

Article 1

All human beings are born free and equal in dignity and rights. They are endowed with reason and conscience and should act towards one another in a spirit of brotherhood.

Article 2

Everyone is entitled to all the rights and freeedoms set forth in this Declaration, without distinction of any kind, such as race, color, sex, language, religion, political or other opinion, national or social origin, birth or other status.

Furthermore, no distinction shall be made on the basis of the political, jurisdictional or international status of the country or.territory to which a person belongs, whether it be independent, trust, non-self-governing or under any other limitation of sovereignty.

Article 3

Everyone has the right to life, liberty, and the security of person.

Article 4

No one shall be held in slavery or servitude; slavery and the slave trade shall be prohibited in all their forms.

Article 5

No one shall be subjected to torture or to cruel, inhuman or degrading treatment or punishment.

Article 6

Everyone has the right to recognition everywhere as a person before the law.

Article 7

All are equal before the law and are entitled without any discrimination to equal protection of the law. All are entitled to equal protection against any discrimination in violation of this Declaration and against any incitement to such discrimination.

Article 8

Everyone has the right to an effective remedy by the competent national tribunals for acts violating the fundamental rights granted him by the constitution or by law.

Article 9

No one shall be subjected to arbitrary arrest, detention or exile. Article 10.Everyone is entitled in full equality to a fair, and public, hearing by an independent and impartial tribunal, in the determination of his rights and obligations and of any criminal charge against him.

Article 11

1. Everyone charged with a penal offence has the right to be presumed innocent until proved guilty according to law in a public trial at which he has had all the guarantees necessary for his defence.

2. No one shall be held guilty of any penal offence on account of any act or omission which did not constitute a penal offence, under national or international law, at the time when it was committed. Nor shall a heavier penalty be imposed than the one that was applicable at the time the penal offence was committed.

Article 12

No one shall be subjected to arbitrary interference with his privacy, family, home or correspondence, not to attacks upon his honour and reputation. Everyone has the right to the protection of the law against such interference or attacks.

Article 13

1. Everyone has the right ot freedom of movement and residence within the borders of each State.

2. Everyone has the right to leave any country, including his own, and to return to his country.

Article 14

1. Everyone has the right to seek and to enjoy in other countries asylum from persecution.
2. This right may not be invoked in the case of prosecutions genuinely arising from non-political crimes or from acts contrary to the purposes and principles of the United Nations.

Article 15

1. Everyone has the right to a nationality.
2. No one shall be arbitrarily deprived of his nationality nor denied the right to change his nationality.

Article 16

1. Men and women of full age, without any limitation due to race, nationality or religion, have the right to marry and to found a family. They are entitled to equal rights as to marriage, during marriage, and at its dissolution.
2. Marriage shall be entered into only with the free and full consent of the intending spouses.
3. The family is the natural and fundamental group unit of society and is entitled to protection by society and the State.

Article 17

1. Everyone has the right to own property alone as well as in association with others.
2. No one shall be arbitrarily deprived of his property.

Article 18

Everyone has the right to freedom of thought, conscience

and religion; this right includes the freedom to change his religion or belief, and freedom, either alone or in community with others and in public or private, to manifest his religion or belief in teaching, practice, worship and observance.

ARTICLE 19

Everyone has the right to freedom of opinion and expression; this right includes freedom to hold opinions without interference and seek, receive and impart information and ideas through any media and regardless of frontiers.

ARTICLE 20

1. Everyone has the right to freedom of peaceful assembly and association.
2. No one may be compelled to belong to an association.

ARTICLE 21

1. Everyone has the right to take part in the government of his country, directly or through freely chosen representatives.
2. Everyone has the right of equal access to public service in his country.
3. The will of the people shall be the basis of the authority of government; this will shall be expressed in periodic and genuine elections which shall be by universal and equal sufferage and shall be held by secret vote or by equivalent free voting procedures.

ARTICLE 22

Everyone, as a member of society, has the right to social

security and is entitled to realization, through national effort and international cooperation and in accordance with the organization and resources of each State, of the economic, social and cultural rights indispensable for his dignity and the free development of his personality.

Article 23

1. Everyone has the right to work, to free choice of employment, to just and favourable conditions of work and protection against unemployment.
2. Everyone, without any discrimination, has the right to equal pay for equal work.
3. Everyone who works has the right to just and favourable remuneration ensuring for himself and his family an existence worthy of human dignity, and supplemented, if necessary, by other means of social protection.
4. Everyone has the right to form and to join trade unions for the protection of his interests.

Article 24

Everyone has the right to rest and leisure, including reasonable limitation of working hours and periodic holidays with pay.

Article 25

1. Everyone has the right to a standard of living adequate for the health and well-being of himself and of his family, including food, clothing, housing and medical care and necessary social services, and the right to security on the event of unemployment, sickness, disability, widowhood, old age or other lack of livelihood in circumstances beyond his control.

2. Motherhood and childhood are entitled to special care and assistance. All children, whether born in or out of wedlock, shall enjoy the same social protection.

Article 26

1. Everyone has the right to education. Education shall be free, at least in the elementary and fundamental stages. Elementary education shall be compulsory. Technical and professional.education shall be made generally available an higher education shall be equally accessible to all on the basis of merit.
2. Education shall be directed to the full development of the human personality and to the strengthening of respect for human rights and fundamental freedoms. It shall promote understanding, tolerance and friendship among all nations, racial or religious groups and shall further the activities of the United Nations for the maintenance of peace.
3. Parents have a prior right to choose the kind of education that shall be given to their children.

Article 27

1. Everyone has the right freely to participate in the cultural life of the community, to enjoy the arts and to share in scientific advancement and its benefits.
2. Everyone has the right to the protection of the moral and material interests resulting from any scientific, literary or artistic production of which he is the author.

Article 28

Everyone is entitled to a social and international order in which the rights and freedoms set forth in this Declaration can be fully realized.

Article 29

1. Everyone has duties to the community in which alone the free and full development of his personality is possible.
2. In the exercise of his rights and freedoms, everyone shall be subject only to such limitations as are determined by law solely for the purpose of securing due recognition and respect for the rights and freedoms of others and of meeting the just requirements of.morality, public order and the general welfare in a democratic society.
3. These rights and freedoms may in no case be exercised contrary to the purposes and principles of the United Nations.

Article 30

Nothing in this Declaration may be interpreted as implying for any State, group or person any right to engage in any activity or to perform any act aimed at the destuction of any of the rights and freedoms set forth herein.

3

Human Rights and Social Justice

Social Justice is the practice in which all people are treated equally. That means that everyone in the country has the same opportunities. Women are allowed to go to school and work as doctors, lawyers and teachers. They can make choices about how they want to spend money and what should be done with their family's land or business. Women are not sold into forced labor or abused physically by their husbands or strangers.

Social justice is when women earn equal pay with men for doing equal work. Just as women have equal opportunities, members of lower castes also have equal opportunities. Dalits, like Biswakarmas and Chamars, can travel anywhere, find any job, go to school and cook and clean in anyone's house without a problem. When they walk down the street people do not look the other way but are happy to shake their hand and let them enter their house.

Social justice means that boy and girl children are not forced to work but rather go to school, are fed well and have time to play with their friends. Individuals are not arrested without good reason and if they are arrested they are given the time and resources to defend themselves properly in an attempt to prove their innocence.

Social justice means that all citizens are able to participate in their political system, speak their minds, demonstrate peacefully and express their opinions. As long as the individual's actions do not hurt others then that individual should be able to move freely throughout the country and say and do what he or she wants.

Social justice is when everyone in the country is treated fairly, given respect and protected by the law. People have the ability to live long and healthy lives and have access to the information and resources needed for a decent standard of living.

Social justice means fairness, and situations can be fair or unfair in different ways. For instance, someone may or may not get their fair share of something that is distributed, like water, food or fodder. Someone may not get a fair chance to explain his or her side of the story. Maybe someone is arrested and jailed without a fair chance to prove his or her innocence or suffers a punishment that is unfair in relation to his or her conduct.

Social Justice derives its authority from the codes of morality prevailing in each culture. In an ideal world, human behaviour could be improved by convincing everyone to adopt the principles of moral philosophy. But the human propensity to evaluate shades of gray becomes the catalyst for a problem that can be stated simply: If a moral code may sometimes require a person to do something that would not be for his or her own benefit, why should that person decide to be "moral" and so act in a correspondingly "just" way?

Humans are vulnerable as individuals. By gathering together into bands and communities, they seek to gain strength and to address their vulnerabilities which, in turn, creates the potential to develop into more complex and evolving civilisations. If simple survival is to be transformed into long-term security, something more than co-ordinating the contribution of everyone's skills will be required. A social organisation will be needed to resolve disputes and offer physical security against attack.

The achievement of community aims will depend upon the co-ordination of many functional specialisations (such as farmers for food, soldiers for protection and rulers for resource management) and a willingness of community members to sacrifice some personal freedom for the greater good. So, would defining or administering justice become one of these specialisations and, as such, be the exclusive responsibility of any one class of citizens? People will not accept the surrender of any of their freedoms unless they perceive real benefits flowing from their decisions.

The key factor is likely to be the emergence of a consensus that the society is working in a fair way, i.e. both that individuals are allowed as much freedom as possible given the role they have within the society and that the rewards compensate adequately for any loss of freedom. Hence, true social justice is attained only through the harmonious co-operative effort of the citizens who, in their own self-interest, accept the current norms of morality as the price of membership in the community.

The next major impetus for the development of the concept came from Christianity. Thomas Aquinas (1225-1274) says, "Justice is a certain rectitude of mind whereby a man does what he ought to do in the circumstances confronting him." As a theologian, Aquinas believed that justice is a form of natural duty owed by one person to another and not enforced by any human-made law. This reflects the Christian view that, before God, all people are equal and must treat each other with respect. Hence, the framework of the argument shifts to require obedience to natural principles of morality to satisfy a duty owed to God, and the outcome of social justice is driven by the tenets of morality embedded in the religion.

A different set of moral tenets, however, produces a different outcome, as in the karmic (Buddhist) principle of justice. In Buddhism, there is no such thing as unexplained, causeless suffering. Every state of existence, good or bad, is caused by ethically good or evil deeds, and karmic justice ultimately rewards good behaviour by allowing escape from suffering into Nirvana. But each individual is judged independently of any other, and actions, good or bad, just or unjust, will have their inescapable consequence.

Consequently, there is no incentive for individuals to engage in collective action to intervene in "unjust" situations. If others are suffering, those responsible for inflicting such injustice will incur bad karma and will be penalised. Further, if anyone misinterprets a situation and, by objective criteria, intervenes to force change on an innocent person, it is the one intervening who will incur bad karma no matter how well-intentioned he or she might be.

John Locke (1632-1704), an early theological utilitarian, argued that people have innate natural goodness and beauty, and so, in the long run, if individuals rationally pursue their private happiness and pleasure, the interests of the society or the general welfare will be looked after fairly. Locke characterised most of Christianity as utilitarian since believers see utility in rewards in the afterlife for their actions on Earth. The Utilitarian School was later associated with Jeremy Bentham (1748-1832) and John Stuart Mill (1806-1873) who judged the morality of an act solely on the basis of its results.

In that era of the Enlightenment, naturalism and any reliance on divine inspiration was rejected. The philosophers believed that through reason and rationality, human nature and society could be perfected. Hence, justice was achieved in any situation where the greatest happiness was achieved by the greatest number of people. Bentham advocated socially-imposed external sanctions of punishment and blame to make the consequences of improper action more obviously painful.

Social Justice was achieved through deterrence which is based on the rational calculation of "equal punishment for equal crime". Mill took the view that human beings are also motivated by such internal sanctions as self-esteem, guilt, and conscience. Because we all have social feelings on behalf of others, the unselfish wish for the good of all is often enough to move us to act morally.

Immanuel Kant (1724-1804) believed that actions are morally right if they are motivated by duty without regard to any personal goal, desire, motive, or self-interest. Kant's moral theory is, therefore, deontological and based on the concept of abject selflessness. In his view, the only relevant feature of moral law is its universalisability, and any rational being understands the categorical imperative to be: "Act only according to that maxim whereby you can at the same time will that it should become a universal law."

For example, the imperative in the proposition that all borrowers should deal honestly with the lenders is that, in the absence of universal acceptance, no-one would be willing to lend. This may be stated as the formula of autonomy, whereby the decision to apply a maxim is actually regarded as having made it a universal law. Here the concern with human dignity is combined with the principle of universalisability to produce a conception of the moral law as self-legislated by each for all.

In the latter part of the twentieth century, the concept of Social Justice has largely been associated with the political philosopher John Rawls (1921-2002) who draws on the utilitarian insights of Bentham and Mill, the social contract ideas of Locke, and the categorical imperative ideas of Kant. His first statement of principle was made in A Theory of Justice (1971) where he proposed that, "Each person possesses an inviolability founded on justice that even the welfare of society as a whole cannot override. For this reason justice denies that the loss of freedom for some is made right by a greater good shared by others.". A deontological proposition that echoes Kant in framing the moral good of justice in absolutist terms. His views are definitively restated in Political Liberalism, where society is seen, "as a fair system of co-operation over time, from one generation to the next."

All societies have a basic structure of social, economic, and political institutions, both formal and informal. In testing how well these elements fit and work together, Rawls based a key test of legitimacy on the theories of social contract. To determine whether any particular system of collectively enforced social arrangements is legitimate, he argued that one must look for agreement by the people who are subject to it. Obviously, not every citizen can be asked to participate in a poll to determine his or her consent to every proposal in which some degree of coercion is involved, so we have to assume that all citizens are reasonable. Rawls constructed an argument for a two-stage process to determine a citizen's hypothetical agreement:

— the citizen agrees to be represented by X for certain purposes; to that extent, X holds these powers as a trustee for the citizen;

— X agrees that a use of enforcement in a particular social context is legitimate; the citizen, therefore, is bound by this decision because it is the function of the trustee to represent the citizen in this way.

This applies to one person representing a small group (e.g. to the organiser of a social event setting a dress code) as equally as it does to national governments which are the ultimate trustees, holding representative powers for the benefit of all citizens within their territorial boundaries, and if those governments fail to provide for the welfare of their citizens according to the principles of justice, they are not legitimate.

To emphasise the general principle that justice should rise from the people and not be dictated by the law-making powers of governments, Rawls asserted that, "There is . . . a general presumption against imposing legal and other restrictions on conduct without sufficient reason. But this presumption creates no special priority for any particular liberty." This is support for an unranked set of liberties that reasonable citizens in all states should respect and uphold - to some extent, the list proposed by Rawls matches the normative human rights that have international recognition and direct enforcement in some nation states where the citizens need encouragement to act in a more objectively just way.

Social Justice as conceived by Rawls is an apolitical philosophical concept (insofar as any philosophical analysis of politics can be free from bias), but many of the ideas, sometimes renamed civil justice, have been adopted by those who lie on the left or center-left of the political spectrum (e.g. Socialists, Social Democrats, etc.), even though there should be general acceptance by all who base their political philosophy on moral values (e.g. in the U.S., Republican voters in the Presidential Election 2004 are said to have exercised preference on moral values).

Similarly, Social Justice is fundamental to Catholic social teaching, and is one of the Four Pillars of the Green Party upheld by the worldwide green parties. As stated by several local branches, this is the principle that all persons are entitled to "basic human needs", regardless of "superficial differences such as economic disparity, class, gender, race, ethnicity, citizenship, religion, age, sexual orientation, disability, or health". This includes the eradication of poverty and illiteracy, the establishment of sound environmental policy, and equality of opportunity for healthy personal and social development.

The concept of Social justice has been politicised and it is sometimes stated proactively as being the promotion of equality through comprehensive government action. In practice, such interventions have not often produced equitable results, resulting in favouritism towards classes of people, restrictions of personal liberty and excessive regulatory burdens. Many critics regard the guarantee of equal outcomes, which is implicit in many social justice movements, as antithetical to the notion of equal opportunity because it frequently requires special, favoured treatment to arbitrary classes of people. Actual justice, they argue, does not penalize success nor reward failure, but holds all persons to the same standards regardless of their race, ethnic origin, financial condition, religion or beliefs.

Still others, more grassroots in orientation, regard social justice "activities" as a moral/ethical balance to less-than-effective government sponsored "legal justice". Many simply believe that a "Social Justice Action" must be initiated by the human individual on his or her own accord to be pure in its "Social Justice" intent. Some people concerned with social justice may hold some or all of the following beliefs:

- Historical inequities insofar as they affect current injustices should be corrected until the actual inequities no longer exist or have been perceptively "negated".
- The redistribution of wealth, power and status for the individual, community and societal good.
- It is government's (or those who hold significant power) responsibility to ensure a basic quality of life for all its citizens.

— A Direct Social Justice Action must be initiated by the individual to be "pure" or remain "virtuous" within its perceived "Social Justice" context, even though other individuals may consciously choose to participate in response (intellectually, emotionally or otherwise) to the initiator's Direct Social Justice Action.

— Vigorous and uncompromising critics of any form or application of "Social Justice" whatsoever, usually have deeper motives for their convictions. For instance, furthering controversial causes like the theories purported in Eugenics. Eugenicists commonly agree that anything "social" or otherwise that could ultimately prove to assist individuals that are perceived by them to be "dysgenic", should be vehemently opposed, dismantled or at the very least contained.

Evolution

One of the ironies of the early twenty-first century is that ideological struggles between and within nations have intensified a decade after the end of the Cold War. Today, proponents of diametrically opposed visions of society, secular and religious, march under the banner of social justice. As desirable social and political goals are depicted in starkly different forms, labels like "good" and "evil" become interchangeable and the meaning of social justice becomes obscured. As it has been for millennia, the concept of social justice is now used as a rationale for maintaining the status quo, promoting far-reaching social reforms, and justifying revolutionary action.

Although fascinating and vitally important, a full exploration of this question is better suited for another essay. This article will focus instead, somewhat more narrowly, on how the concept of social justice in Western societies has influenced contemporary social welfare. The evolution of this concept reflects, in part, the shift towards a secular and materialist culture, and the changes this transformation produced in people's fundamental assumptions about human nature, society, and the state. As the meaning of social justice changed, it became increasingly complex and conflict-ridden, both as an idea and in its applications.

Today, for example, our understanding of social justice is inextricably connected to our definition of terms like equality and freedom, and to sweeping policy questions about the relative responsibilities and obligations of individuals and society. Originally, the idea of social justice was groupspecific-that is, it was applied solely to a particular people or nation with the intention of redressing the effects of hierarchical inequalities, particularly inherited inequalities.

The Bible, for example, introduces the idea of a "jubilee year," when slaves would be freed, debts and obligations liquidated, and land returned to its original owners. In this usage, however, social justice was not regarded as universal in its application. Also, it focused primarily on issues of economic redistribution largely among individuals.

In The Republic, Plato expanded the meaning of justice by equating it with human well-being. He linked the concept of individual and social justice by asserting that justice was derived from the harmony between reason, spirit, and appetite present in all persons. Within this formulation, if a society lacked such harmony, justice could not be achieved.

Yet, Plato's view of justice did not include a belief in equality. In fact, since he regarded class distinctions as essential for the effective functioning of society, he argued that justice would be achieved when each person received those goods they deserved based on their prescribed position in the social order. In other words, that unequals would be treated unequally.

Social justice, therefore, would not involve efforts to transform or transcend existing societal structures, but rather would guarantee that existing institutions would continue to function as intended. Aristotle further developed this concept of justice in The Nicomachian Ethics, where he introduced a view of justice that anticipates modern debates about issues of resource allocation. Aristotle regarded justice, as fulfilled through law, as the principle that ensures social order through the regulation of the allocation and distribution of benefits.

Aristotle states, "equality for the people involved will be the same as for the things involved, since [in a just society] the relation between the people will be the same as the relation between the things involved. For if the people involved are not equal, they will not [justly] receive equal shares; indeed, whenever equals receive unequal shares, or unequals equal shares, ... that is the source of quarrels and accusations". Yet, like Plato and many other philosophers and political leaders over the past 2,000 years, Aristotle did not regard people as fundamentally equal. His view of equality and justice applied only to those individuals who occupied the same stratum of a hierarchical social order-for Aristotle, this meant Athenian men of property.

This interpretation of justice rationalized the coexistence of slavery or oppression for the many with a democratic polls for the few. Universal concepts of justice first appeared between 1,500 and 2,500 years ago in the teachings of most of the world's great religions, such as Judaism, Christianity, Islam, and Buddhism, and in Western literature of this period, such as the Greek tragedies of Sophocles and Aeschylus. The idea of one universal or allpowerful deity became linked with the pursuit of a divine vision for humankind, one in which universal justice was attained, either in this life or the afterlife.

Ironically, as these religions evolved, religious institutions and religiously sanctioned hierarchies emerged that undermined this initial conception of justice. In addition, the exclusivity and competition among proponents of different religions-increasingly linked to states or empires-further undermined the ideal of justice for all. In this context, it is not surprising that the reemergence of the concept of justice in Western societies occurred concurrently with the growth of secular humanism and the spirit of rationalism in the seventeenth and eighteenth centuries. In the early modern period, this conception of justice was initially used to rationalize the consolidation of state power under the authority of absolute monarchs.

Like Aristotle, the foremost proponent of this perspective, the English philosopher Thomas Hobbes, regarded the construction of an external authority-the state or leviathan-as an essential ingredient in the maintenance of a just society. This was not because he considered government the embodiment of the collective will of people who were naturally just, but because he viewed humans as antisocial and driven by their baser instincts-an idea that still resonates in the early twenty-first century.

In Hobbes's conception of justice, the state would create and enforce laws and social norms to preserve peace and restrain individuals from harming each other in the pursuit of their self-interests. This view of justice complemented perfectly the emergence of commercial and industrial capitalism. Through the Elizabethan Poor Laws it shaped Western models of social welfare to the present, particularly in Great Britain and North America.

During the seventeenth and eighteenth centuries, the idea of justice was strongly connected in the West to the scientific revolution (which sought to discover universal nonreligious truths) and the Enlightenment (which sought to apply these scientific discoveries to society and its institutions). As part of their structural analyses of society, political philosophers during the "age of revolution," such as Rousseau (1754/1994), and their nineteenth century successors constructed a series of metanarratives that explained the persistence of injustice. To a considerable extent, the frameworks they constructed over two centuries ago shaped the formation of most modern institutions in the West, including the relationship between the state and social welfare.

The great political and social revolutions of the late eighteenth century also contained a revolutionary idea of justice. Both explicitly and implicitly, the pursuit and realization of social justice were now inextricably linked to the preservation of individual liberty or freedom, the achievement of equality (of rights, opportunities, and outcomes), and the establishment of common bonds of all humanity (fraternity or mutuality). Both the American and French revolutions linked their social justice goals with the "pursuit" or "the perfection of happiness".

In theory, this required the creation of societies that would maximize both individual and collective well-being. Through such documents as the American Declaration of Independence and the French Universal Declaration of the Rights of Man and Citizen, social justice became the unwritten linchpin of so-called "natural rights" that, in rhetoric if not reality, would now be applied to all people. Throughout the nineteenth and twentieth centuries, however, the gap between the ideal of social justice and the reality of persistent inequality and injustice became more apparent, as did the difficulty of reconciling the goal of social equality with the preservation of individual liberties.

The elites that dominated emerging nation-states rationalized their power by distinguishing in both rhetoric and practice between political and economic justice, and separating the abstraction of justice from the legal concept of individual or social rights. This enabled them to withhold political rights from the majority of the population, virtually ignore the issue of social and economic rights. The growing recognition of the gap between social justice as an abstraction and injustice as a fact of life produced a torrent of critical ideas that inspired most of the reform movements and revolutions of the period between 1815 and the outbreak of World War I.

Foremost among the critics of these contradictions was Karl Marx, who applied a rigorous, "scientific" politicaleconomic analysis to the philosophic arguments of those he pejoratively labeled "utopian socialists." In contrast with many contemporary economists (and twentieth century Marxists), Marx expressed a holistic view of the human condition and the social reality from which it emerged. He argued that human beings did not have a fixed, innate nature, but were defined by their social relationships that, in turn, were dependent on the economic structure of society and the classes it produced.

Unlike Hobbes, Marx rejected the idea that injustice was the byproduct of natural human competition, selfishness, and aggression. He asserted that the roots of injustice lie, instead, in the political-economic structure that was based on subjugation, discrimination, exploitation, and privilege. Justice would prevail, therefore, when individuals received what they needed on the basis of their humanity and not merely what they deserved on the basis of their social class origin or productivity.

Thus, in the West, the idea of social justice gradually became closely associated with the concept of a social contract involving mutual rights and obligations. Nineteenth century Liberals and Marxists differed sharply, however, in their interpretation of the terms of this contract. The former emphasized the preservation of individual liberty, including property rights, and the latter stressed the attainment of social equality. In one sense, the debate revolved around distinctions between contributive and distributive views of justice and the implications of these concepts for the allocation of social rights, goods, and responsibilities.

During much of the twentieth century, although differences emerged over the relative balance of these rights and responsibilities, there was broad agreement in the West that a social justice paradigm must incorporate various means of achieving a fair distribution of societal goods-tangible and intangible. In addition, there was agreement that the ways in which society should pursue such goals must be based on some accounting for either the contribution of the individual to society or the individual's past, present, and potential role and status.

In short, Miller asserts that social justice reflects the distribution of benefits and burdens throughout a society, as it results from the major social institutions such as property systems and public organizations. It deals with such matters as the regulations of wages and ... profits, the protections of persons' rights through the legal system, the allocation of housing, medicine, welfare benefits, etc.

Miller's view of social justice is one of "just distribu tion" that is not dependent on the nature of the goods al located or the policy domain, but on "modes of human re lationship". Recently feminist philosophers like Nussbaum and Held have adde a gender dimension to this conception of social justic. Yet, there has been little consensus about the balanc within a social justice framework between individual an group entitlements and social obligations. In brief, then have been six different ways in which distributive justic has been described:

— Equal rights (to intangibles such as freedom) and equal opportunity to obtain social goods, such as property
— Equal distribution to those of equal merit
— Equal distribution to those of equal productivity
— Unequal distribution based upon an individual's needs or requirements
— Unequal distribution based upon an individual's status or position
— Unequal distribution based upon different "contractual" agreements

During the twentieth century, the most popular approach to the problem of distribution was based on utilitarian arguments, whose calculus presupposes the rational ordering of social goods to achieve what John Stuart Mill termed the "greatest net balance of satisfaction" for society. In the late twentieth century, this view was often linked with the assumption that the prioritization of social goals occurs through a process equally accessible to all members of society in a manner that promotes generalized benevolence. Yet, in his contemporary classic, A Theory of Justice, Rawls argues that as a philosophical guide utilitarianism creates no imperative of social justice, since it can be used to rationalize a concentration of goods benefiting the privileged classes of society.

Instead, the justice of a system must be measured, he argued, based "on how fundamental rights and duties are assigned and on the economic opportunities and social conditions in the various sectors of society". Rawls based his conception of distributive justice on the premise that "all social values ... are to be distributed equally unless an unequal distribution of any, or all, of these values is to everyone's advantage". He derived what he called his maximin theory from two fundamental principles:

— Each person has an equal right to the most extensive system of personal liberty compatible with a system of total liberty for all

— Social and economic inequality are to be arranged so that they are both (a) to the greatest benefit to the least advantaged in society and (b) attached to positions open to all under conditions of fair equality of opportunity

From these principles of justice, Rawls articulated a "principle of redress," which established the philosophical basis for social policies directed toward a more just distribution of social goods. Other scholars have applied this principle to support policies like affirmative action and reparations for African Americans. As stated by Rawls, the principle seems particularly well-suited to the social work profession's goal of eliminating racial, gender, and economic inequalities.

Undeserved inequalities call for redress; and since inequalities of birth and natural endowment are undeserved, these inequalities are to be somehow compensated for. Thus, the principle holds that in order to treat all persons equally, to provide genuine equality of opportunity, society must give more attention to those with fewer native assets and to those born into the less favorable social positions. The idea is to redress the bias of contingencies in the direction of equality.

This view of distributive justice found adherents in religious circles as well. In their famous pastoral letter, the U.S. Conference of Catholic Bishops went even finther than Rawls. The bishops asserted that "distributive justice requires that the allocation of income, wealth, and power in society be evaluated in light of its effect on persons whose basic needs are unmet". The document also stated that "social justice implies that persons have an obligation to be active and productive participants in the life of society and that society has a duty to enable them to participate in this way." Thus, the concept of social justice "also includes a duty to organize economic and social institutions so that people can contribute to society in ways that respect their freedom and the dignity of their labor".

Part of the appeal of Rawls' theory and the Bishops' letter is in the .synthesis they forged between two competing meta-analyses-liberalism and socialism-whose conflicting influences have been regarded as central to the development of modern Western social welfare. Rawls' "difference principle" and the duties articulated by the pastoral letter seek to equalize life chances for people across racial, gender, and class lines, but never at the expense of the basic liberal freedoms protected by the "equal liberty principle".

This synthesis is particularly compelling for the social work profession because of its historic emphasis on both the preservation of individual human rights and dignity-best expressed through the concept of self-determination-and the redistribution of resources to promote the well-being of disadvantaged populations. It also offers social reformers a conceptual escape from the trap laid by conservative opponents of social welfare that have often obfuscated appeals for justice-centered social policies by labeling them with antidemocratic rhetoric, such as quotas.

Two fundamental problems are often overlooked, however, in discussions of applying justice principles to contemporary social policy debates. The first is the paradox of attempting to develop principles of justice within a political, economic, and social context based largely, if tacitly, on the preservation of injustice. As Smith argues, "the longstanding history of invidious discrimination in the United States demonstrates that attention must always be paid to the threats [it] poses to liberal values".

The second problem relates to the application of justice concepts based largely on the expansion of individual rights and individual shares of societal resources to the development of policies, programs, and modes of intervention that address group needs and concerns. As Caputo points out, the resolution of this problem is critical to social work's efforts to contribute to the development of a truly multiracial, multicultural society. Throughout the world, but especially in the United States, race and racism are social constructs, deeply rooted in the political-economic system and culture.

Debates over social justice and multiculturalism, therefore, are inextricably linked. They reflect a broader dialogue over the nature of social relations, the concept of community, the structure of the economy, and definitions of what constitutes the public good. The creation of greater social solidarity (fraternity or humanity) implied in the goals of multiculturalism and social justice, requires the reassertion of the ideas of collective responsibility, a community of need, and public virtue. It implies the formulation of citizenship requirements that are "more responsive to our communitarian and collective security needs, without sacrificing our commitment to liberty and justice for all". It also implies the establishment of a societal imperative that promotes full participation of each member of the community in the community's activities.

In the social welfare field, this participation would include the determination of what constitutes individual and social need, the development of alternative conceptions of helping, and the creation of new criteria for evaluating the effectiveness of various modes of intervention. A social justice framework, therefore, can enable the social work profession to develop and refine new practice principles for the difficult years ahead.

In recent decades, postmodern theorists have complicated this picture further through the presentation of powerful challenges to prevailing metanarratives at all ends of the ideological spectrum because of what and whom they exclude. A positive contribution of the postmodernist critique is the expansion of the concept of justice to include other groups long denied the benefits of justice and of other goals of justice, beyond the achievement of economic and social equality. In addition, strongly influenced by feminist theory, postmodernism has defined justice as a process as well as an outcome. It remains to be seen, however, whether the postmodern emphasis on identity can provide the conceptual basis for the formation of powerful social justice-oriented coalitions.

Emergence of Social Work

Since the early twentieth century, the pursuit of social justice has been a core value of the social work profession in the United States, providing an alternative to the concept of social welfare as charity. For a century, the conflict between justice and charitable perspectives was not merely the focus of academic debate. It shaped the evolution of U.S. social policy by forging an awkward synthesis of individualistic and collectivist orientations to society and its problems.

In the Progressive Era, the concept of social justice among social workers emerged through a synthesis of religious ideals (such as the Social Gospel, Quakerism, or Christian socialism), the work of secular philosophers such as Marx, Dewey, and William James, and the political activities of leaders such as Jane Addams, Florence Kelley,

Ellen Gates Starr, and Lillian Wald on behalf of workers' rights, women's suffrage, racial justice, and peace. Settlement workers, in particular, regarded the pursuit of social justice as a necessary response to growing economic inequality and the breakdown of community. Their pursuit of social justice led them to forge alliances with feminist organizations, trade unions, neighborhood-based community associations, civil rights groups, and radicals outside of the social work field, and to advocate for social reforms in areas as diverse as child welfare, housing, and public health.

A generation later, at the height of the Great Depression of the 1930s, the Rank and File Movement in social work articulated "five simple principles" as the basis for developing a justice-centered social work practice. Bertha Reynolds, a leader among the Rank and Filers, summarized these principles:

— The purpose of social work is to serve people in need. If social workers serve other classes who have other purposes, they become too dishonest to be capable of either theoretical or practical development.

— Social work exists to help people help themselves and, therefore, social workers should not be alarmed when people do so by organized means.

— Social work practice operates by communication, listening, and sharing experiences.

— Social workers have to find their place among other movements for human betterment by forming and joining coalitions with clients, community groups, and like-minded colleagues from all disciplines.

— Social workers cannot consider themselves superior to their clients, as if they do not have the same problems.

Beginning in the 1930s, proponents of social justice regarded the establishment and expansion of the welfare state as a primary means of ameliorating the impact of longstanding structural inequalities in society and the market. For nearly half a century after their modest successes during the New Deal, they focused debates over social policy largely on the extent to which they established social rights and provided forms of institutionalized compensation or redress. Since the early 1980s, however, attacks on the concept of entitlement-both legal and social-have undermined the idea of using social welfare as an instrument for achieving social justice, culminating in the United States in the passage of the 1996 Personal Responsibility and Work Opportunity Reconciliation Act (PRWORA).

Contemporary Views

Today's complex environment obscures both the meaning of social justice and the goals of social justice. During the past two decades of welfare cutbacks and retrenchment, social work authors have stated these questions both implicitly and explicitly. Looking for a cause around which to focus the profession's abstract commitment to social justice principles, social workers have linked the pursuit of social justice with a variety of diverse issues. These include the promotion of peace and nuclear disarmament; opposition to U.S. intervention in the political affairs of other nations; support for the rights of women, gays, and lesbians; defense of affirmative action; and the promotion of multiculturalism.

Although the relationships between social workers and other movements for social justice are not as strong as in the past, many observers believe that "far more social workers today think that problems such as poverty are rooted in structural sources than thought so in the 1960s". This demonstrates that even in conservative times the social justice legacy of the profession remains strong.

Influenced by postmodern ideas, social work literature now often links the attainment of social justice with the goals of social diversity or multiculturalism, and with challenges to the normative power structure and the oppression it produces.

Some authors, however, have defined social justice in terms of empowerment practice without specifying the meaning of either term. This ambiguity of meaning is also found in articles about social policy, which recognize that social justice has to be promoted at all levels of government, from local to national but do not explicitly define the concept. Building on the ideas of Reynolds and Freire, other social work scholars have focused on human transformation as part of their critiques of the positivist-empiricist and rationality-centered emphases of social work research and epistemology.

Clinical social workers have struggled with ways of integrating contemporary emphases on the role of narratives within a social justice framework. Some have connected the struggles for social justice and gender or racial equality in a way that "requires an integration of personal, professional, and spiritual-political values and beliefs into a framework that respects the dialectical tensions while striving for wholeness". Swenson provides a clinical perspective on why social justice is considered the organizing value of social work. She identifies several strategies for basing clinical work on a social justice foundation that is derived from the writings of Rawls and Van Soest.

These include recognizing clients' strengths, an awareness of the role of power in professional relationships, and a focus on positionality. Like Wakefield, Mullaly, and others, Swenson argues that clinical social workers can also engage in social justice work through the elimination of oppressive practices in their agencies, the development of new client-centered programs, and the education of colleagues and members of related disciplines about social justice principles.

Van Soest argues that the three different justice theories-libertarianism, utilitarianism, and egalitarianism-could all be used as the basis for reordering national priorities and support people's "valid claim for a share of the resources needed to ensure the provision of adequate food, clothing, and shelter." Gibelman sees the roots of injustice in discrimination and maintains that "social justice refers to conditions in which all members of society have the same basic rights, protections, opportunities, obligations, and social benefits." Using Rawls' conception of justice, FigueiraMcDonough emphasizes the importance of equality in the distribution of social goods. Reflecting the 200year-old tension between individual liberty and social equality, she questions, however, whether social work has been able to attain its dual goals of self-determination and social justice.

Gal elaborates on this issue through an exploration of the different notions of social justice implied in the concept of compensatory social welfare policies. Gal maintains that social justice is defined in two fundamental ways. One definition reflects efforts to reward individuals for past services or contributions, or as a redress for "injuries or losses inflicted unjustly on individuals or groups." This definition is often in conflict with the view of social justice that emphasizes equality. Gal suggests that a way of reconciling this conflict is to use the social welfare system to ensure horizontal equality in meeting needs, while allowing the market to reward people for their efforts by "providing them with their just deserts."

Influenced by Etzioni, McNutt takes a communitarian perspective that seeks to balance individual rights and responsibilities in articulating a definition of social justice. He asserts that social workers today primarily rely upon the definitions of social justice formulated by Rawls, Beverly and McSweeny, or Goulet that are based more on individual rights. As alternatives, McNutt suggests four possible positions on social justice along a continuum from individual to community hegemony:

— The Community Reigns Supreme. Social justice involves individual sacrifice to the common good.

— The Community and the Community Good Position. This view (embraced by communitarians) attempts to link individual rights with community rights.

— The Individual Need Community Position. This is the traditional liberal position in which social justice is assured by state action and the common good is "defined in terms of what will benefit all individuals and that the market cannot deliver."

— The Individual Reigns Supreme Position. The conception of social justice "equates individual self-interest with the common good."

The absence of conceptual or historical clarity or agreement among scholars, however, has not deterred some authors from urging the profession to embrace its social justice responsibilities more fully, as required by the revised Code of Ethics, or to pursue professional unity as a means of reviving the field's interest in social justice goals. NASW can enforce its ethical imperative that "social workers promote social justice" and "challenge social injustice"

Intergenerational Justice

Intergenerational justice—the concern about the well-being of future generations—must be given equal consideration to "social justice" for those we invite here legally. Intergenerational justice must certainly be given higher consideration than social justice and "rights" for those who sneak across our borders.

Who, then, would deny the concept of intergenerational justice? Corporate interests demand only an unending supply of cheap foreign labor. The media are still caught up in promoting open-border agendas. The vast majority of politicians are more concerned about campaign contributions, ethnic vote pandering and the next election.

Generation after generation of Americans traditionally have endeavored to leave their country better than it was. Yet Americans today may be the first to fail this legacy by ignoring the explosive population growth that we see in the daily manifestation of ever-growing symptoms. We are stealing from the future for the sake of present economic gain, just as we are stealing from America's working poor today by replacing them with lower-wage immigrants.

Certainly a tremendous disparity exists between standards of living in the first world and developing countries, including America's overpopulated neighbors to the south. Yet the solution cannot be to invite all of the world's poor into our country, because we can only absorb a small fraction. (And yes, realistic solutions must involve strategies to improve living standards of third world countries - in particular with family planning assistance and micro-loans, which have both proven effective).

We are approaching the point of no return by overpopulating our own country for the sake of corporate greed and a misguided attempt to solve other countries' overpopulation problems. The debate about what kind of nation and society we are leaving to future Americans is not occurring, and the silence is deafening.

America has a right - and indeed an obligation - to openly discuss and shape its demographic future. Yet Americans choose not to confront this terribly important issue, and this selfish action is surely a hate crime against future generations. Future generations of Americans deserve nothing less from us than our full compassion and our every effort to ensure them a sustainable future.

Social Justice and Social Equality

Equality was understood as meaning that people in society are on a par with each other in all respects: politically, economically, and culturally. As a result, the concept of justice was in essence considered as identical to "egalitarian makes flat." Anything not in accord with egalitarianism would be seen as a violation of the justice principle. This wrongful view decreased, even abolished, momentum for socioeconomic development.In fact, however, although the contents of "social justice" and "social equality" are close to one another and may seem identical, they are still different concepts.

Equality means that each person has the same status in society in terms of legal rights. When people are socially equal in all respects, one speaks of total social equality. One important kind of social equality is that of duty and right, of contribution and benefit. This kind of equality is social justice, which is based on the principle that the same contribution equals the same benefit. According to this definition, social justice is a both a form and a concrete expression of social equality, and implementing social justice is implementing a part of social equality.

Social justice is a step on the way to complete social equality; however, it is still not in itself complete social equality. According to Marxist theory, socialism is the first stage of communism. Distribution of goods in that stage is based on the principle that a producer will get from society the amount of consumer goods that is in balance with the value of the labour that he has supplied (after discounting his contribution to social funds).

This is an equal distribution rule, in one sense, because all producers have the same rights to share in the consumption made possible by society if they have made the same contribution. However, implementation of this principle still results in a certain inequality for members of society. That is an inevitable shortcoming of the first stage of communism. Total social equality only occurs in the higher, or second stage of communism. The above discussion shows the difference between social justice and social equality.

Possibilities for Implementation

As mentioned above, the main meaning of social justice is simply that the same contribution equals the same benefit. Therefore, in the current context, when we are still poor, we are not only able but also have to implement social justice by paying more to those who work more to increase labourers' motivation. This principle of justice and its implementation potential need to be clarified:

1. The distribution based on labour as the only criterion of justice; this criterion must now be further expanded. Distribution should be based on:

    — labour;

    — capital sources; and

    — other contributions to society in general (not solely to economic production), especially to the nation's existence and health.

2. Even in labour-based distribution, the justice criterion should not be considered an absolute. This criterion bears a relative characteristic and is established through the experience of daily life.

3. In the transition period from subsidy to market mechanisms, we should not and could not

immediately expect the implementation of absolute justice (total equality in standards of living). We can only obtain this step-by-step and the route is not short.

Social Justice for Socioeconomic Development

At present, social justice is an important force for socioeconomic development in Viet Nam for a number of reasons. Human beings often act for the sake of benefits, especially individual benefits. If we truly carry out the principle "same contribution - same benefit," the labourers will be satisfied because they will not suffer a loss when they contribute to society. As a result, they will try their best to apply intelligence, capital, and other resources for business, production, and other activities needed for socioeconomic development.

Labour and capital are the two basic factors of economic development. Once people who have working capacity eagerly contribute their labour, capital holders will eagerly contribute their funds. All these contributions are important for socioeconomic development. Together with labour and capital, we must count other contributions to society, especially contributions to the existence and health of the nation. These concern one's obligation to create a healthy, harmonious, reliable social psychological atmosphere that will stimulate economic development.

Implementing social justice is a matter of utmost importance at this moment. Sociological survey data show that people are temporarily ready to accept inequality but not to accept unfairness. They agree that the ones who contribute labour, capital, or talent can have an easy life and others who do not will live poorly. But it is unacceptable to see one who is dishonestly trading, embezzling, or abusing power have special privileges and benefits and leading a luxurious overindulgent life, while the ones who work hard day and night still lead a poor life. This is the most difficult problem; if we can solve this problem it will bring about positive effects and encourage working people to boost economic growth.

It is not at all easy to implement the principle "same contribution - same benefit." Previously, most people lived in similar conditions. Although the majority of people agreed to put labour-based distribution into practice, many people, especially those with low-incomes, want to receive equal benefits. Even the managers want to average distributions in order to decrease complexity. This psychology is an obstacle for us in carrying out social justice. In the present situation, implementation of social justice demands a courageous attitude.

4

Social Justice in India

In India, justice is a human expression of a wider universal principle of nature and if man were entirely true to nature, his actions would be spontaneously just. Justice, in the sense of a distributive equity, is experienced by men in three major guises: as moral justice, social justice and legal justice. Each of these forms of justice is viewed as a particularization of the general principle of the universe seen as a total organism. From the broadest to narrowest conception, then, ancient Indian views on justice are inextricably bound up with a sense of economy. The operations of men and the universe itself involve the continual readjustment of particulars to fit the normative balance of the whole.

Human institutions of justice—the state, law, etc.—participate in this overall economy; but the belief has remained strong in India through the centuries that Nature, itself, is the ultimate and final arbiter of justice. Ultimately, justice is cosmic justice. This is to say that to the classical Indian culture the universe is essentially a moral universe. Nature is guided by principles which become translated into ethical terms in the individual and social lives of men. Of course, human life itself is seen as part of this natural process, having a bearing on the functioning of the whole, but not by any means dominating it.

Historical Background

Despite fairly frequent western impressions that India is a society that engulfs its individuals in its various collective units, the status, dignity and autonomy of the individual person have always been held in high value, if not in practice, most definitely in theory. Valorization of the significance of individual life begins with the earliest literature and becomes extremely prominent by the time of the early Upanisads (c. 600 B. C.). Viewing the natural world as an organic whole, all forms of life are seen as interrelated. The thrust of nature is evolutionary and teleological. A single individual may be incarnated at a number of different levels within the order of nature as he progresses (or retrogresses) on the evolutionary scale.

The ultimate perfection of life, moksȧ or spiritual emancipation, is achieved most usually only after the individual passes through a number of animal and human incarnations. The status of man is at the zenith of the chain of existences insofar as opportunity for realization of the final goal is concerned. Even gods and goddesses are "higher beings" only with respect to their greater longevity and power. The central ideal of classical Indian culture in both its orthodox and heterodox forms is decidedly anthropocentric.

A manifest individual is a temporary embodiment or apparent delimitation of the highest spiritual principle, whether this be called jiiva, nirvaa.na, aatman, brahman, puru.sa. et al. It is this principle which underlies universal life and burgeons forth in all the variety of nature. Within man alone, however, can this principle come to full consciousness and realization. Therefore, human life is not simply taken as a "given", but is conceived of as an opportunity to work towards, if not actually achieve, the ultimate teleological fruition.

Most Indian philosophical and religious traditions thus conceive of human status as relatively rare in the overall context of myriads of life forms, and accordingly, existence as a man is invested with seriousness and high purpose. The latter qualities are most apparent among professional religions, but as cultural phenomena they come to inform a broad range of Indian institutions usually regarded as secular, and influence the regulation of collective life.

The individual, then, and not the community is regarded as the locus of the highest spiritual value. Every individual, consciously or not, is on the path to the highest goal and is, therefore, an inviolable center of potential spiritual realization. It is this fundamental notion, cast in a variety of expressions, that becomes the matrix of the Indian sense of justice and of the institutions which embody it.

Man in ancient India could expect perfect equity as he interacted either consciously or unconsciously within his cosmic environment. As part of nature, as a natural power in his own right, the same economic principles of natural balance and normative harmony applied to man's moral behavior as they did to other functions of the universe. The destiny of the individual over a series of lifetimes was determined, as is well known, by the quality of his actions or deeds, by his karma. In the evolutionary process of liberation, man reaps what he sows, even to the extent that the extreme evil-doer can revert to sub-human levels of existence.

The retribution which karma entails has both empirical and non-empirical aspects. It is obviously empirical when catastrophe befalls the evil and honor the good within their present lifetimes. More usually, however, the operations of karma, like other laws of the universe are nonempirical. The evil man is reborn in a lower station in another existence and the good man in a higher.

However, retributive karma is also empirical in the sense that the present condition of the individual is conceived of as the totally inexorable and impersonally just result of his own behavior in past incarnations. This notion is reinforced through its early association with the var.na stratification of Indian society.

A Braahman at the apex of the four varnas was reaping the reward of his past lives. A `suudra, or member of the lowest varna, could be presumed morally as well as socially inferior to the Braahman due to his own past action. But looking forward to future lives, a suudra could hope to improve his position through righteous conduct now according to the dictates of his station. Thus the nearly universal Indian doctrine of karma was used simultaneously to demonstrate the complete moral equity or justice of the status quo as well as to, supply incentive for ethical behavior in hopes of self-advancement.

Self-responsibility for one's own position in society meant that the hierarchy of classes was itself regarded as a reflection of karmic justice. Social inequality is seen as equitable in that the rights and duties, the privileges and responsibilities of a particular class are envisioned as commensurate with the levels of spiritual and moral development of its individual members. Any system of rights and duties which did not take into account the actual differences between these individual levels of advancement on the path of evolution and which advocated indiscriminate equality would itself have been seen as unjust. The salvation of the individual lies in the quality of his performance at the level on which he finds himself. To expect all men to adhere to the same standard or to act in a manner beyond the capacities of their present

Justice in Society

Although man embodies the highest spiritual principle,

he is, nonetheless, embodied. This fact automatically involves the individual in relations with others and places him in an empirical social context which is conceived of as entirely natural and organic. As we have seen, both the fact and the quality of the individual's embodiment are seen as self-determined.

In the tenets of classical Hinduism, then, one's embodiment and one's station in social life according to the var.na classification are the just results of past events. The individual is the result of his past deeds over which he no longer has any control. Yet one's progress in the ladder of evolution is subject to conscious control in the present. A major institution of Indian society is designed around the possibility which exists for the individual to take the harmonious development of his own nature consciously into his own hands.

This institution is the well-known puru saartha-varnaasrama-dharma system, in which an ideal life-program is mapped out in terms of goals to be achieved and progressive stages in life in which they are to be pursued. The goals (Purusaartha) are moral, ethical and social rectitude (dharma), aesthetic and erotic gratification (kaama). material well-being and prosperity (artha) and most important, spiritual liberation and self-realization (moksa). In order to fulfill each of these goals in a balanced and harmonious progress, the Hindu is advised to divide his life into the four stages (aasrama) of the student (brahmacarya), householder (grhastha), forest-dweller (vaanaprastha) and renunciate (sannyaasa).

Like the Creek diakaiosynee of which Professor Manicas speaks, this arrangement of life involves a type of "psychic harmony" or personal order among what might otherwise be conflicting impulses and demands. The pursuit of the puru.saarthas through the aa`sramas is timed slightly differently according to considerations of var.na. Not only individual harmony but also the concepts of social ethics and interpersonal justice revolve around the right of individuals and groups to advance within the teleological structure without interference from their fellows. The ideal society envisioned by Indian sages is an association in which individuals respect and help one another to work out their respective spiritual destinies. In fact, the original condition of man in association with his fellows was seen as a Golden Age (kritayuga).

Legends of the origins of society and the state analogous to and anticipating those of Rousseau, Hobbes, Locke and others are ubiquitous in early Indian literature. These accounts, which bear distinct resemblances to the similar Greek theories in story form can be regarded as representing a culturally widespread substratum of the Indo-European heritage. In effect, the Indian myths of this sort are created more for morally didactic purposes, than as theories in any scientific sense, but this itself serves to indicate a distinctive Indian approach to personal ethics and social justice. In the Indian accounts both society and the state are seen, in an attitude similar to that of Plate's Republic, as both natural and necessary developments informed by an underlying idea of justice.

The sources for Indian ideas concerning the origins of society and the state are as old as Indian literature itself. Already in the Rig Veda are found germinal elements of later, more formal elaborations. The basic ideas are expanded to some extent in the Braahma.na books which follow. In the Aitareya and Taittiriiya Braahma.nas particularly, which can be dated conservatively at c. 700 B.C., there are rudimentary efforts to comment on the origin of the state and kingship in connection with certain rituals which are the main concern of this genre of literature. The Aitareya Braahmana contains what is perhaps the first adumbration of a contractual theory of kingship in the context of warfare between the Asuras ("Titans") and gods: "The gods said, 'Through our lack of a king they conquer us; let us make a king.' " Here the establishment of the state emanates from a social need for self-defense. Later in the same Braahmana.

Indra is elected ruler and consecrated in the Mahaabhisekara ceremony. Indra is chosen for his personal might. "The gods with Prajaapati said 'He is of gods the mightiest, the strongest, the most real, the best to accomplish; let us anoint him.'" Significantly, the ceremony entails ritual objects taken from species of the vegetable world which are deemed appropriate, due to their imputed sovereignty over others of their kind. The selection of a king is a natural human reflection of a hierarchy which already exists in the state of nature. This rudimentary contractual theory is developed and systematized after a fashion in the Paali scriptures of early Buddhism. These afford for the first time a direct view of the ideal of practical justice in the formation of the principal institutions of society and the state.

The principal Paali text, dating from c. 300 B.C., is the Agga~n~na Suttanta, number 27 of the Diigha Nikaaya. As the sutta opens, two novices of the Buddhist order, Braahmans by birth, complain of the opprobrium they have to endure from their fellow Braahmans as a result of their conversion to Buddhism. The Buddha himself takes the opportunity to enunciate a theory of social organization in which he repudiates the arrogant Braahman claims to superiority by dint of having been born from the mouth of the god Brahmaa, while other var.nas were born of lesser organs of the divinity.

The Buddha states quite simply that in their arrogance, the Braahmans have forgotten the origin of things and are born from their mothers' wombs like everyone else. In passing, then, the sutta intimates that the Buddha was quite familiar with such Brahmanical traditions as the creation and gradation of the var.nas which goes back to Hymn X, 90 of the Rig Veda. Although the puru.saarthas are not mentioned at all, the vaanaprastha and sannyaasa aa`sramas seem to be implied as part of the Buddha's awareness of his contemporary social scene.

The Buddha goes on to state that the claims of the Braahmans should not be taken seriously because according to the real teleological norm (dharma) of life, only those who have achieved spiritual liberation are "chief." Although couched in specific Buddhist terminology, the appeal to a cosmic standard as the guarantor of true justice is characteristically Indian. Having forgotten their true origins, continues the Buddha, the Braahmans no longer recall a time (analogous to the Krita Yuga of the Hindus), when all men dwelt in a "Shining World." In this original condition of things there were not the distinctions which apply today. "Beings were counted as beings only."

From this point. the Buddha proceeds to account for the serial appearance of social institutions based on social and economic developments which gradually produce a collective appeal for the administration of justice. The anthropologist can easily read into the figurative account of the sutta various typical stages in the gradual elaboration of the means of subsistence and production. At first man appears in the Golden Age or state of nature as a simple food-gatherer, with no sense of personal property whatsoever. The sutta under discussion and other Paali sources suggest that even the basic institutions of marriage and the family had not yet developed.

Various stages in food-gathering are described until at one point of great moment the process of the domestication of rice begins. At first the rice is simply discovered and gathered as it is needed. In terms of the sutta legend, the Golden Age has not passed entirely, and the rice picked in the evening grows back in the morning without the necessity of cultivation.

The sutta suggests that at this stage men develop a proprietary interest in certain women and a new need for privacy is felt. Together with the growth of the family comes a tendency to harvest more rice than is necessary for immediate use, and the practice of hoarding comes into being. No longer does the rice magically reappear soon after reaping; the natural supply is no longer sufficient for the increased demands brought abut by the new institution of storage. This development sets the stage for the major tarnishing of the Golden Age, viz., the division of the rice fields as private property. Almost automatically, the establishment of private property leads to its violation, and theft becomes commonplace. At first the sutta suggests that the people themselves collectively punish the perpetrators. Society is already organized and can take effective, if inefficient, action on its own behalf.

Finally the situation becomes increasingly severe and the decision is made to administrate the new social sense of equity and justice based on the institutions of family and private property. The person who is elected to be the first king is to be released from the obligation of earning his own living so that he may devote full-time attention to ensuring that others may safely enjoy the fruits of their own labor in a just manner. The king himself is to be supported by the people through contributions of a proportion of their rice. Significantly, especially in relationship to the comments of Professor Manicas' essay, the institutionalization of justice begins only when men rise above the level of daily subsistence and mutually agree to protect the newly found opportunities for personal wealth.

The institution of monarchy gives rise to a "circle of nobles or ksatriyas" (khattiyamandalassa). The Pali word khattiya is even given a fanciful derivation from "khettaanampati" or "lord of the fields" to emphasize the origin of this class of Indian society as protectors of the rights of others once the ownership of private property has been established. The sutta continues with summary descriptions of the origins of the Braahmans as contemplative and religious teachers, of the vai`syas as tradespeople and of the suudras as hunters.

Although the avowed purpose of the Buddha in this dialogue is to demonstrate the original unity of mankind in a Golden Age and also that the social classes arose on the basis of intercooperative function presumably for the benefit of all, even this most liberal of Indian thinkers cannot avoid the interjection of the view that social status, whatever its origins in terms of practical social justice, is also a reflection of individual karmic justice: the sutra closes with a description of the good or bad destinies to which each of the four var.nas is subject on the basis of karmically determinative activity in deed, word or thought.

The ultimate justice is moral and based on natural law; it is not merely an economic convenience. Although the early Buddhists valued moral worth over considerations of caste, rank and wealth, they did not openly militate against the caste system. On the one hand, the legend denies ' the Brahmanical tendency to see the social order as a divine creation, and instead suggests, empirically and rationally, that it is originated out of nothing more exalted than an expedient human concern for justice and protection.

On the other hand, although the legend points out the original undifferentiated (and essential?) equality of all men, it seems that the Buddha implicitly accepts the existence of the four var.nas and implicitly regards the status of rebirth in the hierarchy of var.nas as due to karmic fruition, whether good or bad. However, as the founder of a monastic order, the Buddha has only passing interest in artha, even less in kaama, and addresses himself mainly to the goals of dharma and mok.sa. Being an ascetic he tends to disavow the necessity of gradual progress through the aa`sramas, the doctrine which becomes orthodox in Hinduism, and offers the extra-social alternative of immediate monkshood to members of any and all var.nas.

For the Buddhists, anyone was eligible to drop the concerns of society in an effort to extirpate the conditioning effects of karma altogether, devoting full-time to the realization of the normative teleological goal of nirvaa.na. Thus the early Buddhists were emphatic in their assertion of the equality of all in the context of the extra-social pursuit of the highest spiritual value while, at the same time, not denying social distinctions or their justice as the norm of everyday human association. Indeed, from this point on in Indian social theorizing, economic and social rights are conceived in both orthodox and heterodox schools of thought as inextricably bound up with individual moral and spiritual status.

One of the earliest extant evidences of a developed Brahmanical exposition of the social contract theory is the Arthasaastra attributed to Kautilya. The finished work as it has come down to us probably dates back no further than the Third Century A.D. However, it contains materials which presumably go back to the Kau.tilya who reputedly was minister to King Candragupta Maurya in the Fourth Century B.C., and beyond to other Artha`saastra literature incorporated by Kautilya, but now lost. Kautilya outlines essentially a similar process of increasing anarchy as does the Buddha, a process which leads to the election of the first king Manu Varvasibata in the interests of justice.

Justice and the Role of Law

The ancient Indians were not only idealists but also realists and pragmatists. They were fully aware that the official world-view and the actual ethos of men do not always, in fact, correspond with each other. Even if justice and harmony were spontaneous in the K.rta Yuga, it was unreasonable to expect that they would remain so in the Kali Yuga, the present age of decadence. Therefore the state performed its duty of protection of society and the individual through coercive enforcement of the standards of justice, which are reduced for the purpose into the minutiae of positive law (vyavahaara). Early codes of law, covering every aspect of life, are preserved in the voluminous Dharmasuutra and Dharma`saastra literature, of which perhaps the Maanavadharma`saastra or Laws of Manu is the most well-known.

The books do not betray any overblown estimation of the goodness of men. Their attitude is fully attuned to the actuality of man's frequent failure to act from a sense of his own best interest, and to his frequent total disregard for the karmic repercussions of his deeds. Yet it remains the duty of the state to use coercion to effect adherence to legal statutes which themselves are more or less explicitly directed to maintenance of justice for all and the moral welfare of the individual. As indicated at the end of the last section, through practical law-enforcement the state must actually seek to controvert the ignorance of those men in society who remain unaware or unconvinced of the very purposes for which they themselves, the state, and society exist.

Accordingly, the traditional Indian king has been invested with da.n.da,"the scepter," a symbol of the power and authority of the state which rules inexorably by law and punishment. The practical necessity of da.n.da in the administration of justice in the Kali Yuga is considered a further outgrowth of the ongoing degeneration of the times which, as we have seen, was responsible for the institution of the state in the first place. Manu, as a realist, insists in his discussion of the role of the king that if he does not " . . . inflict punishment on those worthy to be punished, the stronger would roast the weaker like fish on a spit ... " "Having fully considered the time and the place (of the offence), the strength and knowledge (of the offender), let him justly inflict that punishment on men who act unjustly," (Italics mine.) The exercise of the coercive power of da.n.da with regard to law-enforcement is considered just in the highest sense, since particularistic legal codes are considered to be concrete and detailed embodiments of the more abstract and exalted principles of justice (e.g. .rita, dharma) which are fundamental to the cosmos.

The administration of legal justice and redressive punishment was not performed mechanically or indiscriminately without respect for persons, however. Even here the informing vision of man on an evolutionary and hierarchical path to the realization of the highest spiritual value holds full sway and brings us back to our point of departure. Men did not stand as equals before the law. A hypothetical suggestion to the effect that men were equal before the law would. most likely, have been dismissed as unjust. Justice was not blind in ancient India.

Insofar as the varna hierarchy indicated karmic retribution or reward for lifetimes, it was considered only natural to take varna into account in the administration of legal justice. The italicized portion of the above quotation from Manu indicates that the king, acting as judge. should consider "the strength and knowledge" of the defendant. His strength and knowledge are estimated as functions of his var.na. Legal consideration of var.na rank has two main outcomes, one having to do with responsibility, the other with privilege, and one concerning the perpetrators of crime. the other its victims.

In the latter case crimes against persons were adjudicated with reference to the class-status of the victim. Here is reflected. perhaps, some of the Brahmanical hauteur decried by the novices in the Buddhist legend already discussed. The penalty for a crime was increasingly severe the higher the varna of the victim.

For example. in the Dharmasuutras of Baudhaayana and Aapastamba it is stated that the expiatory fine for murdering a ksatriya is a thousand cows and one bull. while that for a suudra is only ten cows and a bull. A similar prescription is recorded in Manu. Yet it should he remembered that what may appear to us as a crass. arrogant and arbitrary assignment of value to human life on the basis of birth and social rank is, in the context of ancient Indian society, another reflection of the assumption of differing and karmically self-determined stages on the ladder of advancement towards the ultimate value.

The same underlying idea is reflected more positively in the legal administration of Indian justice through the notion that the more elevated a man is in terms of var.na, the more responsibility he should bear for his misdeeds. If var.na is determined karmically, then those at the top of the hierarchy should be expected to be morally superior. They were, in fact, considered ritually purer, more knowledgeable and closer to the final enlightenment and beatitude. Their behavior should reflect the long process of spiritual and moral development implied by their higher varna status. This is reflected in law as the requirement of a greater penalty for those of higher station and a milder punishment for the more lowly.

Thus Manu says: When another common man would be fined one kaarshaapana, the king shall be fined one thousand; that is the settled rule. In (a case of) theft the guilt of a `Suudra shall. be eight-fold, that of a Vaisya sixteenfold, that of a Kshatriya two-and-thirtyfold, that of a Braahma.na sixty-fourfold, or quite a hundredfold, or (even) twice four-and-sixtyfold; (each of them) knowing the nature of the offence.

It is only just in this scheme of things that more in the way of a penalty should be expected of those with greater moral capabilities, and who should be expected to know better, while less should be required of those less advanced on the path.

In short, then, we have seen that the varnaasrama dharma system so frequently decried as a form of virtual enslavement especially in some of its modern forms, in classical times was officially regarded as an instrument of both social cooperation and individual emancipation. By following the duty (svadharma) of one's var.na which was clearly detailed in books of law and subject to the just administration of the state, one actually attained the necessary liberty to engage in the universal spiritual quest. Tara Chand describes the intention behind varna as follows:

Society's organization and functioning are so devised as to enable the individual to fulfill his function as an individual - a free spirit associated with the whole apparatus of mental, biological, and rational substructures. This plan contemplates the maximum automatization of the activities of the inferior part so that the maximum opportunity may be available for the consummation of the free self.

One of the chief duties of the king is the maintenance and protection of the var.na system through his power of danda.This is so and the king is obeyed because it is realized that var.na and the state are necessary aids to the achievement of the final goal of life. Stemming from the moral conception of the universe and the axiom of the individual's destiny to self-realization, the ethical, social, state and legal distinctions of ancient India are firmly based on an ideal of equity and justice expressed in terms of natural hierarchy rather than of equality.

SOCIAL JUSTICE AND INDIA'S CONSTITUTION

The Constitution of India makes it clear what kind of a nation we are, highlighting our shared past and shared destiny. Our national commitment is to the values that denote the 'Basic Structure' of our Constitution, as visualised in its Preamble. The success or otherwise, the suitability, viability and justification of any government has to be judged by its readiness to achieve and success in achieving the goals of the Preamble. That is the best guarantee for the nation-building.

Acceptance of the existence of cultural pluralism is an acceptance of the existence of a liberal democracy. It is a realisation that, in a liberal democracy, none of the social groups should have any reason to feel disadvantaged because of any cultural differences. The Constitution of India ensures that, on the one hand, no group is discriminated or disadvantaged and, on the other, that each such group may preserve the identities peculiar to itself.

A dialogue between different identities strengthens their own positions because all of them enjoy similar positions under the Constitution and all of them face similar problems in a democratic plural society. If a dialogue and understanding is there, domination and deprivation are ruled out. A plural society is in greater need of an institutional understanding and consensus over the basic values, of the society, under state protection. This guarantee of protection, for the accepted Indian national values, is provided by the Constitution of India. It is the constitutional restructuring of social relations that has ensured equality among our various identities, basing our pluralism on social equality.

The constitution of India draws extensively from Western legal traditions in its outline of the principles of liberal democracy. It is distinguished from many Western constitutions, however, in its elaboration of principles reflecting the aspirations to end the inequities of traditional social relations and enhance the social welfare of the population. According to constitutional scholar Granville Austin, probably no other nation's constitution "has provided so much impetus toward changing and rebuilding society for the common good." Since its enactment, the constitution has fostered a steady concentration of power in the central government—especially the Office of the Prime Minister.

This centralization has occurred in the face of the increasing assertiveness of an array of ethnic and caste groups across Indian society. Increasingly, the government has responded to the resulting tensions by resorting to the formidable array of authoritarian powers provided by the constitution. Together with the public's perception of pervasive corruption among India's politicians, the state's centralization of authority and increasing resort to coercive power have eroded its legitimacy. However, a new assertiveness shown by the Supreme Court and the Election Commission suggests that the remaining checks and balances among the country's political institutions continue to support the resilience of Indian democracy.

Adopted after some two and one-half years of deliberation by the Constituent Assembly that also acted as India's first legislature, the constitution was put into effect on January 26, 1950. Bhimrao Ramji (B.R.) Ambedkar, a Dalit who earned a law degree from Columbia University, chaired the drafting committee of the constitution and shepherded it through Constituent Assembly debates. Supporters of independent India's founding father, Mohandas Karamchand (Mahatma) Gandhi, backed measures that would form a decentralized polity with strong local administration—known as panchayat—in a system known as panchayati raj , that is rule by panchayats. However, the support of more modernist leaders, such as Jawaharlal Nehru, ultimately led to a parliamentary government and a federal system with a strong central government.

Following a British parliamentary pattern, the constitution embodies the Fundamental Rights, which are similar to the United States Bill of Rights, and a Supreme Court similar to that of the United States. It creates a "sovereign democratic republic" called India, or Bharat (after the legendary king of the Mahabharata), which "shall be a Union of States." India is a federal system in which residual powers of legislation remain with the central government, similar to that in Canada. The constitution provides detailed lists dividing up powers between central and state governments as in Australia, and it elaborates a set of Directive Principles of State Policy as does the Irish constitution.

The 395 articles and ten appendixes, known as schedules, in the constitution make it one of the longest and most detailed in the world. Schedules can be added to the constitution by amendment. The ten schedules in force cover the designations of the states and union territories; the emoluments for high-level officials; forms of oaths; allocation of the number of seats in the Rajya Sabha (Council of States—the upper house of Parliament) per state or territory; provisions for the administration and control of Scheduled Areas and Scheduled Tribes; provisions for the administration of tribal areas in Assam; the union (meaning central government), state, and concurrent (dual) lists of responsibilities; the official languages; land and tenure reforms; and the association of Sikkim with India.

The Indian constitution is also one of the most frequently amended constitutions in the world. The first amendment came only a year after the adoption of the constitution and instituted numerous minor changes. Many more amendments followed, and through June 1995 the constitution had been amended seventy-seven times, a rate of almost two amendments per year since 1950. Most of the constitution can be amended after a quorum of more than half of the members of each house in Parliament passes an amendment with a two-thirds majority vote. Articles pertaining to the distribution of legislative authority between the central and state governments must also be approved by 50 percent of the state legislatures.

Fundamental Rights

The Fundamental Rights embodied in the constitution are guaranteed to all citizens. These civil liberties take precedence over any other law of the land. They include individual rights common to most liberal democracies, such as equality before the law, freedom of speech and expression, freedom of association and peaceful assembly, freedom of religion, and the right to constitutional remedies for the protection of civil rights such as habeas corpus. In addition, the Fundamental Rights are aimed at overturning the inequities of past social practices. They abolish "untouchability"; prohibit discrimination on the grounds of religion, race, caste, sex, or place of birth; and forbid traffic in human beings and forced labor. They go beyond conventional civil liberties in protecting cultural and educational rights of minorities by ensuring that minorities may preserve their distinctive languages and establish and administer their own education institutions.

Originally, the right to property was also included in the Fundamental Rights; however, the Forty-fourth Amendment, passed in 1978, revised the status of property rights by stating that "No person shall be deprived of his property save by authority of law." Freedom of speech and expression, generally interpreted to include freedom of the press, can be limited "in the interests of the sovereignty and integrity of India, the security of the State, friendly relations with foreign States, public order, decency or morality, or in relation to contempt of court, defamation or incitement to an offence".

Directive Principles of State Policy

An important feature of the constitution is the Directive Principles of State Policy. Although the Directive Principles are asserted to be "fundamental in the governance of the country," they are not legally enforceable. Instead, they are guidelines for creating a social order characterized by social, economic, and political justice, liberty, equality, and fraternity as enunciated in the constitution's preamble.

In some cases, the Directive Principles articulate goals that, however admirable, remain vague platitudes, such as the injunctions that the state "shall direct its policy towards securing . . . that the ownership and control of the material resources of the community are so distributed to subserve the common good" and "endeavor to promote international peace and security." In other areas, the Directive Principles provide more specific policy objectives. They exhort the state to secure work at a living wage for all citizens; take steps to encourage worker participation in industrial management; provide for just and humane conditions of work, including maternity leave; and promote the educational and economic interests of Scheduled Castes, Scheduled Tribes, and other disadvantaged sectors of society. The Directive Principles also charge the state with the responsibility for providing free and compulsory education for children up to age fourteen.

The Directive Principles also urge the nation to develop a uniform civil code and offer free legal aid to all citizens. They urge measures to maintain the separation of the judiciary from the executive and direct the government to organize village panchayats to function as units of self-government. This latter objective was advanced by the Seventy-third Amendment and the Seventy-fourth Amendment in December 1992. The Directive Principles also order that India should endeavor to protect and improve the environment and protect monuments and places of historical interest.

The Forty-second Amendment, which came into force in January 1977, attempted to raise the status of the Directive Principles by stating that no law implementing any of the Directive Principles could be declared unconstitutional on the grounds that it violated any of the Fundamental Rights.

The amendment simultaneously stated that laws prohibiting "antinational activities" or the formation of "antinational associations" could not be invalidated because they infringed on any of the Fundamental Rights. It added a new section to the constitution on "Fundamental Duties" that enjoined citizens "to promote harmony and the spirit of common brotherhood among all the people of India, transcending religious, linguistic and regional or sectional diversities."

However, the amendment reflected a new emphasis in governing circles on order and discipline to counteract what some leaders had come to perceive as the excessively freewheeling style of Indian democracy. After the March 1977 general election ended the control of the Congress (Congress (R) from 1969) over the executive and legislature for the first time since independence in 1947, the new Janata-dominated Parliament passed the Forty-third Amendment (1977) and Forty-fourth Amendment (1978). These amendments revoked the Forty-second Amendment's provision that Directive Principles take precedence over Fundamental Rights and also curbed Parliament's power to legislate against "antinational activities".

Group Rights

In addition to stressing the right of individuals as citizens, Part XVI of the constitution endeavors to promote social justice by elaborating a series of affirmative-action measures for disadvantaged groups. These "Special Provisions Relating to Certain Classes" include the reservation of seats in the Lok Sabha (House of the People) and in state legislative bodies for members of Scheduled Castes and Scheduled Tribes. The number of seats set aside for them is proportional to their share of the national and respective state populations.

Part XVI also reserves some government appointments for these disadvantaged groups insofar as they do not interfere with administrative efficiency. The section stipulates that a special officer for Scheduled Castes and Scheduled Tribes be appointed by the president to "investigate all matters relating to the safeguards provided" for them, as well as periodic commissions to investigate the conditions of the Backward Classes. The president, in consultation with state governors, designates those groups that meet the criteria of Scheduled Castes and Scheduled Tribes. Similar protections exist for the small Anglo-Indian community.

The framers of the constitution provided that the special provisions would cease twenty years after the promulgation of the constitution, anticipating that the progress of the disadvantaged groups during that time would have removed significant disparities between them and other groups in society. However, in 1969 the Twenty-third Amendment extended the affirmative-action measures until 1980. The Forty-fifth Amendment of 1980 extended them again until 1990, and in 1989 the Sixty-second Amendment extended the provisions until 2000. The Seventy-seventh Amendment of 1995 further strengthened the states' authority to reserve government-service positions for Scheduled Caste and Scheduled Tribe members.

Emergency Provisions and Authoritarian Powers

Part XVIII of the constitution permits the state to suspend various civil liberties and the application of certain federal principles during presidentially proclaimed states of emergency. The constitution provides for three categories of emergencies: a threat by "war or external aggression" or by "internal disturbances"; a "failure of constitutional machinery" in the country or in a state; and a threat to the financial security or credit of the nation or a part of it. Under the first two categories, the Fundamental Rights, with the exception of protection of life and personal liberty, may be suspended, and federal principles may be rendered inoperative.

A proclamation of a state of emergency lapses after two months if not approved by both houses of Parliament. The president can issue a proclamation dissolving a state government if it can be determined, upon receipt of a report from a governor, that circumstances prevent the government of that state from maintaining law and order according to the constitution. This action establishes what is known as President's Rule because under such a proclamation the president can assume any or all functions of the state government; transfer the powers of the state legislature to Parliament; or take other measures necessary to achieve the objectives of the proclamation, including suspension, in whole or in part, of the constitution.

A proclamation of President's Rule cannot interfere with the exercise of authority by the state's high court. Once approved, President's Rule normally lasts for six months, but it may be extended up to one year if Parliament approves. In exceptional cases, such as the violent revolt in Jammu and Kashmir during the early and mid-1990s, President's Rule has lasted for a period of more than five years.

President's Rule has been imposed frequently, and its use is often politically motivated. During the terms of prime ministers Nehru and Lal Bahadur Shastri, from 1947 to 1966, it was imposed ten times. Under Indira Gandhi's two tenures as prime minister (1966-77 and 1980-84), President's Rule was imposed forty-one times. Despite Mrs. Gandhi's frequent use of President's Rule, she was in office longer (187 months) than any other prime minister except Nehru (201 months). Other prime ministers also have been frequent users: Morarji Desai (eleven times in twenty-eight months), Chaudhury Charan Singh (five times in less than six months), Rajiv Gandhi (eight times in sixty-one months), Vishwanath Pratap (V.P.) Singh (two times in eleven months), Chandra Shekhar (four times in seven months), and P.V. Narasimha Rao (nine times in his first forty-two months in office).

State of emergency proclamations have been issued three times since independence. The first was in 1962 during the border war with China. Another was declared in 1971 when India went to war against Pakistan over the independence of East Pakistan, which became Bangladesh. In 1975 the third Emergency was imposed in response to an alledged threat by "internal disturbances" stemming from the political opposition to Indira Gandhi.

The Indian state has authoritarian powers in addition to the constitution's provisions for proclamations of Emergency Rule and President's Rule. The Preventive Detention Act was passed in 1950 and remained in force until 1970. Shortly after the start of the Emergency in 1962, the government enacted the Defence of India Act. This legislation created the Defence of India Rules, which allow for preventive detention of individuals who have acted or who are likely to act in a manner detrimental to public order and national security. The Defence of India Rules were reimposed during the 1971 war with Pakistan; they remained in effect after the end of the war and were invoked for a variety of uses not intended by their framers, such as the arrests made during a nationwide railroad strike in 1974.

The Maintenance of Internal Security Act promulgated in 1971 also provides for preventive detention. During the 1975-77 Emergency, the act was amended to allow the government to arrest individuals without specifying charges. The government arrested tens of thousands of opposition politicians under the Defence of India Rules and the Maintenance of Internal Security Act, including most of the leaders of the future Janata Party government.

Shortly after the Janata government came to power in 1977, Parliament passed the Forty-fourth Amendment, which revised the domestic circumstances cited in Article 352 as justifying an emergency from "internal disturbance" to "armed rebellion." During Janata rule, Parliament also repealed the Defence of India Rules and the Maintenance of Internal Security Act. However, after the Congress (I) returned to power in 1980, Parliament passed the National Security Act authorizing security forces to arrest individuals without warrant for suspicion of action that subverts national security, public order, and essential economic services. The Essential Services Maintenance Act of 1981 permits the government to prohibit strikes and lockouts in sixteen economic sectors providing critical goods and services. The Fifty-ninth Amendment, passed in 1988, restored "internal disturbance" in place of "armed rebellion" as just cause for the proclamation of an emergency.

The Sikh militant movement that spread through Punjab during the 1980s spurred additional authoritarian legislation. In 1984 Parliament passed the National Security Amendment Act enabling government security forces to detain prisoners for up to one year. The 1984 Terrorist Affected Areas (Special Courts) Ordinance provided security forces in Punjab with unprecedented powers of detention, and it authorized secret tribunals to try suspected terrorists.

The 1985 Terrorist and Disruptive Activities (Prevention) Act imposed the death penalty for anyone convicted of terrorist actions that led to the death of others. It empowered authorities to tap telephones, censor mail, and conduct raids when individuals are alleged to pose a threat to the unity and sovereignty of the nation. The legislation renewing the act in 1987 provided for in camera trials, which may be presided over by any central government officer, and reversed the legal presumption of innocence if the government produces specific evidence linking a suspect to a terrorist act. In March 1988, the Fifty-ninth Amendment increased the period that an emergency can be in effect without legislative approval from six months to three years, and it eliminated the assurance of due process and protection of life and liberty with regard to Punjab found in articles 20 and 21. These rights were restored in 1989 by the Sixty-third Amendment.

Structure of Government

The union government, as India's central government is known, is divided into three distinct but interrelated branches: legislative, executive, and judicial. As in the British parliamentary model, the leadership of the executive is drawn from and responsible to the legislative body. Although Article 50 stipulates the separation of the judiciary from the executive, the executive controls judicial appointments and many of the conditions of work. In addition, one of the more dramatic institutional battles in the Indian polity has been the struggle between elements wanting to assert legislative power to amend the constitution and those favoring the judiciary's efforts to preserve the constitution's basic structure.

The Legislature

Parliament consists of a bicameral legislature, the Lok Sabha (House of the People—the lower house) and the Rajya Sabha (Council of States—the upper house). Parliament's principal function is to pass laws on those matters that the constitution specifies to be within its jurisdiction. Among its constitutional powers are approval and removal of members of the Council of Ministers, amendment of the constitution, approval of central government finances, and delimitation of state and union territory boundaries.

The president has a specific authority with respect to the function of the legislative branch. The president is authorized to convene Parliament and must give his assent to all parliamentary bills before they become law. The president is empowered to summon Parliament to meet, to address either house or both houses together, and to require attendance of all of its members. The president also may send messages to either house with respect to a pending bill or any other matter. The president addresses the first session of Parliament each year and must give assent to all provisions in bills passed.

Lok Sabha

The Lok Sabha in 1995 constitutionally had 545 seats. For a variety of reasons, elections are sometimes not held in all constitutiencies, leaving some seats vacant and giving the appearance of fewer seats in the lower house. A member must be at least twenty-five years of age. Two members are nominated by the president as representatives of the Anglo-Indian community, and the rest are popularly elected. Elections are held on a one-stage, "first-past-the-post" system, similar to that in the United States. As in the United States, candidates from larger parties are favored because each constituency elects only the candidate winning the most votes.

In the context of multiple-candidate elections, most members of Parliament are elected with pluralities of the vote that amount to less than a majority. As a result, political parties can gain commanding positions in the Parliament without winning the support of a majority of the electorate. For instance, Congress has dominated Indian politics without ever winning a majority of votes in parliamentary elections. The best-ever Congress performance in parliamentary elections was in 1984 when Congress (I) won 48 percent of the vote and garnered 76 percent of the parliamentary seats. In the 1991 elections, Congress (I) won 37.6 percent of the vote and 42 percent of the seats.

The usual Lok Sabha term is five years. However, the president may dissolve the house and call for new elections should the government lose its majority in Parliament. Elections must be held within six months after Parliament is dissolved. The prime minister can choose electorally advantageous times to recommend the dissolution of Parliament to the president in an effort to maximize support in the next Parliament.

The term of Parliament can be extended in yearly increments if an emergency has been proclaimed. This situation occurred in 1976 when Parliament was extended beyond its five-year term under the Emergency proclaimed the previous year. The constitution stipulates that the Lok Sabha must meet at least twice a year, and no more than six months can pass between sessions. The Lok Sabha customarily meets for three sessions a year. The Council of Ministers is responsible only to the Lok Sabha, and the authority to initiate financial legislation is vested exclusively in the Lok Sabha.

The powers and authority of the Lok Sabha and the Rajya Sabha are not differentiated. The index of the constitution, for example, has a lengthy list of the powers of Parliament but not for each separate house. The key differences between the two houses lie in their disparate authority in the legislative process.

Rajya Sabha

The Rajya Sabha has a maximum of 250 members. All but twelve are elected by state and territory legislatures for six-year terms. Members must be at least thirty years old. The president nominates up to twelve members on the basis of their special knowledge or practical experience in fields such as literature, science, art, and social service. No further approval of these nominations is required by Parliament. Elections are staggered so that one-third of the members are elected every two years. The number of seats allocated to each state and territory is determined on the basis of relative population, except that smaller states and territories are awarded a larger share than their population justifies.

The Rajya Sabha meets in continuous session. It is not subject to dissolution as is the Lok Sabha. The Rajya Sabha is designed to provide stability and continuity to the legislative process. Although considered the upper house, its authority in the legislative process is subordinate to that of the Lok Sabha.

Legislative Process

The initiative for substantial legislation comes primarily from the prime minister, cabinet members, and high-level officials. Although all legislation except financial bills can be introduced in either house, most laws originate in the Lok Sabha. A legislative proposal may go through three readings before it is voted on. After a bill has been passed by the originating house, it is sent to the other house, where it is debated and voted on. The second house can accept, reject, or amend the bill. If the bill is amended by the second house, it must be returned to the originating house in its amended form. If a bill is rejected by the second house, if there is disagreement about the proposed amendments, or if the second house fails to act on a bill for six months, the president is authorized to summon a joint session of Parliament to vote on the bill. Disagreements are resolved by a majority vote of the members of both houses present in a joint session. This procedure favors the Lok Sabha because it has more than twice as many members as the Rajya Sabha.

When the bill has been passed by both houses, it is sent to the president, who can refuse assent and send the bill back to Parliament for reconsideration. If both houses pass it again, with or without amendments, it is sent to the president a second time. The president is then obliged to assent to the legislation. After receiving the president's assent, a bill becomes an act on the statute book. The legislative procedure for bills involving taxing and spending--known as money bills—is different from the procedure for other legislation. Money bills can be introduced only in the Lok Sabha. After the Lok Sabha passes a money bill, it is sent to the Rajya Sabha.

The upper house has fourteen days to act on the bill. If the Rajya Sabha fails to act within fourteen days, the bill becomes law. The Rajya Sabha may send an amended version of the bill back to the Lok Sabha, but the latter is not bound to accept these changes. It may pass the original bill again, at which point it will be sent to the president for his signature. During the 1950s and part of the 1960s, Parliament was often the scene of articulate debate and substantial revisions of legislation. Prime ministers Indira Gandhi, Rajiv Gandhi, and P.V. Narasimha Rao, however, showed little enthusiasm for parliamentary debate. During the 1975-77 Emergency, many members of Parliament from the opposition as well as dissidents within Indira's own party were arrested, and press coverage of legislative proceedings was censored. It is generally agreed that the quality of discourse and the expertise of members of Parliament have declined since the 1960s. An effort to halt the decline of Parliament through a reformed committee system giving Parliament new powers of oversight over the executive branch has had very limited impact.

Under the constitution, the division of powers between the union government and the states is delimited into three lists: the Union List, the State List, and the Concurrent List. Parliament has exclusive authority to legislate on any of the ninety-seven items on the Union List. The list includes banking, communications, defense, foreign affairs, interstate commerce, and transportation. The State List includes sixty-seven items that are under the exclusive jurisdiction of state legislatures, including agriculture, local government, police, public health, public order, and trade and commerce within the state.

The central-or union-government and state governments exercise concurrent jurisdiction over forty-four items on the Concurrent List, including criminal law and procedure, economic and social planning, electricity, factories, marriage and divorce, price control, social security and social insurance, and trade unions. The purpose of the Concurrent List is to secure legal and administrative unity throughout the country. Laws passed by Parliament relevant to Concurrent List areas take precedence over laws passed by state legislatures.

The Executive

The executive branch is headed by the president, in whom

the constitution vests a formidable array of powers. The president serves as head of state and the supreme commander of the armed forces. The president appoints the prime minister, cabinet members, governors of states and territories, Supreme Court and high court justices, and ambassadors and other diplomatic representatives. The president is also authorized to issue ordinances with the force of acts of Parliament when Parliament is not in session. The president can summon and prorogue Parliament as well as dissolve the Lok Sabha and call for new elections. The president also can dismiss state and territory governments.

Exercise of these impressive powers has been restricted by the convention that the president acts on the advice of the prime minister. In 1976 the Forty-second Amendment formally required the president to act according to the advice of the Council of Ministers headed by the prime minister. The spirit of the arrangement is reflected in Ambedkar's statement that the president "is head of the State but not of the Executive. He represents the nation but does not rule the nation." In practice, the president's role is predominantly symbolic and ceremonial, roughly analogous to the president of Germany or the British monarch.

The president is elected for a five-year term by an electoral college consisting of the elected members of both houses of Parliament and the elected members of the legislative assemblies of the states and territories. The participation of state and territory assemblies in the election is designed to ensure that the president is chosen to head the nation and not merely the majority party in Parliament, thereby placing the office above politics and making the incumbent a symbol of national unity.

Despite the strict constraints placed on presidential authority, presidential elections have shaped the course of Indian politics on several occasions, and presidents have exercised important power, especially when no party has a clear parliamentary majority. The presidential election of 1969, for example, turned into a dramatic test of strength for rival factions when Prime Minister Indira Gandhi put up an opponent to the official Congress candidate. The electoral contest contributed to the subsequent split of the Congress. In 1979, after the Ja-nata Party began to splinter, President Neelam Sanjiva Reddy (1977-82) first selected Janata member Chaudhury Charan Singh as prime minister (1979-80) to form a minority government and then dissolved Parliament and called for new elections while ignoring Jagjivan Ram's claim that he could assemble a stable government and become the country's first Scheduled Caste prime minister.

Tensions between President Giani Zail Singh (1982-87) and Prime Minister Rajiv Gandhi (1984-88) also illustrate the potential power of the president. In 1987 Singh refused to sign the Indian Post Office (Amendment) Bill, thereby preventing the government from having the authority to censor personal mail. Singh's public suggestion that the prime minister had not treated the office of the president with proper dignity and the persistent rumors that Singh was plotting the prime minister's ouster contributed to the erosion of public confidence in Rajiv Gandhi that ultimately led to his defeat in the 1989 elections. In November 1990, President Ramaswami Venkataraman (1987-92) selected Chandra Shekhar as India's eleventh prime minister, even though Chandra Shekhar's splinter Samajwadi Janata Dal held only fifty-eight seats in the Lok Sabha. Chandra Shekhar resigned in June 1991 when the Congress (I) withdrew its support.

In the same manner as the president, the vice president is elected by the electoral college for a five-year term. The vice president is ex officio chairman of the Rajya Sabha and acts as president when the latter is unable to discharge his duties because of absence, illness, or any other reason or until a new president can be elected (within six months of the vacancy) when a vacancy occurs because of death, resignation, or removal. There have been three instances since 1969 of the vice president serving as acting president.

The prime minister is by far the most powerful figure in the government. After being selected by the president, typically from the party that commands the plurality of seats in Parliament, the prime minister selects the Council of Ministers from other members of Parliament who are then appointed by the president. Individuals who are not members of Parliament may be appointed to the Council of Ministers if they become a member of Parliament either through election or appointment within six months of selection.

The Council of Ministers is composed of cabinet ministers (numbering seventeen, representing thirty-one portfolios in 1995), ministers of state (forty-five, representing fifty-three portfolios in 1995), and deputy ministers (the number varies). Cabinet members are selected to accommodate different regional groups, castes, and factions within the ruling party or coalition as well as with an eye to their administrative skills and experience. Prime ministers frequently retain key ministerial portfolios for themselves.

Although the Council of Ministers is formally the highest policy-making body in the government, its powers have declined as influence has been increasingly centralized in the Office of the Prime Minister, which is composed of the top-ranking administrative staff. After the Congress split to form the Congress (R)—R for Requisition—and the Congress (O)—O for Organisation--in 1969, Indira Gandhi (who headed the Congress (R)) increasingly concentrated decision-making authority in the Office of the Prime Minister. When Rajiv Gandhi became prime minister in 1984, he promised to delegate more authority to his cabinet members. However, power rapidly shifted back to the Office of the Prime Minister and a small coterie of Rajiv's personal advisers. Rajiv's dissatisfaction with his cabinet ministers became manifest in his incessant reshuffling of his cabinet. During his five years in office, he changed his cabinet thirty-six times, about once every seven weeks.

When P.V. Narasimha Rao became prime minister in June 1991, he decentralized power, giving Minister of Finance Manmohan Singh, in particular, a large measure of autonomy to develop a program for economic reform. After a year in office, Rao began again to centralize authority, and by the end of 1994, the Office of the Prime Minister had grown to be as powerful as it ever was under Rao's predecessors. As of August 1995, Rao himself held the portfolios in thirteen ministries, including those of defense, industry, and Kashmir affairs.

The Judiciary

Supreme Court

The Supreme Court is the ultimate interpreter of the constitution and the laws of the land. It has appellate jurisdiction over all civil and criminal proceedings involving substantial issues concerning the interpretation of the constitution. The court has the original and exclusive jurisdiction to resolve disputes between the central government and one or more states and union territories as well as between different states and union territories. And the Supreme Court is also empowered to issue advisory rulings on issues referred to it by the president. The Supreme Court has wide discretionary powers to hear special appeals on any matter from any court except those of the armed services. It also functions as a court of record and supervises every high court.

Twenty-five associate justices and one chief justice serve on the Supreme Court. The president appoints the chief justice. Associate justices are also appointed by the president after consultation with the chief justice and, if the president deems necessary, with other associate justices of the Supreme Court and high court judges in the states. The appointments do not require Parliament's concurrence. Justices may not be removed from office until they reach mandatory retirement at age sixty-five unless each house of Parliament passes, by a vote of two-thirds of the members in attendance and a majority of its total membership, a presidential order charging "proved misbehavior or incapacity."

The contradiction between the principles of parliamentary sovereignty and judicial review that is embedded in India's constitution has been a source of major controversy over the years. After the courts overturned state laws redistributing land from zamindar estates on the grounds that the laws violated the zamindars' Fundamental Rights, Parliament passed the first (1951), fourth (1955), and seventeenth amendments (1964) to protect its authority to implement land redistribution. The Supreme Court countered these amendments in 1967 when it ruled in the Golaknath v State of Punjab case that Parliament did not have the power to abrogate the Fundamental Rights, including the provisions on private property. On February 1, 1970, the Supreme Court invalidated the government-sponsored Bank Nationalization Bill that had been passed by Parliament in August 1969. The Supreme Court also rejected as unconstitutional a presidential order of September 7, 1970, that abolished the titles, privileges, and privy purses of the former rulers of India's old princely states.

In reaction to Supreme Court decisions, in 1971 Parliament passed the Twenty-fourth Amendment empowering it to amend any provision of the constitution, including the Fundamental Rights; the Twenty-fifth Amendment, making legislative decisions concerning proper land compensation nonjusticiable; and the Twenty-sixth Amendment, which added a constitutional article abolishing princely privileges and privy purses. On April 24, 1973, the Supreme Court responded to the parliamentary offensive by ruling in the Keshavananda Bharati v the State of Kerala case that although these amendments were constitutional, the court still reserved for itself the discretion to reject any constitutional amendments passed by Parliament by declaring that the amendments cannot change the constitution's "basic structure."

During the 1975-77 Emergency, Parliament passed the Forty-second Amendment in January 1977, which essentially abrogated the Keshavananda ruling by preventing the Supreme Court from reviewing any constitutional amendment with the exception of procedural issues concerning ratification. The Forty-second Amendment's fifty-nine clauses stripped the Supreme Court of many of its powers and moved the political system toward parliamentary sovereignty. However, the Forty-third and Forty-fourth amendments, passed by the Janata government after the defeat of Indira Gandhi in March 1977, reversed these changes. In the Minerva Mills case of 1980, the Supreme Court reaffirmed its authority to protect the basic structure of the constitution. However, in the Judges Transfer case on December 31, 1981, the Supreme Court upheld the government's authority to dismiss temporary judges and transfer high court justices without the consent of the chief justice.

The Supreme Court continued to be embroiled in controversy in 1989, when its US$470 million judgment against Union Carbide for the Bhopal catastrophe resulted in public demonstrations protesting the inadequacy of the settlement. In 1991 the first-ever impeachment motion against a Supreme Court justice was signed by 108 members of Parliament. A year later, a high-profile inquiry found Associate Justice V. Ramaswamy "guilty of willful and gross misuses of office . . . and moral turpitude by using public funds for private purposes and reckless disregard of statutory rules" while serving as chief justice of Punjab and Haryana. Despite this strong indictment, Ramaswamy survived parliamentary impeachment proceedings and remained on the Supreme Court after only 196 members of Parliament, less than the required two-thirds, voted for his ouster.

During 1993 and 1994, the Supreme Court took measures to bolster the integrity of the courts and protect civil liberties in the face of state coercion. In an effort to avoid the appearance of conflict of interest in the judiciary, Chief Justice Manepalli Narayanrao Venkatachaliah initiated a controversial model code of conduct for judges that required the transfer of high court judges having children practicing as attorneys in their courts. Since 1993, the Supreme Court has implemented a policy to compensate the victims of violence while in police custody. On April 27, 1994, the Supreme Court issued a ruling that enhanced the rights of individuals placed under arrest by stipulating elaborate guidelines for arrest, detention, and interrogation.

High Courts

There are eighteen high courts for India's twenty-five states, six union territories, and one national capital territory. Some high courts serve more than one state or union territory. For example, the high court of the union territory of Chandigarh also serves Punjab and Haryana, and the high court in Gauhati (in Meghalaya) serves Assam, Nagaland, Meghalaya, Mizoram, Manipur, Tripura, and Arunachal Pradesh. As part of the judicial system, the high courts are institutionally independent of state legislatures and executives. The president appoints state high court chief justices after consulting with the chief justice of the Supreme Court and the governor of the state. The president also consults with the chief justice of the state high court before he appoints other high court justices. Furthermore, the president may also exercise the right to transfer high court justices without consultation. These personnel matters are becoming more politicized as chief ministers of states endeavor to exert their influence with New Delhi and the prime minister exerts influence over the president to secure politically advantageous appointments.

Each high court is a court of record exercising original and appellate jurisdiction within its respective state or territory. It also has the power to issue appropriate writs in cases involving constitutionally guaranteed Fundamental Rights. The high court supervises all courts within its jurisdiction, except for those dealing with the armed forces, and may transfer constitutional cases to itself from subordinate courts. The high courts have original jurisdiction on revenue matters. They try original criminal cases by a jury, but not civil cases.

Lower Courts

States are divided into districts (zillas), and within each a judge presides as a district judge over civil cases. A sessions judge presides over criminal cases. The judges are appointed by the governor in consultation with the state's high court. District courts are subordinate to the authority of their high court. There is a hierarchy of judicial officials below the district level. Many officials are selected through competitive examination by the state's public service commission. Civil cases at the subdistrict level are filed in munsif (subdistrict) courts. Lesser criminal cases are entrusted to the courts of subordinate magistrates functioning under the supervisory authority of a district magistrate. All magistrates are under the supervision of the high court. At the village level, disputes are frequently resolved by panchayats or lok adalats (people's courts).

The judicial system retains substantial legitimacy in the eyes of many Indians despite its politicization since the 1970s. In fact, as illustrated by the rise of social action litigation in the 1980s and 1990s, many Indians turn to the courts to redress grievances with other social and political institutions. It is frequently observed that Indians are highly litigious, which has contributed to a growing backlog of cases.

Indeed, the Supreme Court was reported to have more than 150,000 cases pending in 1990, the high courts had some 2 million cases pending, and the lower courts had a substantially greater backlog. Research findings in the early 1990s show that the backlogs at levels below the Supreme Court are the result of delays in the litigation process and the large number of decisions that are appealed and not the result of an increase in the number of new cases filed. Coupled with public perceptions of politicization, the growing inability of the courts to resolve disputes expeditiously threatens to erode the remaining legitimacy of the judicial system.

Election Commission

Article 324 of the constitution establishes an independent Election Commission to supervise parliamentary and state elections. Supervising elections in the world's largest democracy is by any standard an immense undertaking. Some 521 million people were eligible to vote in 1991. Efforts are made to see that polling booths are situated no more than two kilometers from a voter's place of residence. In 1991, this objective required some 600,000 polling stations for the country's 3,941 state legislative assembly and 543 parliamentary constituencies. To attempt to ensure fair elections, the Election Commission deployed more than 3.5 million officials, most of whom were temporarily seconded from the government bureaucracy, and 2 million police, paramilitary, and military forces.

Over the years, the Election Commission's enforcement of India's remarkably strict election laws grew increasingly lax. As a consequence, candidates flagrantly violated laws limiting campaign expenditures. Elections became increasingly violent, and voter intimidation and fraud proliferated.

5

Human Rights and Indian Criminal Justice System

India attained independence from the British Crown on August 15, 1947, and became a sovereign democratic republic on January 26, 1950. The Constitution of India provides for a quasi-federal system of government. The President acts as Head of State. A Council of Ministers, headed by the Prime Minister, aid and advise the President. The Council of Ministers is collectively responsible to the Lok Sabha, the lower house of Parliament.

The country is divided into 28 States, each headed by a Governor appointed by the Union Government. A Council of Ministers headed by the Chief Minister aids and advises him or her and is collectively responsible to the State Legislative Assembly. (Article 372 of the Constitution of India protects all the law in force before the commencement of the Constitution until altered, repealed, or amended by the competent Legislature or authority.

It is under this provision that the common law of the land has survived. This includes not only the personal laws such as the Hindu Law and Mohamedan Law, but also the rules of English common law and customary laws.) In addition, there are seven Union Territories (including New Delhi, the national capital city) which are directly administered by the Union Government through its officials.

The Constitution of India clearly limits the law-making power of the Union and State governments in what are known as the Union List, State List and the Concurrent List in Schedule VII. Subjects of relevance to the criminal justice system include the constitution; organization, jurisdiction and powers of the Supreme Court of India; and the extension of the powers and jurisdiction of members of a police force. Public Order, Police, officers and servants of the State High Courts and prisons are within the legislative competence of States. In sum, the criminal Justice System in India is a legacy of the British system. It has four subsystems, those being the Legislature (Parliament), Enforcement (police), Adjudication (courts), and Corrections (prisons, community facilities).

The Indian legal system is a mix of adversarial and accusatorial. In civil law, a conscious attempt has been made to respect and preserve the timeworn tenets of both Hindu and Muslim jurisprudence. (The President of India and Governors act according to the advice of the Council of Ministers.) An informal justice system does operate in the rural areas in civil and family matters.

Historical Background of Criminal Justice System.

The jurisprudence of Ancient India, which was essentially Hindu-ruled, was shaped by the concept of 'Dharma', or rules of right conduct, as outlined in the various manuals explaining the Vedic scriptures such as 'Puranas' and 'Smritis'. The King had no independent authority but derived his powers from 'Dharma' which he was expected to uphold. The distinction between a civil wrong and a criminal offense was clear. While civil wrongs related mainly to disputes arising over wealth, the concept of pataka or sin was the standard against which crime was to be defined.

The Mauryas Dynasty, which had extended to substantial parts of the Central and Eastern regions during the 4th Century, B.C., had a rigorous penal system which prescribed mutilation as well as the death penalty for even trivial offenses. About the 2nd or 3rd Century A.D., the Dharmasahtra code was drawn up by Manu, an important Hindu jurist. The code recognized assault and other bodily injuries and property offenses such as theft and robbery. During the rule of the Gupta Dynasty (4th to 6th Century A.D.), the judicial hierarchy was formed.

The judiciary was comprised of the guild, the folk-assembly or the council and the king himself. Judicial decisions conformed to legal texts, social usage and the edict of the king, who was prohibited from violating the decisions. India was subjected to a series of invasions by the Muslims beginning in the 8th Century A.D. and ending in the 15th century when a mixed race of Persians, Turks and Mongols set up the Moghul Empire. They occupied most of the Northern region and enforced a Mohammedan criminal law that classified all offenses on the basis of the penalty which each merited. These included retaliation (blood for blood), specific penalties (as for theft and robbery) and discretionary penalties.

India became a nation under the British who arrived in the early 17th Century as traders of the East India Company. The Company slowly acquired territory across the sub-continent, strictly for commercial operations in the beginning, but gradually assumed considerable powers of governance. Considering the Muslim criminal law to be irrational and draconian, the Company brought about several reforms through a series of regulations which modified or expanded the definitions of some offenses, introduced new offenses and altered penalties to make them more logical and reasonable.

In 1857, the large possessions and the authority enjoyed by the Company were transferred to the British Monarch by an Act of Parliament. Until this time, India was a loose collection of kingdoms, interactions between whom were nominal, though cultural links were quite pronounced.

An Indian Penal Code (IPC) defining crime and prescribing appropriate punishments was adopted in 1860, following the painstaking work of the First Law Commission, particularly its Chairman Lord Macaulay. Drawing inspiration from the English criminal law, the IPC has stood the test of time. As a sequel to the IPC, a Code of Criminal Procedure was enacted in 1861 and established the rules to be followed in all stages of investigation, trial and sentencing. This code was repealed and a new Code came into effect in 1974. These two codes, along with parts of the Indian Evidence Act of 1872, form the essence of India's criminal law. A large number of special and local laws such as the Arms Act, Prohibition Act, Immoral Traffic (Prevention) Act, etc., take care of various other anti-social activities.

Crime

Classification of Crime

Legal classification. The IPC divides an estimated 300 offenses into two classes. Cognizable crimes are those in which a police officer may arrest the accused or a suspect without a warrant, and includes murder, rioting, rape, kidnapping and abduction, robbery, dacoity, organized robbery, house-breaking and theft. Non- cognizable crimes are those in which a warrant is required for arrest and are generally of a more trivial nature. Crimes can be classified as "bailable" or "non-bailable", depending on their severity.

Age of criminal responsibility: Under the IPC, criminal responsibility starts at the age of seven. However, any act by a child between 7 and 12 years old, which would otherwise be criminal, is free from liability if it is proved that the child had not attained sufficient maturity of understanding to judge the nature and consequences of his or her conduct on the occasion in question.

Drug offenses: The Narcotic Drugs and Psychotropic Substances Act of 1985 promulgated by the Union government is the main legislation dealing with drug offenses. The Act defines narcotic drugs as coca leaf, cannabis (hemp) opium straw, and manufactured drugs, which includes all coca derivatives, medicinal cannabis, opium derivatives and poppy straw concentrate. Psychotropic substances are those listed in the Schedule of the Act and include, among others, LSD, DET, and MDA.

The Act prohibits cultivation of coca plants and the possession, sale, purchase, and use of coca leaves in violation of the Act and in contravention of any license granted under it. A similar prohibition is imposed by the Act for psychotropic substances. Officers empowered under the Act include those of the Union Government (Central Excise, Narcotics, Customs) and the State Government (including Revenue, Drug Control, Excise, and the Police).

Crime Statistics

The National Crime Records Bureau of the Union Ministry of Home Affairs in New Delhi publishes Crime in India annually.

— *Murder*: There were 39,174 murders recorded in 1991. The IPC defines murder as an act by which death is caused intentionally. Attempts are not included.

— *Rape.* There were 10,410 rapes in 1990. The IPC defines rape as sexual intercourse by a man with a woman against her will, without her consent, or with her consent, if her consent has been obtained by putting her or any person in whom she has an interest in fear of death or harm. Attempts are not included.

— *Property crime.* There were 10,831 dacoities recorded in 1990. The IPC defines a dacoity as a robbery committed or attempted to be committed jointly by five or more persons. Attempts are not included.

— *Serious drug offense.* In 1990, there were 5,299 drug offenses, as established by the Narcotic Drugs and Psychotropic Substances Act of 1985. There were 64,234 kilograms of illegal substances seized. Attempts are not included.

— *Crime regions.* In 1991, 8 cities recorded more than 10,000 cognizable IPC offenses each. These were the four metropolitan cities of Bombay, Calcutta, Madras and Delhi and the cities of Ahmedabad, Bangalore, Hydrabad and Pune. The four districts of Patna, Bhopal, Indore, and Jaipur also registered more than 10,000 cognizable IPC offenses.

Murders arising out of land disputes are more common in rural areas. Suburban areas which have isolated housing units and are not intensively policed report a large number of dacoities. Cities tend to report a large number of pocket pickings and forcible snatching of jewelry cases.

Victims

1. *Groups most victimized by crime:* Due to the absence of survey data, it is difficult to say whether a particular ethnic or age group is more victimized than another.
2. *Victims' assistance agencies.* A few private voluntary agencies are active in assisting victims and survivors,

particularly in cases of murder or rape. All of the States have State-sponsored Legal Advice Boards which offer free legal advice to the poor, both in criminal and civil litigation.

3. *Role of the victim.* The victim has no role either in prosecution or in sentencing.
4. *Victims' rights legislation.* Under Section 357 of the Code of Criminal Procedure, when a Court imposes a fine or a sentence which includes a fine, it may order the fine to be awarded to the victim in compensation for any loss or injury caused by the offense. In cases where no fine is imposed, the Court may direct the accused to compensate any person for loss or injury. Section 358 of the Code of Criminal Procedure provides for compensation to a person wrongfully arrested by the police. Until a few years ago, the courts were reluctant to invoke these sections of law. Recently, the Higher Courts have been more inclined to award compensation where no fine has been ordered.

Police

Administration

The Police are a civil authority subordinate to the Executive, represented in the Union Government by the Prime Minister and in the States by the Chief Minister, and their respective Councils of Ministers. Prominent among the Union police forces are the Central Bureau of Investigation (CBI), Border Security Force (BSF), Central Reserve Police Force (CRPF), Central Industrial Security Force (CISF) and the Indo-Tibetan Border Police (ITBP). Each of these forces is headed by a Director/Director-General with the status of a three-star General in the Army. The CBI is controlled by the Department of

Personnel of the Union Government headed by a Minister of State who reports to the Prime Minister. The other forces are controlled by the Union Ministry of Home Affairs headed by a Cabinet Minister.

The bulk of the Indian Police is comprised of forces in the States. Each State has its own force headed by a Director-General of Police (DGP) who is equivalent in rank to his counterpart in the Union Government forces. A number of Additional Directors-General or Inspectors-General of Police (IGP) who look after various portfolios, such as Personnel, Law & Order, Intelligence, Crime, Armed Police, Training, and Technical Services are located at the State Police Headquarters and report directly to the DGP. Major cities in a State are headed by a Commissioner of Police (CP) who, again, reports to the DGP. Areas outside these cities in a State are divided into Districts of varying size. Each district is headed by a Superintendent of Police (SP) and supervised by a Deputy Inspector-General (DIG) whose jurisdiction is called a Range, composed of a group of three or four districts.

In each District and in the city police force, the basic police unit is a Police Station (PS). A few police stations have an Out-post (OP) which is a mini-station for serving remote or trouble-prone localities. The number of police stations depends on the size of the State and the District. The state of Madhya Pradesh, which is the largest state in terms of area (443,447 square kilometers) has 1,101 Police Stations and 554 out-posts. While the larger districts have an average of 22 Police stations, the smaller ones have 15. A medium-sized State such as Tamil Nadu, with an area of 130,058 square kilometers, has 1,090 police stations and 163 out-posts. A medium-sized District covering an area of about 8,000 square kilometers has about 40 police stations.

Each police station is headed by a Sub-Inspector or Inspector referred to as the Station House Officer (SHO).

A designated number of Constables, the lowest rank in the police force, and Head Constables are assigned to each police station. In some States, there are additional ranks, such as Assistant Sub-Inspector or Assistant Police Inspector. While urban police stations often have certain functional divisions such as Law and Order and Crime and Traffic, no such divisions exist in rural or village police stations.

An Armed Reserve at the District Headquarters, under the command of the Superintendent of Police, handles public disturbance problems, such as religious or caste riots and clashes between political rivals. There are a few battalions of the Special Armed Police (SAP) used for more serious situations. The SAP is deployed by the Director General of Police when the situation warrants it. For example, if during a major breakdown of public peace the State Police are outnumbered and unable to cope with the magnitude of the disorder, a State Government may ask for Central forces, especially the Central Reserve Police Force.

The cost of such deployment is usually borne by the State government. The Criminal Investigation Department (CID) is an important arm of every State Police department. Headed by an Additional Director of General Police or Inspector General of Police, it is a specialized agency for conducting sensitive inquiries into allegations against public figures or police personnel. More importantly, it is entrusted with the investigation of important criminal cases which cannot be solved by the District Police.

Resources

Expenditures. There are separate budgets for the Union and State Police forces. A large State such as Madhya Pradesh has an annual police budget of Rupees 3,730 million. A medium-sized State such as Tamil Nadu has an annual police budget of Rupees 3200 million

There are two schemes by which the Union Government assists State Police departments to strengthen police administration: the Police Housing Scheme and the Modernization Scheme. While the Police Housing Scheme funds the construction of housing units for lower levels of police personnel, the Modernization Scheme finances the purchase of equipment in the areas of communication, transport and scientific investigation.

Number of police. As of December 31, 1991, the actual collective police strength in the 25 States and 7 Union Territories was 1,152,586. This figure includes 13,654 female police personnel. Madhya Pradesh, the largest state, has a police force strength of 86,345, including 1,060 female police. The Constabulary, namely, Head Constables and Constables, constitutes more than 90% of the force strength in almost every State. A medium-sized State like Tamil Nadu, with a population of 55 million, has a force strength of about 70,000, which includes 1,275 female police personnel.

As of December 31, 1991, there were 35.1 police officers per 100 square kilometer and 1.4 police officers per 1,000 population in the country. In Madhya Pradesh, there is one police station for every 60,165 persons in the population. In the State of Tamil Nadu, there is now one police officer per 800 persons in the population, and one police station per 52,000 persons in the population.

The Law ensures that the police force is representative of the traditionally poor and underprivileged sections of the society. There is a quota of 22.5% for recruitment in every force for Scheduled Castes and Scheduled Tribes. Additionally, in some States, there is a prescribed quota for those listed as Backward and Most Backward.

Technology

Availability of police automobiles. Considerable attention has been given by both the Union Government and State Governments to increase the mobility of police through the provision of passenger cars, jeeps (including four-wheel drive), trucks, buses and motorcycles. For example, the Tamil Nadu Police force has a fleet strength of 3,980. The fleet strength of the Madhya Pradesh is 3,008. Cars are used for VIP security duty and for senior officers above the level of superintendent. All other vehicles are allotted to teams of personnel at the District or police station level for patrolling or investigation work.

Electronic equipment. Radio communication is very well organized in most of the forces. Very High Frequency (VHF) telephones connected by a large number of relay stations are used to link the police headquarters to the police stations in every State. For instance, in Tamil Nadu, 1,015 police stations out of a total of 1090 have been provided VHF telephones; 101 of the 163 outposts also have this facility. In Madhya Pradesh, 1,062 police stations and 256 outposts have a wireless telegraph facility.

The State Police have 1,516 static and 590 mobile VHF sets. There is also an Inter-State Police Wireless (ISPW) which offers a national grid. At present, the national capital, New Delhi, is connected to the capital cities of States and Union Territories through high frequency radio telegraph and by numerous teleprinter links.

Fax facilities are also available in a number of forces. Computerization of crime information has taken place in a majority of States and is monitored by the National Crime Records Bureau (NCRB) working under the Union Home Ministry in New Delhi. Both mainframe and personal computers are used. Computer-aided dispatch is yet to be introduced. (While the use of computers for personnel management is still limited to a few police forces, there is the distinct possibility of widespread use in the near future.)

Weapons. The most common weapon available at the police station level is the .410 musket. The District Armed Reserve police use .303 rifles and tear-gas guns. The Special Armed Police possess stun-guns, mortars, light machine guns and AK-47 rifles. A few individual police officers on special assignments, such as VIP security, carry revolvers. Bullet-proof vests are generally available to police assigned to protect high dignitaries.

Training and qualifications

There are different recruitment regulations for the Constabulary, Sub-Inspector/Inspector and Assistant Superintendent (ASP)/Deputy Superintendent (DSP) levels. While the minimum educational qualification for the Constabulary and Sub-Inspector/Inspector is a High School diploma, an undergraduate college degree is required for entry into the ASP and DSP level.

Physical requirements include a minimum height of five feet five inches, good eye-sight and minimum attainments in a physical efficiency test consisting of running, jumping, climbing and throwing. Psychological tests are not yet used in a majority of forces. Superintendents of Police (SP) are recruited every year by the Union Government on the basis of a national competitive exam and are appointed into what is known as the Indian Police Service (IPS). (Although IPS officers are recruited by the Union Government, they are assigned to each of the 25 States and collectively to the 7 Union Territories.

Positions in the Central forces are manned partly by IPS officers drawn from the States and partly by recruitment from the open market.) The other levels are recruited by the Union Government forces or by the State

Governments. Superintendents of Police are trained at the National Police Academy, Hyderabad, for about a year. At the end of the year, they also undergo a brief orientation training at the Police Academy of the State to which each is assigned. (IPS officers are exposed to a variety of training programs during their career. These are given at the National Police Academy or at the various management institutions.)

Almost every State and Central Police force has its own training institution. In certain cases, training resources may be pooled, as in the case of the North Eastern Police Academy, which covers the smaller States in that region. The duration of training varies from State to State, and with rank. Generally, DSPs and Sub-Inspectors spend a year at the Academy and Constables are trained for a shorter period (9 months) at Police Recruit Schools. The training faculty are normally police personnel themselves. Only at the NPA, Hyderabad, are outsiders such as lawyers and management consultants associated with training programs.

Discretion

Use of force. The Criminal Procedure Code permits the use of force by the Police to disperse an unlawful assembly that threatens public peace. A police officer acting under this legal authority cannot be prosecuted except with the sanction of the Government. The use of deadly force is permitted as a final resort against an individual accused of an offense punishable with death or with life imprisonment if he forcibly resists or attempts to evade an arrest. The Constabulary, whose duties generally involve patrol, carry a long baton (lathi). Officers may carry a revolver during specific operations or when the occasion otherwise demands it, such as during the tour of a VIP or while patrolling a disturbed area.

Stop/apprehend suspect. A complaint of the commission of a cognizable offense is docketed into what is known as a First Information Report (FIR). An individual could be arrested by the Police on a specific complaint or on suspicion of having committed a cognizable offense. In all such cases, the arrestee has to be brought before the nearest Magistrate within 24 hours of the arrest. Any detention in police custody beyond 24 hours is allowed only with the orders of a Magistrate. The Magistrate has the authority under the Criminal Procedure Code to either release the individual on bail or lodge him in a sub-jail for pre-trial detainees and those under investigation. In certain cases, to facilitate investigation, the Magistrate may permit an arrestee to be retained in police custody for a short period.

After completing the investigation and obtaining legal opinion from the prosecuting personnel, the police investigator either establishes a charge-sheet, accompanied by statements of witnesses, before the competent Magistrate under the appropriate section of law, or, in the event of insufficient evidence, files a Final Report dropping further action. If the defendant is charged, during the trial, it is the responsibility of the investigating officer to assist the Public Prosecutor in every way, including the production of witnesses.

Decision to arrest. Police may arrest, without a warrant and without an order from a Magistrate, any person who has committed or is suspected to have committed a cognizable offense. Police may also arrest persons for the purpose of preventing the commission of such an offense without a warrant or order. Very few arrests are made on the basis of a warrant.

Search and seizure of property. Normally, a warrant is obtained by the Police to search a place. However, when an officer believes that a material needed for investigation is available in a certain place and concludes that the loss of time incurred by obtaining a warrant would be prejudicial to the investigation, he may search the place without a warrant after recording the grounds for his belief. Any police officer may seize any property which is alleged or suspected to be stolen or which is found under circumstances which create suspicion of the commission of any offense.

Confessions. Under Section 25 of the Indian Evidence Act, no confession made to a police officer is admissible as evidence. However, there is a provision in Section 27 which states that when such confession leads to the recovery of a material fact (for example, the weapon used in a murder), the portion of the confession which had directly led to the recovery can be admitted into evidence. Also, during the course of an investigation, a Magistrate may record the confession of any person after warning the person that the recording could be used as evidence against him/her.

Accountability.

Complaints of police misconduct are first handled by the departmental hierarchy. Allegations of torture or death in police custody are often probed by the CID. Charges of corruption are investigated by the Director of Vigilance who is usually a police officer of the rank of DGP or IGP and is stationed outside the department. The Director of Vigilance reports to a Vigilance Commissioner, who is a high ranking civil service officer.

In some States, police standing orders provide for an automatic inquiry into complaints of police torture by a civil authority called the Deputy Collector. Complaints can also be made to a revenue divisional officer who possesses magisterial powers. If the inquiry proves the complaint to be true, a charge-sheet under the IPC may be filed in Court against the delinquent police officers who may ultimately stand trial as offenders.

Prosecutorial and Judicial Process

Rights of the accused. An accused is not required to be physically present in court and may be represented by his pleader. The accused is entitled to receive without delay a copy of the police report, the first information report (FIR), and all statements and confessions on which the prosecution proposes to rely for proving its case. This privilege also extends to cases initiated in a manner other than by a police report. All evidence admitted during a trial shall be recorded in the presence of the accused or his pleader. If the accused pleads guilty, the Judge shall record the plea and may, using his or her discretion, convict him or her thereon. The system of trial by jury was given up decades ago.

Assistance to the accused. Any person accused of an offense before a criminal court has the right to be defended by a pleader of his choice. In cases where the accused has no means of engaging a pleader, it is incumbent on the Court to assign a pleader for his or her defense at State expense.

Procedures

Preparatory procedures for bringing a suspect to trial. A police investigation and the filing of a charge-sheet before a Magistrate precede a criminal trial. If the Magistrate believes that on the basis of the available record there is sufficient ground for prosecution, a summons or warrant is issued. Warrants are used for offenses punishable with death, life imprisonment, or for prison terms exceeding 2 years.

When the accused appears before the Magistrate, the Magistrate ensures that, on the facts of the case, the charges against the accused have been correctly framed. This is done after the Magistrate has furnished a copy of the police report and other records to the accused. At this stage or at any time before judgment is delivered, the Magistrate may alter or add any charge and explain the charge to the accused.

The trial commences thereafter with the Assistant Public Prosecutor (APP) examining prosecution witnesses. However, when the Magistrate finds that a cited offense is in fact triable exclusively by the higher Court, namely, the Court of Sessions, he or she commits the case to that Court after notifying the Prosecutor. Except for minor differences, the trials before Sessions and Magistrate Courts proceed in similar fashion.

Official who conducts prosecution. An Assistant Public Prosecutor, who is usually a full-time Government counsel, conducts the prosecution in the Magistrate's Court. A Public Prosecutor (PP) is also available at every District headquarters to conduct cases before the Sessions Court. The Public Prosecutor is appointed on a contract basis for a specified period.

There is also a Public Prosecutor who is contracted for the whole State and appears on behalf of the Government before the High Court. Any person, including a police officer with a ranking at or above Inspector, who has not investigated the case may conduct the prosecution in a Magistrate's Court. This person may conduct the prosecution after receiving the permission of the court or the Public Prosecutor\ Assistant Public Prosecutor.

Alternatives to trial. Indian criminal law does not provide for plea bargaining.

Proportion of prosecuted cases going to trial. While almost all cases before the Sessions Court proceed to a trial, a substantial number of those before a Magistrate's Court do not. The difference is explained by the severity of the cases before the former.

Pre-trial incarceration conditions. In cases where police investigation cannot be completed within 24 hours of the arrest, the accused is presented to the nearest Judicial Magistrate. If the circumstances warrant custody of the accused, the Magistrate will order a period of detention. For first-time offenders, 15 days is ordered. However, such detention periods can be extended to 90 days if the offense is one punishable by death or imprisonment for more than 10 years or for 60 days for other lesser offenses.

Bail procedure. The First Schedule of the Criminal Procedure Code classifies offenses as non-bailable or bailable. Non-bailable offenses include murder or attempted murder, causing grievous hurt, rape, theft, robbery, and dacoity. A person arrested for a bailable offense may be released by the police or by a court before whom he or she is produced. Based on the discretion of the police or the court, the suspect may be discharged on his/her own recognizance. An individual accused of a non-bailable offense punishable with death or imprisonment for life, may be released on bail only by the High Court or a Court of Session. This provision excludes women, persons below 16 years of age or those who are sick or infirm.

Proportion of pre-trial offenders incarcerated. Nearly 75% of pre-trial offenders are incarcerated, most for 1 or 2 days. Only about 25% of pre-trial offenders may be expected to be in jail during the trial. While no national data exists, the number of prisoners awaiting trial in Tamil Nadu prisons was 607 as of June 1993.

Judicial System

Administration.

Supreme Court. The highest Court of the land is the Supreme Court of India located in New Delhi. Other judicial bodies at the Union level take the form of tribunals whose members may be from the judiciary or from the civil service. The Supreme Court of India is a court of records and hears appeals from any judgments of a High Court. It has the power to issue prerogative writs in the nature of habeas corpus, mandamus, prohibition, quo warranto and certiorari in the enforcement of fundamental rights.

High Courts. Each State or a group of States has a High Court. This is also a court of record which hears appeals from the district courts and has the power to grant writs.

Court of Sessions. Below the High Court is a Court of Sessions of which the Judge, in his or her capacity as District Judge, also handles civil cases. There are a few Additional and Assistant Judges exercising the powers of the Sessions Judge in specified offenses.

District Courts. At the district level, the lower criminal courts (sub-divisional courts) are headed by Magistrates (sub magistrates and sub-divisional magistrates) with jurisdiction over offenses listed in the First Schedule to the Criminal Procedure Code. One of the Magistrates in a District is appointed as the Chief Judicial Magistrate. Magistrates commit for trial to the Court of Sessions certain offenses, such as murder, which are exclusively triable by Sessions Judges. Magistrates are competent to try and dispose of lesser offenses.

Special courts

The Criminal Procedure Code empowers the High Court, upon being requested by the Union or State Government, to confer on any person the powers of a Judicial Magistrate to try particular cases or classes of cases. Special courts exist for handling a variety of problems, including terrorist violence, family disputes, juvenile delinquency, theft of forest wealth, corruption among public officials, and various socio-economic offenses (such as adulteration, hoarding and black-marketing of essential food articles). Judges presiding over such courts sometimes look after IPC offenses.

Judges

Number of judges. Including the Chief Justice, the Supreme Court of India has 26 Judges. The number of judges varies in the State High Courts. One of the medium-sized High Courts is Madras with 24. Increasingly, female judges are being appointed at all levels. At present, there is one female on the Supreme Court. There is no regional or ethnic quota for the higher judiciary.

Appointment, training, and qualifications. Judges of the Supreme Court and the High Courts are appointed by the President of India acting on the advice of the Executive and after a process of consultation with the existing Judges. Judges who have sat on a High Court for at least 5 years, or have practiced as an Advocate in a High Court for 10 years, or a person who, in the opinion of the President, is a distinguished jurist, are all eligible for the Supreme Court.

Anyone who has held a judicial office for 10 years or has been an Advocate in a High Court for 10 years is eligible for a position on the High court. Sessions Judges are appointed by the State Governor in consultation with the High Court. Other judicial appointments are made by the Governor after consultation with the State Public Service Commission and the High Court.

Penalities and Sentencing

Sentencing Process.

— Who Determines the sentence? The trial judge determines the sentence.

— Is there a special sentencing hearing? There is no special sentencing hearing. At the end of a trial, the sentence is wholly determined by the Judge, who delivers the sentence. The accused is required to be present in Court at this time, unless absence at the trial had been previously approved or if the sentence is a fine.

— Which persons have input into the sentencing process? No other person (social worker, psychiatrist or victim) has input in the sentencing process.

Types of Penalties

Range of penalties. Available penalties include the death sentence, life imprisonment, imprisonment, forfeiture of property, and fines. Under certain circumstances, a person under 21 years of age who is convicted of an offense punishable with a fine or with imprisonment for 7 years or less may be released on probation. Community-based treatment is also available. Probation with and without supervision is the primary community based treatment. The probation department functions under the Home Department in most states and under the welfare department in the other states. Generally, punishment takes the form of a term of imprisonment or fine or some combination of both.

Death penalty. A death sentence can be imposed for murder and for specified offenses against the State which include waging war against the Government of India, attempting or abetting war or mutiny. Special reasons have to be given for imposing the death penalty. For instance, in addition to the above circumstances, the death penalty can be imposed for abetting the suicide of a child, an insane or delirious person, an idiot, or an intoxicated person. The death penalty can also be imposed when an individual serving a life sentence attempts to murder, even if a non-fatal injury results from the attempt.

Execution is by hanging. While nationwide figures on executions are not available, inquiries indicate that in Tamil Nadu, two to three persons are hanged each year.

Prison

Number of prisons and type. As of April 1, 1992, there were 1,155 prisons in India. These included 86 Central Prisons, 252 District Prisons and 718 sub-jails. In a typical State, such as Tamil Nadu, there are five categories of prisons. In Tamil Nadu there are 8 central prisons, which are used for convicts serving one month or more, 2 special prisons for women, which are used for female convicts serving more than 1 month; 113 sub-jails, which are used for convicts serving less than 1 month or awaiting trial; 1 Borstal School used for adolescent convicts from 16 to 23 years old; and one Open Air Prison. In addition, some States have a District Prison which accommodates convicts serving a term of 1 year or less.

Number of prison beds. As of April 1, 1992, the total prison capacity of India was 193,987. The State of Tamil Nadu is at 50% capacity, with a prison population of 18,228. Women account for less than 5% of the total Indian prison population.

Number of annual admissions. Information not obtained.

Average daily population/number of prisoners Information not obtained.

Actual or estimated proportions of inmates incarcerated. Information not obtained.

Administration

Administration. The administration of Prisons in India is the sole responsibility of the States. All prisons are managed by State governments or by the Union Territory administration. The Central Government is largely concerned with policy formulation and planning services. In each State, the head of prison administration is an Inspector- General who is usually a police officer. He has a few Deputy Inspectors-General to look after the jails in each of the various geographical ranges into which the State is divided.

In the state of Tamil Nadu there are four such Ranges. Prisoners are classified on the basis of age, sex, mental health, nature of offense (criminal, civil, or security), and the frequency of the commission of crime. In Tamil Nadu prisons, prisoners are categorized into A and B classes. The criteria for A class are social status, education, style of living, character and antecedents. Those convicted for offenses involving gross depravity of character or for offenses against society are not eligible for A class.

The Central Prisons and the jails have both custodial and treatment staff who include medical doctors, psychologists, welfare officers, social workers, teachers and vocational instructors. The hierarchy of custodial staff in the prison system takes the following form: superintendent, jailer, deputy jailer, assistant jailer, head warders, warders.

Number of prison guards. Prison guards are known as warders, who are supervised by head warders. While no national data is available, as of 1993, the state of Tamil Nadu had 2,108 warders, 347 head warders, and 33 chief head warders, of which 76 were female.

Training and qualifications. While no national data is available, the basic qualification for recruitment of warders in the state of Tamil Nadu is a High School diploma. They are put through a six-month training program in discipline, the principles of prison administration, and the practice of correctional procedure.

Expenditure on Prison system. While no national data is available, during the fiscal year 1992-93, the Tamil Nadu Prison Department had a budget of Rupees 238 million.

Prison conditions

Remissions. Different scales of remission exist. For instance, 2 days per month for good conduct or work done while in prison can be given. Convicts employed in prison services such as cooking and sweeping and who must work on Sundays and other holidays get 3 days of remission every quarter. There is also a Special remission of 30 days a year for maintaining prison discipline.

Parole is allowed in the form of emergency leave (15 days yearly) and ordinary leave (30 days yearly) for participating in family ceremonies, such as marriages or funerals and for attending to domestic problems like enrollment of children into school and repairs to one's home.

Work/education. Prisoners sentenced to rigorous imprisonment are assigned the appropriate class of hard, medium, or light labor under recommendation of the medical officer. Purposeless and non-productive forms of labor are avoided. Prisoners are often taught trades such as carpentry, tailoring, weaving, and book binding. Every central prison has an elementary school with qualified teachers. Adult education is available for all prisoners. Attendance is optional. Prisoners can also enroll in distance education programs, such as university correspondence courses. There are many instances of prisoners receiving under-graduate and graduate degrees.

Amenities and Privileges. Vegetarian and non-vegetarian food is provided at fixed costs, which are slightly higher for A class prisoners. A special diet is available to women and their babies, and to sick prisoners on medical advice. Each central prison has a hospital with a part-time medical officer. Writing and receiving letters and interviews with relatives are permitted. Recreation in the form of games, yoga, television watching and meditation classes are also available.

Extraditoin and Treaties

Extradition. India has entered into bilateral extradition treaties with Nepal, the United States of America, Uganda, Bhutan, The Netherlands, Belgium, Canada and the United Kingdom (including Northern Ireland). India is a member of the South Asia Association for Regional Cooperation (SAARC) Convention on Suppression of Terrorism along with Pakistan, Sri Lanka, Bangla Desh, Nepal and the Maldives. The Convention provides for the extradition of fugitive offenders.

Exchange and transfer of prisoners. Information not obtained.

Specified conditions. As a general rule, offenses of a political nature are excluded from the purview of extradition. Also, the return of a fugitive criminal to India is sought only if the offense with which he is charged is recognized by the extradition treaty with the country from which such extradition is sought.

Recommendations for Reforms in Indian Criminal Justice System

In November 2000 the Government of India set up the Committee on Reforms of the Criminal Justice System, purportedly to fairly assess and propose changes to the way criminal trials are conducted in India. The Committee submitted its report in April 2003. It was constituted by the Ministry of Home Affairs of the Government of India in November 2000 and headed by former Chief Justice of Kerala and Karnataka, and former member of the National Human Rights Commission (NHRC), Justice V.S. Malimath.

There has been sporadic media coverage of selected recommendations in the report, and on 11 August 2003 it was reported that the government was introducing a Bill to amend the Code of Criminal Procedure, reflecting a few of the Committee's recommendations. While there has been no official government response to the report., a common thread in most of the Committee's recommendations is an absolute disregard for human rights - both constitutional and international standards.

The recommendations of the Committee cover are wide ranging, from making confessions to the police admissible to courts to making matrimonial cruelty a bailable offence; they include placing a police officer as head of the prosecution and adding provisions from the Prevention of Terrorism Act (POTA) into the regular penal law. This article focuses on the manner in which the 'proposed reforms' were arrived at, by examining the report's methodology, interrogating its premises and unraveling its exclusions and silences.

A criminal justice system (CJS) does not function in a vacuum. The system and the actors, be they police, prosecutors, judges or lawyers, are all embedded in specific social, economic, political and cultural contexts. In India, like elsewhere, class, caste, gender, religious, ethnic and sexual identity and other (dis)abilities greatly influence the working of the criminal justice system. Thus it is critical that the purpose, sincerity and significance of any proposed reforms of the criminal justice system be judged by: the extent to which the process of drawing up the reforms was participatory and inclusive; and the extent to which they address social vulnerability and disadvantage and enable the system to better protect the rights of those most discriminated against.

Given the importance of the issue of reform of the CJS and the impact of any such reforms on all members of society, there is a need for transparency and consultation in the process of reform. The Malimath Committee appears to share a similar view when it voices its opinion that there is need for a reform of penal law in

India and this should "not be an exercise to be carried out only by lawyers and Judges. Public men and women representing different walks of life and different schools of thoughts, social scientists, politicians etc should be on such a committee to recommend to the Parliament a better and progressive penal law for the country."

However the Committee ignores the fact that its own constitution and membership fails these inclusive and representative standards. The members of the Committee, besides the former judge as chairperson were: an Advocate, a serving bureaucrat, a retired IAS official, a retired DGP of Police and a legal academician. That this Committee was addressing the entire criminal justice system (not just the penal law) only made it more important that it be constituted with broader representation.

Another aspect in which the question of representation is valid is in authorship of the "research papers" that the Committee appears to have commissioned from various 'experts'. Six of the sixteen papers were written by serving or retired Police and other security agency officials (including the serving Inspector General of Police, Rajasthan and the serving Director of the Central Bureau of Investigation). The remaining ten papers are covered by a spattering of legal academics and lawyers and judges. Once again the Committee fails to live up to its own set standards.

The committee sent a questionnaire sent to over 3000 individuals, and received 264 responses. There has been no categorization of responses into the different sectors of society they came from. There is also little input from criminal lawyers dealing with cases on the ground. The Committee claims to have consulted broadly in drawing up its report and recommendations. These claims are suspect. The body organised four seminars on specific issues and its various members attended another eight seminars organised by different organisations. There is little in the Report however to indicate that the Committee indeed drew from these limited discussions.

Volume II of the Report of the Committee also contains a copy of a questionnaire sent to 3,164 individuals, along with an analysis of the 264 responses (less than 10%) received. There is no mention on how many of the 264 responses to the questionnaire came from non-governmental individuals or groups. There is little input from criminal lawyers dealing with cases within the criminal justice system on the ground. Members of the Committee conducted a whirlwind visit of France and this trip appears to have given them in-depth knowledge of the French system that they rely on heavily later in the report.

Unfortunately the report itself does not provide the material on the basis of which the bulk of the recommendations appear to have been made. Recommendations are made without independent analysis of specific areas of the criminal justice system. This is evident from the Committee's treatment of the prosecution system and summary trials - where it suggests major changes without referring to any studies that identify problems. In other places, the Committee is extremely selective in its reference to studies on the criminal justice system.

This lack of research leads to several very broad and vague recommendations - for example tagging of pregnant women prisoners and the videoing of confessional statements made to police - without providing any detailed analysis of how such recommendations could be implemented. Though the Committee claims to have applied its mind to the "grave problems facing the country", there is little to suggest that it considered the grave problems facing the most vulnerable sections of Indian society vis-à-vis the criminal justice system. There is a deafening silence in the report on the criminalisation of poverty, the crisis in legal aid and the abject failures of the criminal justice system in protecting the human rights of the poor, dalits, minorities and other vulnerable sections of society. The most vulnerable endure enormous challenges in seeking redress from the criminal justice system. The Malimath Committee ignores this.

Furthermore, there is sufficient material to suggest that the poor constitute a disproportionately large number of the criminal defendants going in and out of the criminal justice system. A large percentage of the 2.7 lakh prisoners in India belongs to the economically weaker section of society, is by and large illiterate and unaware of the law or working of the legal system. The Committee on the other hand believes that "the accused now-a-days are more educated and well informed and use sophisticated weapons and advance techniques to commit offences without leaving any trace of evidence"; "the accused is normally represented by very competent lawyer of his choice".

Needless to say, the Committee does not back these observations with any empirical evidence. For example, there is no substantive discussion in the Malimath Committee report on the challenges faced by dalits in ensuring protections from the criminal justice system. Institutional prejudices within the police and the judiciary or the problems with the implementation of the Schedules Castes/Schedules Tribes (Prevention of) Atrocities Act or the working of the Special Courts and many other issues significant to the protection of dalit human rights have not been of the least significance to the Malimath Committee. Neither is the Committee interested in police inaction and even direct complicity and participation in atrocities against dalits. The extent of the failure of the criminal justice system to combat caste discrimination seems to have totally escaped the Malimath Committee.

There have been repeated failures in ensuring effective protection, investigation, prosecution and justice to victims and survivors of communal violence. The Committee finds no space in its report to discuss these concerns. The failure to provide equal protection of the law to and safeguard the rights of minorities has been a major human rights issue dogging the criminal justice system for decades now. In early 2002, while the Committee was contemplating the "grave problems facing the country" and engaged in drawing up "comprehensive criminal justice reforms" more than 2000 people were massacred in Gujarat, thanks in no small measure to a criminal justice system that seemed more criminal than just.

Despite repeated failures in ensuring effective protection, investigation, prosecution and justice to victims and survivors of communal violence it the Committee finds no space in its report to discuss these concerns. Instead the Report prefers to project communal violence as a phenomenon that is largely engineered by the Pakistan's Inter-services Intelligence and pro-Pakistani terrorist outfits.

The Committee's silence on the protection of human rights are by no means the only ones. A "comprehensive reform" of the criminal justice system was an opportunity to overhaul the system in a manner that could also address major human rights concerns of other vulnerable groups. These include criminalizing child sexual abuse, decriminalizing consensual same sex relations and addressing the serious challenges faced by the mentally ill, all areas in which the prevailing standards are way behind internationally accepted standards of protection.

6

International Covenant on Civil and Political Rights

(Adopted by General Assembly resolution 2200A (XXI) of 16 December 1966)

PREAMBLE

The States Parties to the present Covenant,

Considering that, in accordance with the principles proclaimed in the Charter of the United Nations, recognition of the inherent dignity and of the equal and inalienable rights of all members of the human family is the foundation of freedom, justice and peace in the world,

Recognizing that these rights derive from the inherent dignity of the human person,

Recognizing that, in accordance with the Universal Declaration of Human Rights, the ideal of free human beings enjoying civil and political freedom and freedom from fear and want can only be achieved if conditions are created whereby everyone may enjoy his civil and political rights, as well as his economic, social and cultural rights,

Considering the obligation of States under the Charter of the United Nations to promote universal respect for, and observance of, human rights and freedoms,

Realizing that the individual, having duties to other individuals and to the community to which he belongs, is under a responsibility to strive for the promotion and observance of the rights recognized in the present Covenant,

Agree upon the following articles:

PART I

Article 1 General Comment on its Implementation

1. All peoples have the right of self-determination. By virtue of that right they freely determine their political status and freely pursue their economic, social and cultural development.
2. All peoples may, for their own ends, freely dispose of their natural wealth and resources without prejudice to any obligations arising out of international economic cooperation, based upon the principle of mutual benefit, and international law. In no case may a people be deprived of its own means of subsistence.
3. The States Parties to the present Covenant, including those having responsibility for the administration of Non-Self-Governing and Trust Territories, shall promote the realization of the right of self-determination, and shall respect that right, in conformity with the provisions of the Charter of the United Nations.

PART II

Article 2 General Comment on its Implementation

1. Each State Party to the present Covenant undertakes to respect and to ensure to all individuals within its territory and subject to its jurisdiction the rights

recognized in the present Covenant, without distinction of any kind, such as race, colour, sex, language, religion, political or other opinion, national or social origin, property, birth or other status.

2. Where not already provided for by existing legislative or other measures, each State Party to the present Covenant undertakes to take the necessary steps, in accordance with its constitutional processes and with the provisions of the present Covenant, to adopt such laws or other measures as may be necessary to give effect to the rights recognized in the present Covenant.

3. Each State Party to the present Covenant undertakes:

   (a) To ensure that any person whose rights or freedoms as herein recognized are violated shall have an effective remedy, notwithstanding that the violation has been committed by persons acting in an official capacity;

   (b) To ensure that any person claiming such a remedy shall have his right thereto determined by competent judicial, administrative or legislative authorities, or by any other competent authority provided for by the legal system of the State, and to develop the possibilities of judicial remedy;

   (c) To ensure that the competent authorities shall enforce such remedies when granted.

Article 3 General Comment on its Implementation

The States Parties to the present Covenant undertake to ensure the equal right of men and women to the enjoyment of all civil and political rights set forth in the present Covenant. General comment on its implementation

Article 4 General Comment on its Implementation

1. In time of public emergency which threatens the life

of the nation and the existence of which is officially proclaimed, the States Parties to the present Covenant may take measures derogating from their obligations under the present Covenant to the extent strictly required by the exigencies of the situation, provided that such measures are not inconsistent with their other obligations under international law and do not involve discrimination solely on the ground of race, colour, sex, language, religion or social origin.

2. No derogation from articles 6, 7, 8 (paragraphs I and 2), 11, 15, 16 and 18 may be made under this provision.

3. Any State Party to the present Covenant availing itself of the right of derogation shall immediately inform the other States Parties to the present Covenant, through the intermediary of the Secretary-General of the United Nations, of the provisions from which it has derogated and of the reasons by which it was actuated. A further communication shall be made, through the same intermediary, on the date on which it terminates such derogation.

Article 5

1. Nothing in the present Covenant may be interpreted as implying for any State, group or person any right to engage in any activity or perform any act aimed at the destruction of any of the rights and freedoms recognized herein or at their limitation to a greater extent than is provided for in the present Covenant.

2. There shall be no restriction upon or derogation from any of the fundamental human rights recognized or existing in any State Party to the present Covenant pursuant to law, conventions, regulations or custom on the pretext that the present Covenant does not

recognize such rights or that it recognizes them to a lesser extent.

PART III

Article 6 General comment on its implementation

1. Every human being has the inherent right to life. This right shall be protected by law. No one shall be arbitrarily deprived of his life.
2. In countries which have not abolished the death penalty, sentence of death may be imposed only for the most serious crimes in accordance with the law in force at the time of the commission of the crime and not contrary to the provisions of the present Covenant and to the Convention on the Prevention and Punishment of the Crime of Genocide. This penalty can only be carried out pursuant to a final judgement rendered by a competent court.
3. When deprivation of life constitutes the crime of genocide, it is understood that nothing in this article shall authorize any State Party to the present Covenant to derogate in any way from any obligation assumed under the provisions of the Convention on the Prevention and Punishment of the Crime of Genocide.
4. Anyone sentenced to death shall have the right to seek pardon or commutation of the sentence. Amnesty, pardon or commutation of the sentence of death may be granted in all cases.
5. Sentence of death shall not be imposed for crimes committed by persons below eighteen years of age and shall not be carried out on pregnant women.
6. Nothing in this article shall be invoked to delay or to prevent the abolition of capital punishment by any State Party to the present Covenant.

Article 7 General comment on its implementation

No one shall be subjected to torture or to cruel, inhuman or degrading treatment or punishment. In particular, no one shall be subjected without his free consent to medical or scientific experimentation.

Article 8

1. No one shall be held in slavery; slavery and the slave-trade in all their forms shall be prohibited.
2. No one shall be held in servitude.
3.
   (a) No one shall be required to perform forced or compulsory labour;

   (b) Paragraph 3 (a) shall not be held to preclude, in countries where imprisonment with hard labour may be imposed as a punishment for a crime, the performance of hard labour in pursuance of a sentence to such punishment by a competent court;

   (c) For the purpose of this paragraph the term "forced or compulsory labour" shall not include:

      (i) Any work or service, not referred to in subparagraph (b), normally required of a person who is under detention in consequence of a lawful order of a court, or of a person during conditional release from such detention;

      (ii) Any service of a military character and, in countries where conscientious objection is recognized, any national service required by law of conscientious objectors;

      (iii) Any service exacted in cases of emergency or calamity threatening the life or well-being of the community;

(iv) Any work or service which forms part of normal civil obligations.

Article 9 General Comment on its Implementation

1. Everyone has the right to liberty and security of person. No one shall be subjected to arbitrary arrest or detention. No one shall be deprived of his liberty except on such grounds and in accordance with such procedure as are established by law.
2. Anyone who is arrested shall be informed, at the time of arrest, of the reasons for his arrest and shall be promptly informed of any charges against him.
3. Anyone arrested or detained on a criminal charge shall be brought promptly before a judge or other officer authorized by law to exercise judicial power and shall be entitled to trial within a reasonable time or to release. It shall not be the general rule that persons awaiting trial shall be detained in custody, but release may be subject to guarantees to appear for trial, at any other stage of the judicial proceedings, and, should occasion arise, for execution of the judgement.
4. Anyone who is deprived of his liberty by arrest or detention shall be entitled to take proceedings before a court, in order that court may decide without delay on the lawfulness of his detention and order his release if the detention is not lawful.
5. Anyone who has been the victim of unlawful arrest or detention shall have an enforceable right to compensation.

Article 10 General comment on its implementation

1. All persons deprived of their liberty shall be treated

with humanity and with respect for the inherent dignity of the human person.

2.

(a) Accused persons shall, save in exceptional circumstances, be segregated from convicted persons and shall be subject to separate treatment appropriate to their status as unconvicted persons;

(b) Accused juvenile persons shall be separated from adults and brought as speedily as possible for adjudication. 3. The penitentiary system shall comprise treatment of prisoners the essential aim of which shall be their reformation and social rehabilitation. Juvenile offenders shall be segregated from adults and be accorded treatment appropriate to their age and legal status.

Article 11

No one shall be imprisoned merely on the ground of inability to fulfil a contractual obligation.

Article 12 General Comment on its Implementation

1. Everyone lawfully within the territory of a State shall, within that territory, have the right to liberty of movement and freedom to choose his residence.
2. Everyone shall be free to leave any country, including his own.
3. The above-mentioned rights shall not be subject to any restrictions except those which are provided by law, are necessary to protect national security, public order (ordre public), public health or morals or the rights and freedoms of others, and are consistent with the other rights recognized in the present Covenant.

4. No one shall be arbitrarily deprived of the right to enter his own country.

Article 13

An alien lawfully in the territory of a State Party to the present Covenant may be expelled therefrom only in pursuance of a decision reached in accordance with law and shall, except where compelling reasons of national security otherwise require, be allowed to submit the reasons against his expulsion and to have his case reviewed by, and be represented for the purpose before, the competent authority or a person or persons especially designated by the competent authority.

Article 14 General comment on its implementation

1. All persons shall be equal before the courts and tribunals. In the determination of any criminal charge against him, or of his rights and obligations in a suit at law, everyone shall be entitled to a fair and public hearing by a competent, independent and impartial tribunal established by law. The press and the public may be excluded from all or part of a trial for reasons of morals, public order (ordre public) or national security in a democratic society, or when the interest of the private lives of the parties so requires, or to the extent strictly necessary in the opinion of the court in special circumstances where publicity would prejudice the interests of justice; but any judgement rendered in a criminal case or in a suit at law shall be made public except where the interest of juvenile persons otherwise requires or the proceedings concern matrimonial disputes or the guardianship of children.
2. Everyone charged with a criminal offence shall have the right to be presumed innocent until proved guilty according to law.

3. In the determination of any criminal charge against him, everyone shall be entitled to the following minimum guarantees, in full equality:

   (a) To be informed promptly and in detail in a language which he understands of the nature and cause of the charge against him;

   (b) To have adequate time and facilities for the preparation of his defence and to communicate with counsel of his own choosing;

   (c) To be tried without undue delay;

   (d) To be tried in his presence, and to defend himself in person or through legal assistance of his own choosing; to be informed, if he does not have legal assistance, of this right; and to have legal assistance assigned to him, in any case where the interests of justice so require, and without payment by him in any such case if he does not have sufficient means to pay for it;

   (e) To examine, or have examined, the witnesses against him and to obtain the attendance and examination of witnesses on his behalf under the same conditions as witnesses against him;

   (f) To have the free assistance of an interpreter if he cannot understand or speak the language used in court;

   (g) Not to be compelled to testify against himself or to confess guilt.

4. In the case of juvenile persons, the procedure shall be such as will take account of their age and the desirability of promoting their rehabilitation.

5. Everyone convicted of a crime shall have the right to his conviction and sentence being reviewed by a higher tribunal according to law.

6. When a person has by a final decision been convicted of a criminal offence and when subsequently his conviction has been reversed or he has been pardoned on the ground that a new or newly discovered fact shows conclusively that there has been a miscarriage of justice, the person who has suffered punishment as a result of such conviction shall be compensated according to law, unless it is proved that the non-disclosure of the unknown fact in time is wholly or partly attributable to him.

7. No one shall be liable to be tried or punished again for an offence for which he has already been finally convicted or acquitted in accordance with the law and penal procedure of each country.

Article 15

1. No one shall be held guilty of any criminal offence on account of any act or omission which did not constitute a criminal offence, under national or international law, at the time when it was committed. Nor shall a heavier penalty be imposed than the one that was applicable at the time when the criminal offence was committed. If, subsequent to the commission of the offence, provision is made by law for the imposition of the lighter penalty, the offender shall benefit thereby.

2. Nothing in this article shall prejudice the trial and punishment of any person for any act or omission which, at the time when it was committed, was criminal according to the general principles of law recognized by the community of nations.

Article 16

Everyone shall have the right to recognition everywhere as a person before the law.

Article 17 General comment on its implementation

1. No one shall be subjected to arbitrary or unlawful interference with his privacy, family, home or correspondence, nor to unlawful attacks on his honour and reputation.

2. Everyone has the right to the protection of the law against such interference or attacks.

Article 18 General Comment on its Implementation

1. Everyone shall have the right to freedom of thought, conscience and religion. This right shall include freedom to have or to adopt a religion or belief of his choice, and freedom, either individually or in community with others and in public or private, to manifest his religion or belief in worship, observance, practice and teaching.

2. No one shall be subject to coercion which would impair his freedom to have or to adopt a religion or belief of his choice.

3. Freedom to manifest one's religion or beliefs may be subject only to such limitations as are prescribed by law and are necessary to protect public safety, order, health, or morals or the fundamental rights and freedoms of others. 4. The States Parties to the present Covenant undertake to have respect for the liberty of parents and, when applicable, legal guardians to ensure the religious and moral education of their children in conformity with their own convictions.

Article 19 General Comment on its Implementation

1. Everyone shall have the right to hold opinions without interference.

2. Everyone shall have the right to freedom of expression; this right shall include freedom to seek, receive and impart information and ideas of all kinds, regardless of frontiers, either orally, in writing or in print, in the form of art, or through any other media of his choice.

3. The exercise of the rights provided for in paragraph 2 of this article carries with it special duties and responsibilities. It may therefore be subject to certain restrictions, but these shall only be such as are provided by law and are necessary:

   (a) For respect of the rights or reputations of others;

   (b) For the protection of national security or of public order (ordre public), or of public health or morals.

Article 20 General Comment on its Implementation

1. Any propaganda for war shall be prohibited by law.

2. Any advocacy of national, racial or religious hatred that constitutes incitement to discrimination, hostility or violence shall be prohibited by law.

Article 21

The right of peaceful assembly shall be recognized. No restrictions may be placed on the exercise of this right other than those imposed in conformity with the law and which are necessary in a democratic society in the interests of national security or public safety, public order (ordre public), the protection of public health or morals or the protection of the rights and freedoms of others.

Article 22

1. Everyone shall have the right to freedom of association with others, including the right to form and join trade unions for the protection of his interests.

2. No restrictions may be placed on the exercise of this right other than those which are prescribed by law and which are necessary in a democratic society in the interests of national security or public safety, public order (ordre public), the protection of public health or morals or the protection of the rights and freedoms of others. This article shall not prevent the imposition of lawful restrictions on members of the armed forces and of the police in their exercise of this right.

3. Nothing in this article shall authorize States Parties to the International Labour Organisation Convention of 1948 concerning Freedom of Association and Protection of the Right to Organize to take legislative measures which would prejudice, or to apply the law in such a manner as to prejudice, the guarantees provided for in that Convention.

Article 23 General comment on its implementation

1. The family is the natural and fundamental group unit of society and is entitled to protection by society and the State.
2. The right of men and women of marriageable age to marry and to found a family shall be recognized.
3. No marriage shall be entered into without the free and full consent of the intending spouses.
4. States Parties to the present Covenant shall take appropriate steps to ensure equality of rights and responsibilities of spouses as to marriage, during marriage and at its dissolution. In the case of dissolution, provision shall be made for the necessary protection of any children.

Article 24 General comment on its implementation

1. Every child shall have, without any discrimination as

to race, colour, sex, language, religion, national or social origin, property or birth, the right to such measures of protection as are required by his status as a minor, on the part of his family, society and the State.

2. Every child shall be registered immediately after birth and shall have a name.

3. Every child has the right to acquire a nationality.

Article 25 General comment on its implementation

Every citizen shall have the right and the opportunity, without any of the distinctions mentioned in article 2 and without unreasonable restrictions:

(a) To take part in the conduct of public affairs, directly or through freely chosen representatives;

(b) To vote and to be elected at genuine periodic elections which shall be by universal and equal suffrage and shall be held by secret ballot, guaranteeing the free expression of the will of the electors;

(c) To have access, on general terms of equality, to public service in his country.

Article 26

All persons are equal before the law and are entitled without any discrimination to the equal protection of the law. In this respect, the law shall prohibit any discrimination and guarantee to all persons equal and effective protection against discrimination on any ground such as race, colour, sex, language, religion, political or other opinion, national or social origin, property, birth or other status.

Article 27 General comment on its implementation

In those States in which ethnic, religious or linguistic minorities exist, persons belonging to such minorities shall not be denied the right, in community with the other members of their group, to enjoy their own culture, to profess and practise their own religion, or to use their own language.

PART IV

Article 28

1. There shall be established a Human Rights Committee (hereafter referred to in the present Covenant as the Committee). It shall consist of eighteen members and shall carry out the functions hereinafter provided.
2. The Committee shall be composed of nationals of the States Parties to the present Covenant who shall be persons of high moral character and recognized competence in the field of human rights, consideration being given to the usefulness of the participation of some persons having legal experience.
3. The members of the Committee shall be elected and shall serve in their personal capacity.

Article 29

1. The members of the Committee shall be elected by secret ballot from a list of persons possessing the qualifications prescribed in article 28 and nominated for the purpose by the States Parties to the present Covenant.
2. Each State Party to the present Covenant may nominate not more than two persons. These persons shall be nationals of the nominating State.

3. A person shall be eligible for renomination.

Article 30

1. The initial election shall be held no later than six months after the date of the entry into force of the present Covenant.

2. At least four months before the date of each election to the Committee, other than an election to fill a vacancy declared in accordance with article 34, the Secretary-General of the United Nations shall address a written invitation to the States Parties to the present Covenant to submit their nominations for membership of the Committee within three months.

3. The Secretary-General of the United Nations shall prepare a list in alphabetical order of all the persons thus nominated, with an indication of the States Parties which have nominated them, and shall submit it to the States Parties to the present Covenant no later than one month before the date of each election.

4. Elections of the members of the Committee shall be held at a meeting of the States Parties to the present Covenant convened by the Secretary General of the United Nations at the Headquarters of the United Nations. At that meeting, for which two thirds of the States Parties to the present Covenant shall constitute a quorum, the persons elected to the Committee shall be those nominees who obtain the largest number of votes and an absolute majority of the votes of the representatives of States Parties present and voting.

Article 31

1. The Committee may not include more than one national of the same State.

2. In the election of the Committee, consideration shall be given to equitable geographical distribution of

membership and to the representation of the different forms of civilization and of the principal legal systems.

Article 32

1. The members of the Committee shall be elected for a term of four years. They shall be eligible for re-election if renominated. However, the terms of nine of the members elected at the first election shall expire at the end of two years; immediately after the first election, the names of these nine members shall be chosen by lot by the Chairman of the meeting referred to in article 30, paragraph 4.
2. Elections at the expiry of office shall be held in accordance with the preceding articles of this part of the present Covenant.

Article 33

1. If, in the unanimous opinion of the other members, a member of the Committee has ceased to carry out his functions for any cause other than absence of a temporary character, the Chairman of the Committee shall notify the Secretary-General of the United Nations, who shall then declare the seat of that member to be vacant.
2. In the event of the death or the resignation of a member of the Committee, the Chairman shall immediately notify the Secretary-General of the United Nations, who shall declare the seat vacant from the date of death or the date on which the resignation takes effect.

Article 34

1. When a vacancy is declared in accordance with article 33 and if the term of office of the member to be replaced does not expire within six months of the

declaration of the vacancy, the Secretary-General of the United Nations shall notify each of the States Parties to the present Covenant, which may within two months submit nominations in accordance with article 29 for the purpose of filling the vacancy.

2. The Secretary-General of the United Nations shall prepare a list in alphabetical order of the persons thus nominated and shall submit it to the States Parties to the present Covenant. The election to fill the vacancy shall then take place in accordance with the relevant provisions of this part of the present Covenant.

3. A member of the Committee elected to fill a vacancy declared in accordance with article 33 shall hold office for the remainder of the term of the member who vacated the seat on the Committee under the provisions of that article.

Article 35

The members of the Committee shall, with the approval of the General Assembly of the United Nations, receive emoluments from United Nations resources on such terms and conditions as the General Assembly may decide, having regard to the importance of the Committee's responsibilities.

Article 36

The Secretary-General of the United Nations shall provide the necessary staff and facilities for the effective performance of the functions of the Committee under the present Covenant.

Article 37

1. The Secretary-General of the United Nations shall convene the initial meeting of the Committee at the Headquarters of the United Nations.

2. After its initial meeting, the Committee shall meet at such times as shall be provided in its rules of procedure.

3. The Committee shall normally meet at the Headquarters of the United Nations or at the United Nations Office at Geneva.

Article 38

Every member of the Committee shall, before taking up his duties, make a solemn declaration in open committee that he will perform his functions impartially and conscientiously.

Article 39

1. The Committee shall elect its officers for a term of two years. They may be re-elected.

2. The Committee shall establish its own rules of procedure, but these rules shall provide, inter alia, that:

   (a) Twelve members shall constitute a quorum;

   (b) Decisions of the Committee shall be made by a majority vote of the members present.

Article 40

1. The States Parties to the present Covenant undertake to submit reports on the measures they have adopted which give effect to the rights recognized herein and on the progress made in the enjoyment of those rights:

   (a) Within one year of the entry into force of the present Covenant for the States Parties concerned;

   (b) Thereafter whenever the Committee so requests.

2. All reports shall be submitted to the Secretary-General of the United Nations, who shall transmit them to the Committee for consideration. Reports shall indicate the factors and difficulties, if any, affecting the implementation of the present Covenant.

3. The Secretary-General of the United Nations may, after consultation with the Committee, transmit to the specialized agencies concerned copies of such parts of the reports as may fall within their field of competence.

4. The Committee shall study the reports submitted by the States Parties to the present Covenant. It shall transmit its reports, and such general comments as it may consider appropriate, to the States Parties. The Committee may also transmit to the Economic and Social Council these comments along with the copies of the reports it has received from States Parties to the present Covenant.

5. The States Parties to the present Covenant may submit to the Committee observations on any comments that may be made in accordance with paragraph 4 of this article.

Article 41 General comment on its implementation

1. A State Party to the present Covenant may at any time declare under this article that it recognizes the competence of the Committee to receive and consider communications to the effect that a State Party claims that another State Party is not fulfilling its obligations under the present Covenant. Communications under this article may be received and considered only if submitted by a State Party which has made a declaration recognizing in regard to itself the competence of the Committee. No communication shall be received by the Committee if it concerns a

State Party which has not made such a declaration. Communications received under this article shall be dealt with in accordance with the following procedure:

(a) If a State Party to the present Covenant considers that another State Party is not giving effect to the provisions of the present Covenant, it may, by written communication, bring the matter to the attention of that State Party. Within three months after the receipt of the communication the receiving State shall afford the State which sent the communication an explanation, or any other statement in writing clarifying the matter which should include, to the extent possible and pertinent, reference to domestic procedures and remedies taken, pending, or available in the matter;

(b) If the matter is not adjusted to the satisfaction of both States Parties concerned within six months after the receipt by the receiving State of the initial communication, either State shall have the right to refer the matter to the Committee, by notice given to the Committee and to the other State;

(c) The Committee shall deal with a matter referred to it only after it has ascertained that all available domestic remedies have been invoked and exhausted in the matter, in conformity with the generally recognized principles of international law. This shall not be the rule where the application of the remedies is unreasonably prolonged;

(d) The Committee shall hold closed meetings when examining communications under this article;

(e) Subject to the provisions of subparagraph ©, the Committee shall make available its good offices to the States Parties concerned with a view to a friendly solution of the matter on the basis of respect for human rights and fundamental freedoms as recognized in the present Covenant;

(f) In any matter referred to it, the Committee may call upon the States Parties concerned, referred to in subparagraph (b), to supply any relevant information;

(g) The States Parties concerned, referred to in subparagraph (b), shall have the right to be represented when the matter is being considered in the Committee and to make submissions orally and/ or in writing;

(h) The Committee shall, within twelve months after the date of receipt of notice under subparagraph (b), submit a report:

(i) If a solution within the terms of subparagraph (e) is reached, the Committee shall confine its report to a brief statement of the facts and of the solution reached;

(ii) If a solution within the terms of subparagraph (e) is not reached, the Committee shall confine its report to a brief statement of the facts; the written submissions and record of the oral submissions made by the States Parties concerned shall be attached to the report. In every matter, the report shall be communicated to the States Parties concerned.

2. The provisions of this article shall come into force when ten States Parties to the present Covenant have made declarations under paragraph I of this article. Such declarations shall be deposited by the States Parties with the Secretary-General of the United Nations, who shall transmit copies thereof to the other States Parties. A declaration may be withdrawn at any

time by notification to the Secretary-General. Such a withdrawal shall not prejudice the consideration of any matter which is the subject of a communication already transmitted under this article; no further communication by any State Party shall be received after the notification of withdrawal of the declaration has been received by the Secretary-General, unless the State Party concerned has made a new declaration.

Article 42

1.

(a) If a matter referred to the Committee in accordance with article 41 is not resolved to the satisfaction of the States Parties concerned, the Committee may, with the prior consent of the States Parties concerned, appoint an ad hoc Conciliation Commission (hereinafter referred to as the Commission). The good offices of the Commission shall be made available to the States Parties concerned with a view to an amicable solution of the matter on the basis of respect for the present Covenant;

(b) The Commission shall consist of five persons acceptable to the States Parties concerned. If the States Parties concerned fail to reach agreement within three months on all or part of the composition of the Commission, the members of the Commission concerning whom no agreement has been reached shall be elected by secret ballot by a two-thirds majority vote of the Committee from among its members.

2. The members of the Commission shall serve in their personal capacity. They shall not be nationals of the States Parties concerned, or of a State not Party to the present Covenant, or of a State Party which has not made a declaration under article 41.

3. The Commission shall elect its own Chairman and adopt its own rules of procedure.

4. The meetings of the Commission shall normally be held at the Headquarters of the United Nations or at the United Nations Office at Geneva. However, they may be held at such other convenient places as the Commission may determine in consultation with the Secretary-General of the United Nations and the States Parties concerned.

5. The secretariat provided in accordance with article 36 shall also service the commissions appointed under this article.

6. The information received and collated by the Committee shall be made available to the Commission and the Commission may call upon the States Parties concerned to supply any other relevant information. 7. When the Commission has fully considered the matter, but in any event not later than twelve months after having been seized of the matter, it shall submit to the Chairman of the Committee a report for communication to the States Parties concerned:

(a) If the Commission is unable to complete its consideration of the matter within twelve months, it shall confine its report to a brief statement of the status of its consideration of the matter;

(b) If an amicable solution to the matter on tie basis of respect for human rights as recognized in the present Covenant is reached, the Commission shall confine its report to a brief statement of the facts and of the solution reached;

(c) If a solution within the terms of subparagraph (b) is not reached, the Commission's report shall embody its findings on all questions of fact relevant to the issues between the States Parties concerned, and its views on the possibilities of an amicable solution of the matter. This report shall also contain the written submissions and a record of the oral submissions made by the States Parties concerned;

(d) If the Commission's report is submitted under subparagraph ©, the States Parties concerned shall, within three months of the receipt of the report, notify the Chairman of the Committee whether or not they accept the contents of the report of the Commission.

8. The provisions of this article are without prejudice to the responsibilities of the Committee under article 41.

9. The States Parties concerned shall share equally all the expenses of the members of the Commission in accordance with estimates to be provided by the Secretary-General of the United Nations.

10. The Secretary-General of the United Nations shall be empowered to pay the expenses of the members of the Commission, if necessary, before reimbursement by the States Parties concerned, in accordance with paragraph 9 of this article.

Article 43

The members of the Committee, and of the ad hoc conciliation commissions which may be appointed under article 42, shall be entitled to the facilities, privileges and immunities of experts on mission for the United Nations as laid down in the relevant sections of the Convention on the Privileges and Immunities of the United Nations.

Article 44

The provisions for the implementation of the present Covenant shall apply without prejudice to the procedures prescribed in the field of human rights by or under the constituent instruments and the conventions of the United Nations and of the specialized agencies and shall not prevent the States Parties to the present Covenant from having recourse to other procedures for settling a dispute in accordance with general or special international agreements in force between them.

Article 45

The Committee shall submit to the General Assembly of the United Nations, through the Economic and Social Council, an annual report on its activities.

PART V

Article 46

Nothing in the present Covenant shall be interpreted as impairing the provisions of the Charter of the United Nations and of the constitutions of the specialized agencies which define the respective responsibilities of the various organs of the United Nations and of the specialized agencies in regard to the matters dealt with in the present Covenant.

Article 47

Nothing in the present Covenant shall be interpreted as impairing the inherent right of all peoples to enjoy and utilize fully and freely their natural wealth and resources.

PART VI

Article 48

1. The present Covenant is open for signature by any State Member of the United Nations or member of

any of its specialized agencies, by any State Party to the Statute of the International Court of Justice, and by any other State which has been invited by the General Assembly of the United Nations to become a Party to the present Covenant.

2. The present Covenant is subject to ratification. Instruments of ratification shall be deposited with the Secretary-General of the United Nations.

3. The present Covenant shall be open to accession by any State referred to in paragraph 1 of this article.

4. Accession shall be effected by the deposit of an instrument of accession with the Secretary-General of the United Nations.

5. The Secretary-General of the United Nations shall inform all States which have signed this Covenant or acceded to it of the deposit of each instrument of ratification or accession.

Article 49

1. The present Covenant shall enter into force three months after the date of the deposit with the Secretary-General of the United Nations of the thirty-fifth instrument of ratification or instrument of accession.

2. For each State ratifying the present Covenant or acceding to it after the deposit of the thirty-fifth instrument of ratification or instrument of accession, the present Covenant shall enter into force three months after the date of the deposit of its own instrument of ratification or instrument of accession.

Article 50

The provisions of the present Covenant shall extend to all

parts of federal States without any limitations or exceptions.

Article 51

1. Any State Party to the present Covenant may propose an amendment and file it with the Secretary-General of the United Nations. The Secretary-General of the United Nations shall thereupon communicate any proposed amendments to the States Parties to the present Covenant with a request that they notify him whether they favour a conference of States Parties for the purpose of considering and voting upon the proposals. In the event that at least one third of the States Parties favours such a conference, the Secretary-General shall convene the conference under the auspices of the United Nations. Any amendment adopted by a majority of the States Parties present and voting at the conference shall be submitted to the General Assembly of the United Nations for approval.
2. Amendments shall come into force when they have been approved by the General Assembly of the United Nations and accepted by a two-thirds majority of the States Parties to the present Covenant in accordance with their respective constitutional processes.
3. When amendments come into force, they shall be binding on those States Parties which have accepted them, other States Parties still being bound by the provisions of the present Covenant and any earlier amendment which they have accepted.

Article 52

Irrespective of the notifications made under article 48,

paragraph 5, the Secretary-General of the United Nations shall inform all States referred to in paragraph I of the same article of the following particulars:

(a) Signatures, ratifications and accessions under article 48;

(b) The date of the entry into force of the present Covenant under article 49 and the date of the entry into force of any amendments under article 51.

Article 53

1. The present Covenant, of which the Chinese, English, French, Russian and Spanish texts are equally authentic, shall be deposited in the archives of the United Nations.

2. The Secretary-General of the United Nations shall transmit certified copies of the present Covenant to all States referred to in article 48.

7

International Covenant on Economic, Social and Cultural Rights (ICESCR)

The International Covenant on Economic, Social and Cultural Rights was adopted and opened for signature, ratification and accession by General Assembly resolution 2200 A (XXI) of 16 December 1966, following almost 20 years of drafting debates. It finally gained the force of law a decade later, entering into force on 3 January 1976.

The Covenant contains some of the most significant international legal provisions establishing economic, social and cultural rights, including rights relating to work in just and favourable conditions, to social protection, to an adequate standard of living, to the highest attainable standards of physical and mental health, to education and to enjoyment of the benefits of cultural freedom and scientific progress.

As on 12 April 1996, 133 States had ratified the Covenant, thereby voluntarily undertaking to implement its norms and provisions.

Compliance by States parties with their obligations under the Covenant and the level of implementation of the rights and duties in question is monitored by the Committee on Economic, Social and Cultural Rights.

The Committee works on the basis of many sources of information, including reports submitted by States parties and information from United Nations specialised agencies--International Labour Organisation, United Nations Educational, Scientific and Cultural Organisation, World Health Organisation, Food and Agriculture Organisation of the United Nations—from the Office of the United Nations High Commissioner for Refugees, and from the United Nations Centre for Human Settlements (Habitat) and others. It also receives information from non-governmental and community-based organisations working in States which have ratified the Covenant, from international human rights and other non-governmental organisations, from other United Nations treaty bodies, and from generally available literature.

Substantive Provisions of the International Covenant on Economic, Social and Cultural Rights Self-determination

Article 1

1. All peoples have the right of self-determination. By virtue of that right they freely determine their political status and freely pursue their economic, social and cultural development.
2. All peoples may, for their own ends, freely dispose of their natural wealth and resources without prejudice to any obligations arising out of international economic cooperation, based upon the principle of mutual benefit, and international law. In no case may a people be deprived of its own means of subsistence.
3. The States Parties to the present Covenant, including those having responsibility for the administration of

> Non-Self-Governing and Trust Territories, shall promote the realisation of the right of self-determination, and shall respect that right, in conformity with the provisions of the Charter of the United Nations.

Article one of the Covenant is worded in precisely the same terminology as article one of its sister text, the International Covenant on Civil and Political Rights. The self-determination provisions in common article one are particularly important because the realisation of this right is a fundamental prerequisite for the effective guarantee and observance of individual human rights and is pivotal in securing and strengthening human rights protection measures.

The right to self-determination is a cornerstone of the international legal system, and has been a premier concern of the international community since the creation of the United Nations in 1945, particularly in regard to issues such as independence, non-interference and democracy. This right has both external and internal dimensions and has been the subject of some controversy in recent years, as it is increasingly asserted by groups within countries, as distinct from ex-colonies and occupied countries.

As far as the rights contained in the Covenant are concerned, the right of peoples freely to pursue their economic, social and cultural development includes freedom to carry on economic, social and cultural activities.

Obligations of States Parties

Article 2

1. Each State Party to the present Covenant undertakes to take steps, individually and through international assistance and cooperation, especially economic and technical, to the maximum of its available resources,

with a view to achieving progressively the full realisation of the rights recognised in the present Covenant by all appropriate means, including particularly the adoption of legislative measures.

2. The States parties to the present Covenant undertake to guarantee that the rights enunciated in the present Covenant will be exercised without discrimination of any kind as to race, colour, sex, language, religion, political or other opinion, national or social origin property, birth or other status.

3. Developing countries, with due regard to human rights and their national economy, may determine to what extent they would guarantee the economic rights recognised in the present Covenant to non-nationals.

Article 2 is one of the most important articles of the Covenant because it outlines the nature of States parties' legal obligations under the Covenant and determines how they must approach the implementation of the substantive rights contained in articles 6 to 15.

Any analysis of obligations relating to economic, social and cultural rights cannot be isolated from the obligations inherent in securing the individual entitlements of the beneficiaries of the right(s) in question. Most frequently, obligations are divided into 'layers' reflecting duties to (a) respect, (b) protect, (c) promote, and (d) fulfil each of the rights contained in the Covenant. Each of these legal responsibilities can take on more specific obligations of 'conduct' (e.g., action or inaction) and obligations of 'result' (e.g., ends).

The provision from article 2, paragraph 1, requires all States parties to begin immediately to take measures towards the full enjoyment by everyone of all the rights in the Covenant. The adoption of legislation will, in many cases, be indispensable if economic, social and cultural rights are to be made real, but laws alone are not a sufficient response at the national level. Administrative, judicial, policy, economic, social and educational measures and many other steps will be required by governments in order to ensure these rights to all.

Under article 2, paragraph 1, States parties are legally obliged to undertake legislative action in some instances, particularly when existing laws are clearly incompatible with the obligations assumed under the Covenant. This would be the case when, for instance, a law in a given country was patently discriminatory or had the express effect of preventing the enjoyment of any of the rights in the Covenant, or when legislation allowed the violation of rights, especially in terms of negative duties of States. Laws allowing governments forcibly to remove people from their homes, evicting them without due process of law, would have to be amended in order to bring domestic legislation into conformity with the Covenant.

The 'progressive obligation' component of the Covenant is often mistakenly taken to imply that only once a State reaches a certain level of economic development must the rights established under the Covenant be realised. This is not the intent of this clause. Rather, the duty in question obliges all States parties, notwithstanding their level of national wealth, to move immediately and as quickly as possible towards the realisation of economic, social and cultural rights. This clause should never be interpreted as allowing States to defer indefinitely efforts to ensure the enjoyment of the rights laid down in the Covenant.

Whereas certain rights, by their nature, may be more apt to be implemented in terms of the 'progressive obligation' rule, many obligations under the Covenant are clearly required to be implemented immediately. This would apply especially to non-discrimination provisions and to the obligation of States parties to refrain from actively violating economic, social and cultural rights or withdrawing legal and other protection relating to those rights.

The Committee on Economic, Social and Cultural Rights has asserted that this duty exists independently of an increase in available resources and thus recognises that all existing resources must be devoted in the most effective way possible to the realisation of the rights enshrined in the Covenant.

Like the 'progressive realisation' provision, this standard is also used to justify the non-enjoyment of rights. However, as recognised in the Limburg Principles on the Implementation of the International Covenant on Economic, Social and Cultural Rights, this requirement obliges States parties to ensure minimum subsistence rights for everyone, regardless of the level of economic development in a given country.

The term 'available resources' applies both to domestic resources and to any international economic or technical assistance or cooperation available to a State party. In the use of available resources, due priority should be given to the realisation of rights recognised in the Covenant, considering the need to assure to everyone the satisfaction of subsistence requirements, as well as the provision of essential services.

Importantly, the grounds of discrimination mentioned in this provision are not exhaustive and thus certain other forms of unfair discrimination negatively affecting the enjoyment of the rights enunciated in the Covenant (for instance, on the basis of sexual orientation) must be prevented.

According to the Limburg Principles, special measures taken for the sole purpose of securing adequate advancement of certain groups or individuals requiring protection in order to ensure their equal enjoyment of economic, social and cultural rights are not considered discrimination, provided that such measures do not lead to the maintenance of separate rights for different groups and are not continued after their objectives have been achieved. This applies, for example, to affirmative-action programme.

This provision not only obliges governments to desist from discriminatory behaviour and to alter laws and practices which allow discrimination, it also applies to the duty of States parties to prohibit private persons and bodies (third parties) from practising discrimination in any field of public life.

Equal Rights for Men and Women

Article 3

The States parties to the present Covenant undertake to ensure the equal right of men and women to the enjoyment of all economic, social and cultural rights set forth in the present Covenant.

Women often suffer substantial and disproportionate difficulties in securing human rights, including economic, social and cultural rights. Article 3 guarantees that men and women possess precisely the same legal entitlement to the rights set forth in the Covenant and that, if necessary, special measures will be employed by States parties to ensure that this position of equality is attained.

The Covenant provides a framework for instigating progressive and immediate measures such that women may enjoy on an equal footing rights which have often been denied them. For instance, the housing rights provisions in article 11, paragraph 1, of the Covenant must apply to men and women equally, and thus women must be accorded equal rights to housing inheritance—

something which is still not the case in many countries. Together, article 3 and article 2, paragraph 2, thus provide significant legal protection against all forms of discrimination in the pursuit of economic, social and cultural rights.

LIMITATIONS

Article 4

The States parties to the present Covenant recognise that, in the enjoyment of those rights provided by the State in conformity with the present Covenant, the State may subject such rights only to such limitations as are determined by law only in so far as this may be compatible with the nature of these rights and solely for the purpose of promoting the general welfare in a democratic society.

Article 5

1. Nothing, in the present Covenant may be interpreted as implying for any State group or person any right to engage in any activity or to perform any act aimed at the destruction of any of the rights or freedoms recognised herein, or at their limitation to a greater extent than is provided for in the present Covenant.
2. No restriction upon or derogation from any of the fundamental human rights recognised or existing in any country in virtue of law, conventions, regulations or custom shall be admitted on the pretext that the present Covenant does not recognise such rights or that it recognises them to a lesser extent.

Articles 4 and 5 were not intended by the drafters of the Covenant to be overly permissive of the imposition of limitations by the state on the rights provided for. Rather, these provisions are formulated in such a manner as to be protective of the rights of individuals. They are also not designed to introduce limitations on rights affecting the subsistence or survival of the individual or the integrity of the person.

If a State party finds it necessary to invoke the provisions of these articles, it may do so only if this is provided for by law and only if the measures in question are consistent with the Covenant. Such measures cannot be applied in an arbitrary, unreasonable or discriminatory way. Moreover, individuals should have legal safeguards and effective remedies against illegal or abusive imposition of limitations on economic, social and cultural rights.

The term 'democratic society' (art. 4) further restricts the imposition of limitations under the Covenant and thus the burden rests on the State to prove that any limitations do not impair the democratic functioning of society.

None of the provisions in the law relating to any limitation may be interpreted in such a way as to nullify any of the rights or freedoms recognised in the Covenant. The main purpose of article 5, paragraph 2, is to ensure that no provision of the Covenant is interpreted so as to prejudice provisions of domestic law or any other legal instrument already in force, or which may come into force, under which more favourable treatment would be accorded to persons protected.

The Right to Work

Article 6

1. The States parties to the present Covenant recognise the right to work, which includes the right of everyone to the opportunity to gain his living by work which he freely chooses or accepts, and will take appropriate steps to safeguard this right.

2. The steps to be taken by a State party to the present Covenant to achieve the full realisation of this right shall include technical and vocational guidance and training programmes, policies and techniques to achieve steady economic, social and cultural development and full and productive employment under conditions safeguarding, fundamental political and economic freedoms to the individual.

Freely chosen work remains an essential part of being human. For many people, whether employed in the formal or informal sectors, work represents the primary source of income on which subsistence, survival and life depend. The right to work is fundamental to the enjoyment of certain subsistence and livelihood rights such as food, clothing, housing, etc. Moreover, one's working status may easily affect the enjoyment of other rights relating to health and education. The right to work is increasingly important as governments the world over continue to withdraw from the provision of basic services, leaving these to market forces and non-governmental actors.

The right to work is fundamental to ensuring the dignity and self-respect of the beneficiaries of the rights contained in the Covenant. Article 6 obliges States parties to refrain from instigating or allowing forced labour. The Committee on Economic, Social and Cultural Rights has examined this article in terms of the implementation of policies and measures aimed at securing work for all who are available to work. This right encompasses, therefore, both the right to enter into employment and the right not to be unjustly deprived of work. Although unemployment persists in all States parties, these States must apply the basic principles set out in article 2 for ensuring the full realisation of the right to work.

THE RIGHT TO JUST AND FAVOURABLE CONDITIONS OF WORK

Article 7

The States parties to the present Covenant recognise the right of everyone to the enjoyment of just and favourable conditions of work which ensure, in particular:

a) Remuneration which provides all workers, as a minimum, with:

   i) Fair wages and equal remuneration for work of equal value without distinction of any kind, in particular women being guaranteed conditions of work not inferior to those enjoyed by men, with equal pay for equal work;

   ii) A decent living for themselves and their families in accordance with the provisions of the present Covenant.

b) Safe and healthy working, conditions;

c) Equal opportunity for everyone to be promoted in his employment to an appropriate higher level, subject to no considerations other than those of seniority and competence;

d) Rest, leisure and reasonable limitation of working hours and periodic holidays with pay, as well as remuneration for public holidays.

Article 7 establishes a right to a minimum remuneration for employment, stipulating fair wages sufficient to guarantee a decent living, as well as working conditions that are just and favourable. Wages must be equitable and just in order to be considered fair.

This article relates closely to a large number of conventions adopted by the International Labour Organisation, including the Minimum Wage Fixing

Convention (No. 131, 1970) and the Equal Remuneration Convention (No. 100, 1951).

People must be afforded minimum conditions of occupational health and safety, and States parties are responsible for adopting policies and laws to that end. A coherent national policy in this regard is incumbent on all States parties.

The standards laid down in article 7 also relate to the duties of States parties to reduce the working week in a progressive manner and to ensure that workers enjoy adequate rest and holidays. For all aspects of this article, States parties must establish a baseline or minimum standard below which the working conditions of no worker should be allowed to fall; they must also develop enforcement measures guaranteeing these rights.

The Right to Form and Join Trade Unions

Article 8

1. The States Parties to the present Covenant undertake to ensure:

   a) The right of everyone to form trade unions and join the trade union of his choice, subject only to the rules of the organisation concerned, for the promotion and protection of his economic and social interests. No restrictions may be placed on the exercise of this right other than those prescribed by law and which are necessary in a democratic society in the interests of national security or public order or for the protection of the rights and freedoms of others;

   b) The right of trade unions to establish national federations or confederations and the right of the latter to form or join international trade-union organisations;

c) The right of trade unions to function freely subject to no limitations other than those prescribed by law and which are necessary in a democratic society in the interests of national security or public order or for the protection of the rights and freedoms of others;

d) The right to strike, provided that it is exercised in conformity with the laws of the particular country.

2. This article shall not prevent the imposition of lawful restrictions on the exercise of these rights by members of the armed forces or of the police or of the administration of the State.

3. Nothing in this article shall authorise States parties to the International Labour Organisation Convention of 1948 concerning Freedom of Association and Protection of the Right to Organise to take legislative measures which would prejudice, or apply the law in such a manner as would prejudice, the guarantees provided for in that Convention.

The right to form and join trade unions is closely linked to the right to freedom of association, which is widely recognised throughout international human rights law. These rights, combined with the right to strike, are fundamental if the rights of workers and other citizens under the Covenant are to be implemented.

Article 8 provides for a right not to be compelled to join a particular trade union, in accordance with the term of his choice' (para. 1(a)). It also includes the right to federate or confederate, which should not be subject to state control. The right to collective bargaining, the right to protection from dissolution or suspension and the right to strike are also protected.

States parties are allowed some measure of discretion concerning the implementation of article 8, as evidenced by the language concerning limitations in the interests of national security, public order and the rights and freedoms of others. These grounds for exemption, however, must be interpreted narrowly by States parties seeking to invoke them.

With regard to national security concerns, for instance, the Limburg Principles on the Implementation of the International Covenant on Economic, Social and Cultural Rights stress that the systematic violation of economic, social and cultural rights undermines true national security and may jeopardise international peace and security. A State responsible for such violation shall not invoke national security as a justification for measures aimed at suppressing opposition to such violation or at perpetrating repressive practices against its population.

The Right to Social Security and Social Insurance

Article 9

The States parties to the present Covenant recognise the right of everyone to social security, including social insurance.

A large number of States do not maintain adequate social security or social insurance provisions under domestic laws protecting people in circumstances such as old age, disability, ill-health or other situations not allowing them to earn a decent living. At the same time, many countries which do provide such protection are beginning to transfer responsibility for these matters from the state to the private sector. These issues raise serious concerns regarding enjoyment of the rights contained in the Covenant.

The Committee on Economic, Social and Cultural Rights specifically asks States parties whether they maintain social security schemes in the following areas: medical care, cash sickness benefits, maternity benefits, old-age benefits, invalidity benefits, survivors' benefits, employment injury benefits, unemployment benefits and family benefits.

The Committee has devoted particular attention to enjoyment of the rights provided for in article 9 by women, older persons (General Comment No. 6 (1995)), and persons with disabilities (General Comment No. 5 (1994)).

Protection and Assistance for the Family

Article 10

The States parties to the Present Covenant recognise that:

1. The widest possible protection and assistance should be accorded to the family, which is the natural and fundamental group unit of society, particularly for its establishment and while it is responsible for the care and education of dependent children. Marriage must be entered into with the free consent of the intending spouses.

2. Special protection should be accorded to mothers during a reasonable period before and after childbirth. During such period working mothers should be accorded paid leave or leave with adequate social security benefits.

3. Special measures of protection and assistance should be taken on behalf of all children and young persons without any discrimination for reasons of parentage or other conditions. Children and young persons should be protected from economic and social exploitation. Their employment in work harmful to

> their morals or health or dangerous to life or likely to hamper their normal development should be punishable by law. States should also set age limits below which the paid employment of child labour should be prohibited and punishable by law.

Article 10 provides protection for the family, mothers and children. It includes the right to enter freely into marriage, raising doubts as to the situation in countries where marriage occurs without the free and informed consent of one or another spouse, almost invariably the woman. Mothers are to be accorded substantial protection before and after childbirth. The Committee on Economic, Social and Cultural Rights regularly requests information from States parties as to whether any particular groups of women lack such protection.

The Committee has not spent a great deal of time examining situations relating to family rights, but has devoted increased attention to the rights of the child as they are established under article 10, paragraph 3. It has paid particular attention to child labour and the living conditions of children. The most intensive work within the United Nations system on children's rights is carried out by the Committee on the Rights of the Child, with which the Committee on Economic, Social and Cultural Rights works closely.

The Right to an Adequate Standard of Living

Article 11

1. The States parties to the present Covenant recognise the right of everyone to an adequate standard of living for himself and his family, including adequate food, clothing and housing, and to the continuous improvement of living conditions. The States parties

will take appropriate steps to ensure the realisation of this right, recognising to this effect the essential importance of international cooperation based on free consent.

2. The States parties to the present Covenant, recognising the fundamental right of everyone to be free from hunger, shall take, individually and through international cooperation, the measures, including specific programmes, which are needed :

   a) To improve methods of production, conservation and distribution of food by making full use of technical and scientific knowledge, by disseminating knowledge of the principles of nutrition and by developing or reforming agrarian systems in such a way as to achieve the most efficient development and utilisation of natural resources;

   b) Taking into account the problems of both food-importing and food-exporting countries, to ensure an equitable distribution of world food supplies in relation to need.

Article 11 incorporates a broad range of concerns relating to the lives and livelihoods of residents of States parties, in particular food, clothing and housing. The Committee on Economic, Social and Cultural Rights has devoted extensive attention to this article, particularly as it relates to the human right to adequate housing. To date, the right to adequate housing is the only right in the Covenant which has had an entire general comment devoted to it (General Comment No. 4 (1991)).

General Comment No. 4 reveals the extensive nature of the protection included under article 11 and elaborates legal interpretations of the right to adequate housing which go far beyond restricted visions of this right as simply a right to shelter. In it, the Committee, which has given more attention to the right to housing than to any other right under the Covenant, states :

> . . . the right to housing, should not be interpreted in a narrower restrictive sense which equates it with, for example, the shelter provided by merely having a roof over one's head . . . Rather it should be seen as the right to live somewhere in security, peace and dignity . . . . (Para. 7.)

The Committee has defined the term 'adequate housing' to comprise security of tenure, availability of services, affordability, habitability, accessibility, location and cultural adequacy.

Article 11 does not imply a stagnant state of affairs, but also includes a right 'to the continuous improvement of living conditions' (para. 1) and the possibilities associated with international cooperation in the event of States parties being unable to guarantee the rights in question. This is particularly relevant in times of food crises or famine.

The Committee has decided on several occasions that certain States parties had violated provisions of article 11, particularly as a result of the practice of forced evictions. This is indicative of the seriousness which the Committee accords article 11.

The Right to the Highest Attainable Standard of Physical and Mental Health

Article 12

1. The States parties to the present Covenant recognise the right of everyone to the enjoyment of the highest attainable standard of physical and mental health.

2. The steps to be taken by the States parties to the present Covenant to achieve the full realisation of this right shall include those necessary for:

   a) The provision for the reduction of the stillbirth-rate and of infant mortality and for the healthy development of the child;

   b) The improvement of all aspects of environmental and industrial hygiene;

   c) The prevention, treatment and control of epidemic, endemic, occupational and other diseases;

   d) The creation of conditions which would assure to all medical service and medical attention in the event of sickness.

Recognition of the right to health obviously does not mean that beneficiaries of this right have a right to be healthy. Rather, the Covenant stresses the obligation of States parties to ensure for their citizens "the highest attainable standard of . . . health".

Article 12 therefore places emphasis on equal access to health care and minimum guarantees of health care in the event of sickness.

The Committee on Economic, Social and Cultural Rights has spent increasing energy on clarifying and monitoring health rights, having held a general discussion on the topic and adopted a general comment on the rights of persons with disabilities (General Comment No. 5 (1994)). The rights of people with HIV/AIDS have also received increasing attention from the Committee in recent years.

The Right to Education

Article 13

1. The States parties to the present Covenant recognise the right of everyone to education. They agree that education shall be directed to the full development of the human personality and the sense of its dignity, and shall strengthen the respect for human rights and fundamental freedoms. They further agree that education shall enable all persons to participate effectively in a free society, promote understanding, tolerance and friendship among all nations and all racial, ethnic or religious groups, and further the activities of the United Nations for the maintenance of peace.

2. The States parties to the present Covenant recognise that, with a view to achieving the full realisation of this right:

   a) Primary education shall be compulsory and available free to all;

   b) Secondary education in its different forms, including technical and vocational secondary education, shall be made generally available and accessible to all by every appropriate means, and in particular by the progressive introduction of free education;

   c) Higher education shall be made equally accessible to all, on the basis of capacity, by every appropriate means, and in particular by the progressive introduction of free education;

   d) Fundamental education shall be encouraged or intensified as far as possible for those persons who have not received or completed the whole period of their primary education;

e) The development of a system of schools at all levels shall be actively pursued, an adequate fellowship system shall be established, and the material conditions of teaching staff shall be continuously improved.

3. The States parties to the present Covenant undertake to have respect for the liberty of parents and, when applicable, legal guardians to choose for their children schools, other than those established by the public authorities, which conform to such minimum educational standards as may be laid down or approved by the State and to ensure the religious and moral education of their children in conformity with their own convictions.

4. No part of this article shall be construed so as to interfere with the liberty of individuals and bodies to establish and direct educational institutions, subject always to the observance of the principles set forth in paragraph one of this article and to the requirement that the education given in such institutions shall conform to such minimum standards as may be laid down by the State.

Compulsory and Free Primary Education

Article 14

Each State party to the present Covenant which, at the time of becoming a Party, has not been able to secure in its metropolitan territory or other territories under its jurisdiction compulsory primary education, free of charge, undertakes within two years, to work out and adopt a detailed plan of action for the progressive implementation, within a reasonable number of years, to be fixed in the plan, of the principle of compulsory education free of charge for all.

Articles 13 and 14 recognise that education is a fundamental precondition for the enjoyment and assertion of human rights and that education strengthens human rights and basic democratic principles. The international community has long recognised these basic truths and has proclaimed the decade 1995-2004 as the United Nations Decade for Human Rights Education. The Committee on Economic, Social and Cultural Rights held a general discussion on this topic in 1994.

These two articles guarantee all children a right to free and compulsory primary education, wherever they may live. They also enshrine the right to equal access to education and equal enjoyment of education facilities; the freedom to choose education and to establish educational institutions; the protection of pupils against inhuman disciplinary measures and academic freedom.

The Right to Culture and to Benefit from Scientific Progress

Article 15

1. The States parties to the present Covenant recognise the right of everyone:

    a) To take part in cultural life;

    b) To enjoy the benefits of scientific progress and its applications;

    c) To benefit from the protection of the moral and material interests resulting from any scientific, literary or artistic production of which he is the author.

2. The steps to be taken by the States parties to the present Covenant to achieve the full realisation of this right shall include those necessary for the

conservation, the development and the diffusion of science and culture.

3. The States parties to the present Covenant undertake to respect the freedom indispensable for scientific research and creative activity.

4. The States parties to the present Covenant recognise the benefits to be derived from the encouragement and development of international contacts and cooperation in the scientific and cultural fields.

The rights to enjoy culture, to participate in cultural life and to benefit from technological and scientific progress form the foundation of article 15. Although these issues may not seem to be matters of human rights, they are of fundamental importance to the principles of equality of treatment, freedom of expression, the right to receive and impart information, and the right to the full development of the human personality.

Cultural attributes can often be attacked or derided by States in attempts to favour one national, racial or ethnic group over another, to cite but one example of how important the rights in question are. Moreover, these rights include the right to participate in the life of society, giving a wide reading to the term 'culture'.

The right to benefit from scientific progress and its applications is designed to ensure that everyone in society can enjoy advances in this regard, in particular disadvantaged groups. It includes the right of everyone to seek and receive information about such advances resulting from new scientific insights and to have access to any developments which could enhance their enjoyment of the rights contained in the Covenant.

Vienna Declaration and Programme of Action

Although the Committee on Economic, Social and Cultural

Rights can assist in the implementation of the Covenant from an international perspective, the ultimate effectiveness of this instrument is contingent on the measures taken by governments to give actual effect to their international legal obligations. In this regard, the Committee has recognised the essential importance of the adoption by States of appropriate legislative measures and the provision of judicial remedies, indicating the very real legal nature of economic, social and cultural rights.

The necessity of implementing the provisions of the Covenant through domestic legislation is consistent with article 27 of the 1969 Vienna Convention on the Law of Treaties, which states that "a party may not invoke the provisions of its internal law as justification for its failure to perform a treaty." Indeed, the Covenant often requires legislative action to be taken in cases where existing legislation is in violation of the obligations assumed under the Covenant.

The Limburg Principles on the Implementation of the International Covenant on Economic, Social and Cultural Rights emphasise that "States parties shall provide for effective remedies, including, where appropriate, judicial remedies" (Principle 19). Because there does not yet exist an individual complaints procedure under the Covenant, the full implementation of the rights which this instrument contains is all the more dependent on the provision of appropriate laws and remedies at the national level.

At minimum, the national and local judiciaries of States parties must consider international human rights laws such as the Covenant an interpretative aid to domestic law and ensure that domestic law is interpreted and applied in a manner consistent with the provisions of international human rights instruments ratified by the State. From the perspective of international law, the underlying principle is that courts should avoid placing their government in violation of the terms of an international treaty which it has ratified.

Regarding the justifiability of the rights contained in the Covenant—i.e., the possibility of their being subjected to judicial review—the Committee has stated in its General Comment No. 3 (1990):

> Among, the measures which might be considered appropriate, in addition to legislation, is the provision of judicial remedies with respect to rights which may, in accordance with the national legal system, be considered justifiable . . . (Para. 5.)

In this regard, the Committee has indicated that a number of articles in the Covenant are capable of immediate implementation, including article 3, article 7, subparagraph (a) (i), article 8, article 10, paragraph 3, article 13, paragraphs 2 (a), 3 and 4, and article 15, paragraph 3. It has also stressed, with respect to the right to adequate housing, for example, that "instances of forced eviction are *prima facie* incompatible with the requirements of the Covenant and can only be justified in the most exceptional circumstances, and in accordance with the relevant principles of international law." In order to put such obligations into effect domestically, national courts would obviously have an important role to play in ensuring respect for the rights in question.

Monitoring the Implementation of the Covenant: the Committee on Economic, Social and Cultural Rights

Creation and Composition of the Committee

Unlike the five other human rights treaty bodies, the Committee on Economic, Social and Cultural Rights was not established by its corresponding instrument. Rather, the Economic and Social Council (ECOSOC) created the Committee, following the less than ideal performance of two previous bodies entrusted with monitoring the Covenant.

The Committee was established in 1985, met for the first time in 1987 and has to date held 14 sessions. Meeting initially on an annual basis, the Committee currently convenes twice a year, holding two three-week sessions, generally in May and November/December. It holds all its meetings at the United Nations Office at Geneva.

The Committee comprise 18 members who are experts with recognised competence in the field of human rights. Members of the Committee are independent and serve in their personal capacity, not as representatives of Governments. At present, the Committee is made up of 13 men and five women. The Committee itself selects its chairperson, three vice-chairpersons and rapporteur.

Members of the Committee are elected by ECOSOC for four-year terms, and are eligible for re-election if renominated. The Committee is thus a subsidiary organ of ECOSOC and derives its formal authority from that body. Elections take place in a secret ballot from a list of nominees proposed by States parties to the Covenant. States which have not ratified the Covenant cannot, therefore, nominate their own nationals for positions on the Committee. The principles of equitable geographical distribution and the representation of different social and legal systems guide the selection process. The Committee is serviced by the United Nations Centre for Human Rights.

The primary function of the Committee is to monitor the implementation of the Covenant by States parties. It strives to develop a constructive dialogue with States parties and seeks to determine through a variety of means whether or not the norms contained in the Covenant are being adequately applied in States parties and how the implementation and enforcement of the Covenant could be improved so that all people who are entitled to the rights enshrined in the Covenant can actually enjoy them in full.

Drawing on the legal and practical expertise of its members, the Committee can also assist governments in fulfilling their obligations under the Covenant by issuing specific legislative, policy and other suggestions and recommendations such that economic, social and cultural rights are more effectively secured.

How do States Parties Report to the Committee?

Under articles 16 and 17 of the Covenant, States parties undertake to submit periodic reports to the Committee-within two years of the entry into force of the Covenant for a particular State party, and thereafter once every five years—outlining the legislative, judicial, policy and other measures which they have taken to ensure the enjoyment of the rights contained in the Covenant. States parties are also requested to provide detailed data on the degree to which the rights are implemented and areas where particular difficulties have been faced in this respect.

The Committee has assisted the reporting process by providing States parties with a detailed 22-page set of reporting guidelines specifying the types of information the Committee requires in order to monitor compliance with the Covenant effectively.

The reporting requirement is much more than simply a formalistic commitment. Although the reporting process is imbued with a number of difficulties, not the least of which are the non-submission of reports by a large number of States parties and problems relating to resource constraints of States, this mechanism has a number of important functions. Among these are the initial review function, the monitoring function, the policy formulation function, the public scrutiny function, the evaluation function, the function of acknowledging problems and the information-exchange function.

The Committee has emphasised that reporting obligations under the Covenant fulfil seven key objectives. In its General Comment No. 1 (1989), the Committee stated these objectives as follows:

1. to ensure that a State party undertakes a comprehensive review of national legislation, administrative rules and procedures, and practices in order to assure the fullest possible conformity with the Covenant;

2. to ensure that the State party regularly monitors the actual situation with respect to each of the enumerated rights in order to assess the extent to which the various rights are being enjoyed by all individuals within the country;

3. to provide a basis for government elaboration of clearly stated and carefully targeted policies for implementing the Covenant;

4. to facilitate public scrutiny of government policies with respect to the Covenant's implementation, and to encourage the involvement of the various sectors of society in the formulation, implementation and review of relevant policies;

5. to provide a basis on which both the State party and the Committee can effectively evaluate progress towards the realisation of the obligations contained in the Covenant;

6. to enable the State party to develop a better understanding of problems and shortcomings

impeding the realisation of economic, social and cultural rights;

7. to facilitate the exchange of information among States parties and to help develop a fuller appreciation of both common problems and possible solutions in the realisation of each of the rights contained in the Covenant.

The Committee typically considers some five or six reports of States parties during any given session. If a State party which has submitted a report that is scheduled for the Committee's consideration at a given session seeks to defer the presentation of the report at the last minute, the Committee does not grant such a request, and proceeds with its consideration, even in the absence of a State party representative.

The Committee has also had to grapple with problems relating to the non-submission of reports and reports which are considerably overdue. In response to such situations, the Committee has notified States parties whose reports are long overdue of its intention to consider these reports at specified future sessions. If no report is forthcoming, the Committee then proceeds to consider the status of economic, social and cultural rights in the States concerned in the light of all available information.

Submission of Reports and the Pre-sessional Working Group

When States parties submit their reports, a standard procedure of consideration is followed by the Committee. Once received, processed and translated by the Secretariat, States parties' reports are initially reviewed by the Committee's five-person pre-sessional working group, which meets six months prior to a report being considered by the full Committee. The pre-sessional working group gives a preliminary consideration to the report, appoints one member to give particular consideration to each report, and develops written lists of questions based on disparities found in the reports which are submitted to the States parties concerned. The States parties are then required to reply in writing to these questions prior to their appearance before the Committee.

Presentation of Reports

Representatives of reporting States are strongly encouraged to be present at meetings when the Committee considers their reports. Such delegations are virtually always present during this process, which is generally carried out over a two-day period. Delegations first provide introductory comments and responses to the pre-sessional working group's written questions. This is followed by the provision of information by the United Nations specialised agencies relevant to the report under consideration. Committee members then put questions and observations to the State party appearing before it. A further period of time is then allowed for representatives of States parties to respond, generally not on the same day, to the questions and views put to them, as precisely as possible. If the questions cannot be adequately dealt with, the Committee often requests a State party to provide it with additional information for its consideration at forthcoming sessions.

Concluding Observations: The Committee Decides

Upon completion by the Committee of its analysis of reports and the appearance by States parties, the Committee concludes its consideration of States parties' reports by issuing 'concluding observations', which constitute the decision of the Committee regarding the status of the Covenant in a given State party. Concluding observations are divided into five sections: (a) introduction; (b) positive aspects; (c) factors and difficulties impeding the implementation of the Covenant; (d) principal subjects of concern; and (e) suggestions and recommendations. Concluding observations are adopted in private session, and are released to the public on the final day of each session.

On a number of occasions, the Committee has concluded that violations of the Covenant had taken place, and subsequently urged States parties to desist from any further infringements of the rights in question.

All human rights are subject to violation, and economic, social and cultural rights are no exception. The Limburg Principles on the Implementation of the International Covenant on Economic, Social and Cultural Rights list the following circumstances amounting to violations of the Covenant by a State party (principle 72): (a) it fails to take a step which the Covenant requires it to take; (b) it fails to remove promptly obstacles which it is obligated to remove to permit the immediate fulfilment of a right; (c) it fails to implement without delay a right which the Covenant requires it to provide immediately; (d) it wilfully fails to meet a generally accepted international minimum standard of achievement, which is within its powers to meet; (e) it applies a limitation to a right recognised in the Covenant in a manner not in accordance with the Covenant; (f) it deliberately retards or halts the progressive realisation of a right, unless it is acting within a limitation permitted by the Covenant or it does so because of a lack of available resources; and (g) it fails to submit reports as required under the Covenant.

While the Committee's concluding observations, in particular suggestions and recommendations, may not carry legally binding status, they are indicative of the opinion of the only expert body entrusted with and capable of making such pronouncements. Consequently, for States parties to ignore or not act on such views would be to show bad faith in implementing their Covenant-based obligations. In a number of instances, changes in policy, practice and law have been registered at least partly in response to the Committee's concluding observations.

In addition to concluding observations, letters from the chairperson are occasionally addressed to States parties informing them of the Committee's concerns.

The Committee also adopts draft decisions for eventual adoption by ECOSOC, when such approval is required. This is generally the case when the Committee requests a State party to issue it with an invitation to visit the country and provide the government with technical and other assistance which it may require in order to implement more fully and enforce the norms of the Covenant. The Committee has to date twice requested invitations to visit the territories of States parties (Dominican Republic and Panama). Only in one of these instances (Panama), however, did the State issue the requisite invitation, and a mission took place in April 1995.

Generating Interpretative Clarity

a) General Comments

The Committee decided in 1988 to begin preparing 'general comments' on the rights and provisions contained in the Covenant with a view to assisting States parties in fulfilling their reporting obligations and to provide greater interpretative clarity as to the intent, meaning and content of the Covenant. The Committee further views the adoption of general comments as a means of promoting the implementation of the Covenant, by drawing the attention of States parties to insufficiencies disclosed by a large number of States parties' reports, and by inducing renewed attention to particular provisions of the Covenant on the part of States parties, United Nations agencies and others with a view to achieving progressively the full realisation of the rights established under the Covenant.

General comments are a crucial means of generating jurisprudence, providing a method by which members of the Committee may come to an agreement by consensus regarding the interpretation of norms embodied in the Covenant.

As of April 1996, the Committee has adopted six general comments. These are:

— General Comment No. 1 (1989) on reporting by States parties;

— General Comment No. 2 (1990) on international technical assistance measures (art. 22);

— General Comment No. 3 (1990) on the nature of States parties' obligations (art. 2, para. 1, of the Covenant);

— General Comment No. 4 (1991) on the right to adequate housing (art. 11, para. 1, of the Covenant);

— General Comment No. 5 (1994) on persons with disabilities;

— General Comment No. 6 (1995) on the economic, social and cultural rights of older persons.

It is likely that the Committee will consider the adoption of additional general comments in the near future on issues such as the right to health; the domestic application of the Covenant; forced evictions and the Covenant; the non-discrimination clauses of the Covenant (art. 2, para. 2); the right to food; and others.

b) General Discussions

At each of its sessions, the Committee holds a 'day of general discussion' on particular provisions of the Covenant, particular human rights or other themes of direct relevance to the Committee in order to develop its understanding of the issues concerned. The Committee has sought to draw on a wide range of expertise during these discussions and has, therefore, engaged in dialogue with United Nations special rapporteurs, experts from relevant non-governmental organisations and representatives of United Nations specialised agencies.

General discussions to date have been held on the right to food (1989); the right to housing (1990); economic and social indicators (1991); the right to take part in cultural life (1992); the rights of the ageing and elderly (1993); the right to health (1993); the role of social safety nets as a means of protecting economic, social and cultural rights, with particular reference to situations involving major structural adjustment and/or transition to a free market economy (1994); human rights education (1994); the interpretation and practical application of the obligations incumbent on States parties (1995); and a draft optional protocol to the Covenant (1995).

Civil Society and the Work of the Committee

The World Conference on Human Rights affirms that extreme poverty and social exclusion constitute a violation of human dignity and that urgent steps are necessary to achieve better knowledge of extreme poverty and its causes, including those related to the problem of development, in order to promote the human rights of the poorest, and to put an end to extreme poverty and social exclusion and to promote the enjoyment of the fruits of social progress. It is essential for States to foster participation by the poorest people in the decision-making process and the community in which they live, the promotion of human rights and efforts to combat extreme poverty.

Relevance of NGOs and CBOs

The Committee has long recognised the important contribution which can be made by civil society in the provision of information concerning the status of the Covenant within States parties. The Committee was the first treaty body to provide non-governmental organisations (NGOs) with the opportunity to submit written statements and make oral submissions dealing with issues relating to the enjoyment or non-enjoyment of the rights contained in the Covenant in specific countries.

On the first day of each session of the Committee, the afternoon meeting is set aside to give international and national NGOs and community-based organisations (CBOs) an opportunity to express their views about how the Covenant is or is not implemented by States parties. The Committee will receive oral testimony from NGOs as long as the information focuses specifically on the provisions of the Covenant, is of direct relevance to matters under consideration by the Committee, is reliable and is not abusive. In recent years, NGOs and CBOs have taken increased advantage of this procedure and provided the Committee with written, audio and video materials alleging the non-enjoyment of economic, social and cultural rights in States parties.

The Committee has indicated that the purposes of the NGO procedure are to enable it to inform itself as fully as possible, to examine the accuracy and pertinence of information which would most probably be available to it anyway, and to put the process of receiving NGO information on a more transparent basis.

NGOs and CBOs wishing to provide reliable and new information to the Committee may write to the secretariat of the Committee several months prior to the beginning of a particular session, with a specific request to intervene during the NGO procedure. Groups with written materials may also send these to the secretariat, and may attend Committee sessions. NGOs in consultative status with the United Nations or other groups which have relations with such NGOs also may attend Committee sessions. NGOs with consultative status may, in accordance with the relevant ECOSOC resolutions, submit written submissions to the Committee at any time. Committee sessions are generally held in public, with the exception of meetings at which it prepares its concluding observations, which are held privately.

The active participation of NGOs in the work of the Committee has also proven fundamental in ensuring the wide distribution of information about the Covenant and the Committee at the national and local levels. In many instances, these organisations have generated substantial media attention in their countries following the adoption of concluding observations regarding the States in question.

Towards a Formal Complaints Procedure (Optional Protocol)

At present it is not possible for individuals or groups who feel that their rights under the Covenant have been violated to submit formal complaints to the Committee. The absence of such procedure places significant constraints on the ability of the Committee to develop jurisprudence or case-law and, of course, greatly limits the chances of victims of abuses of the Covenant obtaining international redress.

There are numerous arguments supporting the adoption of a complaints procedure under the Covenant. These include the improved enjoyment by people of economic, social and cultural rights; a strengthening of international accountability of States parties; increased congruence in the legal standing and seriousness accorded to both International Covenants; a refinement of the rights and duties emerging from the provisions of the International Covenant on Economic, Social and Cultural Rights; and a structural and concrete affirmation of the indivisibility and interdependence of all human rights. It is also argued that such a procedure would encourage States parties to provide similar remedies at the local and national levels.

The Committee has devoted increasing attention to the possibility of elaborating such an optional protocol since 1990 and has discussed the issue at length on several occasions. (20) At its sixth session, in 1991, the Committee supported the drafting of an optional protocol "since that would enhance the practical implementation of the Covenant as well as the dialogue with States parties and would make it possible to focus the attention of public opinion to a greater extent on economic, social and cultural rights."

The World Conference on Human Rights, held at Vienna in June 1993, gave added impetus to this initiative by asserting, in the Vienna Declaration and Programme of Action which it adopted, that the Committee should continue its efforts towards this end. The Committee has prepared a draft optional protocol, but it has yet to be officially adopted by the relevant United Nations organs.

Many other initiatives have also addressed the desirability of including a complaints procedure under the

International Covenant on economic, Social and Cultural Rights, and these have given added support to this means of strengthening this pivotal human rights treaty.

Pending the addition of an optional protocol, beneficiaries of the rights contained in the Covenant may still have recourse to the general procedures of the Committee, and may utilise what has been called an unofficial petition procedure" based on the modalities of the Committee.

NGO Participation in the Activities of the Committee on Economic, Social and Cultural Rights

At its eighth session, in May 1993, the Committee adopted the following procedure regarding the participation of non-governmental organisations in its activities:

A. Written information

1. The Committee reiterates its long-standing invitation to NGOs to submit to it in writing, at any time, information regarding any aspect of its work.

B. Oral information

2. In addition to the receipt of written information, a short period of time will be made available at the beginning of each session of the pre-sessional working group to provide NGOs with an opportunity to submit relevant oral information to the members of the working group.

3. Furthermore, the Committee will set aside part of the first afternoon at each of its sessions to enable it to receive oral information provided by NGOs. Such information should: (a) focus specifically on the provisions of the International Covenant on Economic, Social and Cultural Rights; (b) be of direct relevance

to matters under consideration by the Committee; (c) be reliable; (d) not be abusive. The relevant meeting, will be open and will be provided with interpretation services, but will not be covered by summary records. The purposes are: to enable the Committee to inform itself as fully as possible; to probe the accuracy and pertinence of information which would most probably be available to it anyway; and to put the process of receiving NGO information on a more transparent and open basis than is permitted by the current approach.

4. NGOs wishing to present oral information should inform the Committee in advance. In cases in which the Committee receives more expressions of interest than can be dealt with in the limited time available, the Chairperson of the Committee, in consultation with the Bureau, shall determine on an objective basis which NGOs will be invited to make an oral presentation.

5. To the extent that information provided to the Committee in writing, under these procedures is referred to by any member of the Committee in questions posed to the State party, the relevant information should be available for consultation by the government concerned and all other interested parties.

6. The Committee requests its Chairperson, in conjunction with the secretariat, to make these procedures as widely known as possible.

8

Human Rights and the Indian Constitution

The Constitution of India, one of the world's lengthier written constitutions (with 395 articles and 12 schedules in 117369 words in English) was passed by the Constituent Assembly on November 26, 1949. It has been in effect since January 26, 1950, which is celebrated as Republic Day in India.

Features

The constitution of India draws extensively from Western legal traditions in its outline of the principles of liberal democracy. It is distinguished from many Western constitutions, however, in its elaboration of principles reflecting the aspirations to end the inequities of traditional social relations and enhance the social welfare of the population. According to constitutional scholar Granville Austin, probably no other nation's constitution "has provided so much impetus toward changing and rebuilding society for the common good." Since its enactment, the constitution has fostered a steady concentration of power in the central government—especially the Office of the Prime Minister. This centralization has occurred in the face of the increasing assertiveness of an array of ethnic and caste groups across Indian society.

Increasingly, the government has responded to the resulting tensions by resorting to the formidable array of authoritarian powers provided by the constitution. Together with the public's perception of pervasive corruption among India's politicians, the state's centralization of authority and increasing resort to coercive power have eroded its legitimacy. However, a new assertiveness shown by the Supreme Court and the Election Commission suggests that the remaining checks and balances among the country's political institutions continue to support the resilience of Indian democracy. Also, regional parties are increasingly gaining popularity at the expense of national parties which has led to coalition governments at the centre. As a consequence, the power is getting more decentralised.

Adopted after some two and one-half years of deliberation by the Constituent Assembly that also acted as India's first legislature, the constitution was put into effect on January 26, 1950. Bhimrao Ramji Ambedkar, a Dalit who earned a law degree from Columbia University, chaired the drafting committee of the constitution and shepherded it through Constituent Assembly debates. However, the Constitution in its final form owes much to the indoctrination of different principles from various Constitutions as well the general structure of the democratic framework to B. N. Rau, a constitutional scholar of international standing.

Supporters of independent India's founding father, Mohandas K. Gandhi, backed measures that would form a decentralized polity with strong local administration - known as panchayat - in a system known as panchayati raj, that is rule by panchayats. However, the support of more modernist leaders, such as Jawaharlal Nehru, ultimately led to a parliamentary government and a federal system with a strong central government. Following a British parliamentary pattern, the constitution embodies the Fundamental Rights, which are similar to the United States Bill of Rights, and a Supreme Court similar to that of the United States.

It creates a "sovereign democratic republic" called India, or Bharat (after the legendary king Bharata, son of king Dushyanta), which "shall be a Union of States." India is a federal system in which residual powers of legislation remain with the central government, similar to that in Canada. The constitution provides detailed lists dividing up powers between central and state governments as in Australia, and it elaborates a set of Directive Principles of State Policy as does the Irish constitution.

Schedules

Schedules can be added to the constitution by amendment. The twelve schedules in force cover the designations of the states and union territories; the emoluments for high-level officials; forms of oaths; allocation of the number of seats in the Rajya Sabha (Council of States—the upper house of Parliament) per state or territory; provisions for the administration and control of Scheduled Areas and Scheduled Tribes (tribes and areas needing special protection due to disadvantageous conditions); provisions for the administration of tribal areas in Assam; the union (meaning central government), state, and concurrent (dual) lists of responsibilities; the official languages; land and tenure reforms; the association of Sikkim with India; rural developmet; and urban planning.

Human Rights Issues in India

The new coalition government led by the Congress party, which replaced the Hindu nationalist Bharatiya Janta Party (BJP) after elections in May 2004, has taken some important positive steps with regard to respect for human rights. These include repeal of the oft-abused Prevention of Terrorism Act (POTA) and a re-evaluation of federal government educational policies that have fostered communitarian resentments.

Attacks on civilians by militant groups and Indian security forces continued unabated before and after the change in government. Notwithstanding the repeal of POTA, the government continues to use other legislation to shield security forces from accountability. Indian military, paramilitary, and police forces have engaged in serious human rights abuses not just in conflict-zones such as Kashmir, but also when dealing with criminal suspects and detainees.

The Gujarat government's failure to bring to justice those responsible for massive communitarian riots in the state, in which thousands of Muslims were killed and left homeless, continues to be a source of tension throughout the entire country. However, the Supreme Court and the National Human Rights Commission have taken several positive steps to secure justice for the victims of the riots. The new government of Manmohan Singh also has to contend with the Indian government's systematic failure to protect the rights of Dalits, other marginalized castes and religious minorities. The Congress Party itself has failed to provide any justice to the victims of serious abuses against the Sikh community in Delhi and Punjab twenty years ago. India faces a burgeoning HIV/AIDS problem, as people with HIV and their families face government and social discrimination.

Rights of Dalits and Indigenous Tribal Groups

Despite legislative measures to protect marginalized groups, discrimination based on caste, social, or religious grounds continues widely in practice. Local police often fail to implement the special laws set up to protect Dalits and members of tribal groups. Dalits, or so-called untouchables, continue to face violence and discrimination in nearly every sphere of their lives. Abuses against Dalits range from harassment and use of excessive force by security forces in routine matters, to mutilations and killings by members of other castes for attempting to cross caste barriers. Dalit women are targeted with sexual violence.

Not only do authorities regularly tolerate such discrimination and violence, in some instances they actively encourage it. In one widely noted incident in July 2004, for example, police used excessive force against Dalits who tried to participate in a religious festival in Tamil Nadu. Indigenous peoples, or Adivasis, have suffered from high rates of displacement. Scheduled Tribes that make up 8 percent of the total population constitute 55 percent of displaced people. This has had a serious effect on the overall development of these communities, particularly tribal children.

The government continues to use the Land Acquisition Act of 1894 to displace the indigenous peoples from their lands without sufficient compensation, as is evident in the Narmada Valley Development Project. Tribal groups who have converted to Christianity have been targeted for attack by extremist Hindu organizations.

Impunity of Security Forces

Indian security forces, including the military, paramilitary forces, and the police, routinely abuse human rights with impunity. The Indian federal government rarely prosecutes army and paramilitary troops in a credible and transparent manner. The result has been an increase in serious violations by security forces throughout the country.

The government's repeal of the controversial Prevention of Terrorism Act (POTA) was a major step forward for civil liberties in India. POTA empowered security forces to hold individuals for up to 180 days without filing charges, broadening the scope of the death penalty, dispensing with the presumption of innocence by placing the burden of proof on suspects, and admitting confessions into evidence despite the frequent use of torture. The law was often used against marginalized communities such as Dalits, indigenous groups, Muslims, and the political opposition.

But POTA's repeal has not ended the legal impunity that security agencies enjoy. Laws such as the National Security Act, the Disturbed Areas Act, the Armed Forces Special Powers Act or the Armed Forces (Jammu and Kashmir) Special Powers Act have spawned abuses in various parts of the country, including many deaths in custody and widespread allegations of torture. These laws give security agencies unchecked powers of detention that often foster torture during interrogation.

For instance in Kashmir and Manipur states, the sites of long-standing insurgencies, Indian military and paramilitary forces have held suspects in army camps and barracks and have routinely tortured them, in violation of domestic and international laws. In July 2004, Manipur state witnessed unprecedented civilian protests against the Armed Forces Special Powers Act after army troops sexually assaulted and killed a woman in custody. That Act provides security forces virtual immunity for crimes committed in the course of duty. The new government recently agreed to review the act.

Other laws such as the Public Safety Act and section 197 of the Criminal Code of Procedure also raise human rights concerns. Section 197 extends immunity to public servants by requiring government authorization to initiate the prosecution of public servants for crimes that result from the discharge of their official functions. In effect, it allows the government to shield security forces from any legal accountability.

In Kashmir, military, paramilitary, and police forces continue their practice of torturing detainees and custodial killings. There has also been a nationwide rise in allegations of extrajudicial executions by security forces, who typically justify their actions by claiming to have killed suspects in an exchange of gunfire.

Kashmir Conflict

Since November 2003, a cease-fire along the Line of Control in Kashmir has provided tremendous relief to residents on both sides of the de facto border. During the intermittent shelling, however, neither Pakistan nor India took adequate precautions to protect civilians. The violence inside Indian-controlled Kashmir continued.

Bomb and grenade attacks by militants in crowded market places constituted the intentional targeting of civilians. Attacks, apparently by separatist militants, on moderate Kashmiri leaders have hindered the peace process. Indian police and security services often use excessive force, and have been responsible for arbitrary detention, torture, and extrajudicial execution. Since 1989, when the insurgency began, thousands of people have disappeared at the hands of both militant and government forces.

Legacy of Communal Violence

Large-scale episodes of communal violence remain unpunished. This injustice continues to foster communal resentments throughout India. There has still been no accountability for the deaths of more than two thousand Muslims in the western state of Gujarat during communal violence that erupted following an attack on a train carrying Hindu pilgrims in 2002. In Discouraging Dissent, a report released in August 2004, Human Rights Watch documented the continued discrimination, intimidation of witnesses, faulty investigation, and apparent interference from members of the BJP state government in efforts to prosecute those responsible for the anti-Muslim violence.

The Indian Supreme Court has already ordered two Gujarat cases to be retried in another state. The criminal justice system in Gujarat, the Supreme Court concluded, had been "abused, misused and mutilated by subterfuge." Human rights activists and lawyers have petitioned for fresh investigations and trials in a number of cases where it was felt that the local courts, prosecutors and police were hostile to Muslim complainants. Despite these positive developments, rights activists in Gujarat continue to be harassed on the basis of what police claim are their "anti-national activities." Witnesses, however, remain vulnerable to threats.

2004 marked the twentieth anniversary of Operation Blue Star, a focal point in the conflict between Sikh nationalists and state security apparatus in the Punjab in the 1980s; and the anti-Sikh riots in New Delhi, which resulted in more than three thousand Sikh deaths. In July, the National Human Rights Commission called for claims in cases of summary execution in Punjab. The assignment of individual criminal responsibility for those and other crimes committed during the period, however, remains elusive. Also in July, the Nanavati Commission of inquiry served former prime minister P.V. Narasimha Rao, who was home minister in the Congress Party government in 1984, a notice for his failure to act to prevent the attacks on Sikhs. Two others who have similarly been served notices have recently been appointed ministers in the new Congress government.

Rights of Children

India has the largest number of working children in the world, millions of whom work in the worst forms of child labor, including bonded labor. The Indian government knows about these children and is required by its own laws to protect them. Instead, for reasons of apathy, caste bias, and corruption, many government officials deny that they exist at all. Both literacy and school enrollment rates overall have improved in the last decade, but according to UNESCO, approximately half of students completed grade five. Proportionately fewer girls than boys attend school, and those that do, drop out at higher rates. Dalits also have higher illiteracy and drop-out rates and face significant discrimination in education.

Rights of Those Living with HIV/AIDS

The government estimates that 5.1 million people in India are living with HIV/AIDS, though many experts suggest the number is much higher. People with AIDS, as well as those traditionally at highest risk-sex workers, injection drug users, and men who have sex with men-face widespread stigmatization and discrimination. People with AIDS are denied employment and access to education and healthcare. Those at high risk face police harassment and other state-sponsored abuse that undermines HIV prevention and AIDS care services for them. Married women are also at risk because they are frequently unable to demand condom use of their husbands, who may have extramarital sexual partners.

At least hundreds of thousands of children are living with HIV/AIDS. Many more are otherwise seriously affected by India's burgeoning epidemic-when they are forced to withdraw from school to care for sick parents, are forced to work to replace their parents' income, or are orphaned (losing one or both parents to AIDS). Children affected by HIV/AIDS are being discriminated against in education and health services, denied care by orphanages, and pushed onto the streets and into the worst forms of child labor. Gender discrimination makes girls more vulnerable to HIV transmission and makes it more difficult for them to get care. Many children, especially the most vulnerable as well as the professionals who care for them, are not getting the information about HIV they need to protect themselves or to combat discrimination.

Protection against Gender-Based Discrimination and Violence

Women and girls confront discrimination and violence in practically every aspect of life. A strong preference for sons over daughters has led to sharply skewed gender ratios in several states. Sex-selective abortions, female feticide, and inadequate provision of food and health care to girls has led to ratios of less than eight hundred women for every one thousand men in some places.

Despite several legal provisions for gender equality, women still struggle to realize equal rights to property, marriage, divorce, and protection under the law. Gender-based violence, including domestic violence, sexual harassment, sexual assault, and trafficking into forced labor and forced prostitution remain serious and pervasive problems in India. Domestic violence includes dowry-related abuses and "bride-burning."

Activists continue to campaign for reform of rape laws to protect women and children from all forms of sexual violence. The pervasive understanding of 'rape' is that it occurs only when a stranger uses force on a woman. A marital exemption protects men from being prosecuted for raping their wives. Marital rape is not recognized or penalized unless the wife is under the age of fifteen or if she lives separately from her husband.

There is inadequate legal protection for abuse against girls, boys, and men, or for sexual violence between spouses. In the absence of a more suitable law, section 377 of the Indian Penal Code, which penalizes consensual sexual activity deemed "unnatural," is also used to prosecute the sexual abuse of children and women. This provision has also been used to penalize men having sex with men, and has been used as justification for harassment of HIV/AIDS educators. The Delhi High Court dismissed a legal challenge to section 377, dealing a disappointing set back for activists working to improve the rights of gay and lesbian people in India.

Key International Actors

India receives 60 percent of its aid from multilateral donors such as the World Bank. India decided in 2003 to stop receiving bilateral assistance from all but six countries, including the United States, the United Kingdom, and Russia. The decision is widely perceived as an effort to bolster India's image as a world power. Increasingly, India has been providing significant amounts of financial and military aid to its smaller neighbors, but has not used its increasing influence to make public calls for better compliance with human rights standards.

The thawing of relations between India and Pakistan began in earnest in November 2003 with a ceasefire across the line-of-control. That was followed by a meeting between then-Prime Minister Vajpayee and President Pervez Musharraf of Pakistan in January 2004. The Congress government continued its predecessor's policy of dialogue with Pakistan to resolve outstanding issues of conflict. The two countries' leaders met in New York in September, where Singh and Musharraf reiterated a commitment to the bilateral dialogue to restore normalcy and a peaceful negotiated settlement in Kashmir.

The easing of tensions between India and Pakistan has allowed the United States to focus its dialogue with India on strengthening bilateral relations between New Delhi and Washington. U.S. Secretary of State Colin Powell visited India in March 2004. Human rights issues were not discussed. The increasingly warm relations between the two countries, despite the U.S. conferring the status of "major non-NATO ally" upon Pakistan, will likely continue under Congress Party leadership. Deputy Secretary of State Richard Armitage visited New Delhi in July, reaffirming to Indian leaders that the United States sees India as an important partner. India has also been strengthening its military-to-military ties, conducting joint exercises with United States and other NATO forces.

India is the largest provider of military assistance to Nepal, which is in the midst of a brutal civil war. India has not used its position of influence to push the Nepalese government to improve its human right records, and has resisted calls for a multilateral peace conference, presumably to avoid similar calls for resolving the Kashmir dispute. India has been increasingly close to the brutal military government of Burma.

A delegation of Burma's political opposition was not allowed to enter India to attend a conference on human rights. In September 2004, the Indian government welcomed a delegation from the Burmese military government, but did not raise any concerns about Burma's dismal human rights record. Thousands of Burmese continue to seek refuge in India, where they are not granted proper protections under international law.

Fundamental Rights Guaranties by Indian Constitution

The fundamental rights guaranties by Indian constitution is given below

PART III OF INDIAN CONSTITUTION

Fundamental Rights

General

Article 12. Definition: In this Part, unless the context otherwise requires, "the State" includes the Government and Parliament of India and the Government and the Legislature of each of the States and all local or other authorities within the territory of India or under the control of the Government of India.

Article 13. Laws of inconsistent with or in derogation of the fundamental rights:

(1) All laws in force in the territory of India immediately before the commencement of this Constitution, in so far as they are inconsistent with the provisions of this Part, shall, to the extent of such inconsistency, be void.

(2) The State shall not make any law which takes away or abridges the rights conferred by this Part and any law made in contravention of this clause shall, to the extent of the contravention, be void.

(3) In this article, unless the context otherwise requires,-

  (a) "law" includes any Ordinance, order, bye-law, rule, regulation, notification, custom or usage having in the territory of India the force of law;

  (b) "laws in force" includes laws passed or made by a Legislature or other competent authority in the territory of India before the commencement of this Constitution and not previously repealed, notwithstanding that any such law or any part thereof may not be then in operation either at all or in particular areas.

[(4) Nothing in this article shall apply to any amendment of this Constitution made under article 368.]

Right to equality

Article 14. Equality before law: The State shall not deny to any person equality before the law or the equal protection of the laws within the territory of India.

Article 15. Prohibition of discrimination on grounds of religion,race,caste,sex or place of birth:

(1) The State shall not discriminate against any citizen on grounds only of religion, race, caste, sex, place of birth or any of them.

(2) No citizen shall, on grounds only of religion, race, caste, sex, place of birth or any of them, be subject to any disability, liability, restriction or condition with regard to-

(a) access to shops, public restaurants, hotels and places of public entertainment; or

(b) the use of wells, tanks, bathing ghats, roads and places of public resort maintained wholly or partly out of State funds or dedicated to the use of the general public.

(3) Nothing in this article shall prevent the State from making any special provision for women and children.

[(4) Nothing in this article or in clause (2) of article 29 shall prevent the State from making any special provision for the advancement of any socially and educationally backward classes of citizens or for the Scheduled Castes and the Scheduled Tribes.]

Article 16. Equality of opportunity in matters of public employment:

(1) There shall be equality of opportunity for all citizens in matters relating to employment or appointment to any office under the State.

(2) No citizen shall, on grounds only of religion, race, caste, sex, descent, place of birth, residence or any of them, be ineligible for, or discriminated against in respect of, any employment or office under the State.

(3) Nothing in this article shall prevent Parliament from making any law prescribing, in regard to a class or classes of employment or appointment to an office [under the Government of, or any local or other authority within, a State or Union territory, any requirement as to residence within that State or Union territory] prior to such employment or appointment.

(4) Nothing in this article shall prevent the State from making any provision for the reservation of appointments or posts in favour of any backward class of citizens which, in the opinion of the State, is not adequately represented in the services under the State.

[(4A) Nothing in this article shall prevent the State from making any provision for reservation [in matters of promotion, with consequential seniority, to any class] or classes of posts in the services under the State in favour of the Scheduled Castes and the Scheduled Tribes which, in the opinion of the State, are not adequately represented in the services under the State.]

[(4B) Nothing in this article shall prevent the State from considering any unfilled vacancies of a year which are reserved for being filled up in that year in accordance with any provision for reservation made under clause (4) or clause (4A) as a separate class of vacancies to be filled up in any succeeding year or years and such class of vacancies shall not be considered together with the vacancies of the year in which they are being filled up for determining the ceiling of fifty per cent. reservation on total number of vacancies of that year.].

(5) Nothing in this article shall affect the operation of any law which provides that the incumbent of an office

in connection with the affairs of any religious or denominational institution or any member of the governing body thereof shall be a person professing a particular religion or belonging to a particular denomination.

Article 17. Abolition of Untouchability "Untouchability" is abolished and its practice in any form is forebidden: The enforcement of any disability rising out of "Untouchability" shall be an offence punishable in accordance with law.

Article 18. Abolition of titles:

(1) No title, not being a military or academic distinction, shall be conferred by the State.

(2) No citizen of India shall accept any title from any foreign State.

(3) No person who is not a citizen of India shall, while he holds any office of profit or trust under the State, accept without the consent of the President any title from any foreign State.

(4) No person holding any office of profit or trust under the State shall, without the consent of the President, accept any present, emolument, or office of any kind from or under any foreign State.

Right to freedom

Article 19. Protection of certain rights regarding freedom of speech, etc:

(1) All citizens shall have the right-

(a) to freedom of speech and expression;

(b) to assemble peaceably and without arms;

(c) to form associations or unions;

(d) to move freely throughout the territory of India;

(e) to reside and settle in any part of the territory of India; [and]

* * * * *

(g) to practise any profession, or to carry on any occupation, trade or business.

[(2) Nothing in sub-clause (a) of clause (1) shall affect the operation of any existing law, or prevent the State from making any law, in so far as such law imposes reasonable restrictions on the exercise of the right conferred by the said sub-clause in the interests of [the sovereignty and integrity of India,] the security of the State, friendly relations with foreign States, public order, decency or morality, or in relation to contempt of court, defamation or incitement to an offence.]

(3) Nothing in sub-clause (b) of the said clause shall affect the operation of any existing law in so far as it imposes, or prevent the State from making any law imposing, in the interests of [the sovereignty and integrity of India or] public order, reasonable restrictions on the exercise of the right conferred by the said sub-clause.

(4) Nothing in sub-clause (c) of the said clause shall affect the operation of any existing law in so far as it imposes, or prevent the State from making any law imposing, in the interests of [the sovereignty and integrity of India or] public order or morality, reasonable restrictions on the exercise of the right conferred by the said sub-clause.

(5) Nothing in [sub-clauses (d) and (e)] of the said clause shall affect the operation of any existing law in so far as it imposes, or prevent the State from making any law imposing, reasonable restrictions on the exercise of any of the rights conferred by the said sub-clauses either in the interests of the general public or for the protection of the interests of any Scheduled Tribe.

(6) Nothing in sub-clause (g) of the said clause shall affect the operation of any existing law in so far as it imposes, or prevent the State from making any law imposing, in the interests of the general public, reasonable restrictions on the exercise of the right conferred by the said sub-clause, and, in particular, [nothing in the said sub-clause shall affect the operation of any existing law in so far as it relates to, or prevent the State from making any law relating to,-

(i) the professional or technical qualifications necessary for practising any profession or carrying on any occupation, trade or business, or

(ii) the carrying on by the State, or by a corporation owned or controlled by the State, of any trade, business, industry or service, whether to the exclusion, complete or partial, of citizens or otherwise].

Article 20. protection in respect of conviction for offences.

(1) No person shall be convicted of any offence except for violation of a law in force at the time of the commission of the Act charged as an offence, nor be subjected to a penalty greater than that which might have been inflicted under the law in force at the time of the commission of the offence.

(2) No person shall be prosecuted and punished for the same offence more than once.

(3) No person accused of any offence shall be compelled to be a witness against himself.

Article 21. Protection of life and personal liberty: No person shall be deprived of his life or personal liberty except according to procedure established by law.

Article 22. Protection against arrest and detention in certain cases:

(1) No person who is arrested shall be detained in custody without being informed, as soon as may be, of the grounds for such arrest nor shall he be denied the right to consult, and to be defended by, a legal practitioner of his choice.

(2) Every person who is arrested and detained in custody shall be produced before the nearest magistrate within a period of twenty-four hours of such arrest excluding the time necessary for the journey from the place of arrest to the court of the magistrate and no such person shall be detained in custody beyond the said period without the authority of a magistrate.

(3) Nothing in clauses

(1) and

(2) shall apply-

(a) to any person who for the time being is an enemy alien; or

(b) to any person who is arrested or detained under any law providing for preventive detention.

(4) No law providing for preventive detention shall authorise the detention of a person for a longer period than three months unless-

(a) an Advisory Board consisting of persons who are, or have been, or are qualified to be appointed as, Judges of a High Court has reported before the expiration of the said period of three months that there is in its opinion sufficient cause for such detention: Provided that nothing in this sub-clause shall authorise the detention of any person beyond the maximum period prescribed by any law made by Parliament under sub-clause

(b) of clause (7); or (b) such person is detained in accordance with the provisions of any law made by Parliament under sub-clauses (a) and (b) of clause (7).

(5) When any person is detained in pursuance of an order made under any law providing for preventive detention, the authority making the order shall, as soon as may be, communicate to such person the grounds on which the order has been made and shall afford him the earliest opportunity of making a representation against the order.

(6) Nothing in clause (5) shall require the authority making any such order as is referred to in that clause to disclose facts which such authority considers to be against the public interest to disclose.

(7) Parliament may by law prescribe-

(a) the circumstances under which, and the class or classes of cases in which, a person may be detained for a period longer than three months under any law providing for preventive detention without obtaining the opinion of an Advisory Board in accordance with the provisions of sub-clause (a) of clause (4);

(b) the maximum period for which any person may in any class or classes of cases be detained under any law providing for preventive detention; and

(c) the procedure to be followed by an Advisory Board in an inquiry under sub-clause (a) of clause (4).

Right against exploitation

Article 23. Prohibition of traffic in human beings and forced labour: 23. Prohibition of traffic in human beings and forced labour.-

(1) Traffic in human beings and begar and other similar forms of forced labour are prohibited and any contravention of this provision shall be an offence punishable in accordance with law.

(2) Nothing in this article shall prevent the State from imposing compulsory service for public purposes, and in imposing such service the State shall not make any discrimination on grounds only of religion, race, caste or class or any of them.

Article 24. Prohibition of employment of children in factories, etc. No child below the age of fourteen years shall be employed to work in any factory or mine or engaged in any other hazardous employment.

Right to freedom of religion

Article 25. Freedom of conscience and free profession, practice and propagation of religion:

(1) Subject to public order, morality and health and to the other provisions of this Part, all persons are equally entitled to freedom of conscience and the right freely to profess, practise and propagate religion.

(2) Nothing in this article shall affect the operation of any existing law or prevent the State from making any law-

(a) regulating or restricting any economic, financial, political or other secular activity which may be associated with religious practice;

(b) providing for social welfare and reform or the throwing open of Hindu religious institutions of a public character to all classes and sections of Hindus.

Explanation I.- The wearing and carrying of kirpans shall be deemed to be included in the profession of the Sikh religion.

Explanation II.- In sub-clause (b) of clause (2), the reference to Hindus shall be construed as including a reference to persons professing the Sikh, Jaina or Buddhist religion, and the reference to Hindu religious institutions shall be construed accordingly.

Article 26. Freedom to manage religious affairs:

Subject to public order, morality and health, every religious denomination or any section thereof shall have the right-

(a) to establish and maintain institutions for religious and charitable purposes;

(b) to manage its own affairs in matters of religion;

(c) to own and acquire movable and immovable property; and

(d) to administer such property in accordance with law.

Article 27. Freedom as to payment of taxes for promotion of any particular religion: No person shall be compelled to pay any taxes, the proceeds of which are specifically appropriated in payment of expenses for the promotion or maintenance of any particular religion or religious denomination.

Article 28. Freedom as to attendance at religious instruction or religious worship in certain education institutions:

(1) No religious instruction shall be provided in any educational institution wholly maintained out of State funds.

(2) Nothing in clause (1) shall apply to an educational institution which is administered by the State but has been established under any endowment or trust which requires that religious instruction shall be imparted in such institution.

(3) No person attending any educational institution recognised by the State or receiving aid out of State funds shall be required to take part in any religious instruction that may be imparted in such institution or to attend any religious worship that may be conducted in such institution or in any premises attached thereto unless such person or, if such person is a minor, his guardian has given his consent thereto.

Cultural and educational rights

Article 29. Protection of interests of minorities:

(1) Any section of the citizens residing in the territory of India or any part thereof having a distinct language, script or culture of its own shall have the right to conserve the same.

(2) No citizen shall be denied admission into any educational institution maintained by the State or receiving aid out of State funds on grounds only of religion, race, caste, language or any of them.

Article 30. Right of minorities to establish and administer educational institutions:

(1) All minorities, whether based on religion or language, shall have the right to establish and administer educational institutions of their choice.

[(1A) In making any law providing for the compulsory acquisition of any property of any educational institution established and administered by a minority, referred to in clause (1), the State shall ensure that the amount fixed by or determined under such law for the acquisition of such property is such as would not restrict or abrogate the right guaranteed under that clause.]

(2) The State shall not, in granting aid to educational institutions, discriminate against any educational institution on the ground that it is under the

management of a minority, whether based on religion or language.

[* * *

Article 31. [Repealed.]: [Compulsory acquisition of property.] Rep. by the Constitution (Forty-fourth Amendment) Act, 1978, s. 6 (w.e.f. 20-6-1979).

Saving of certain laws

31A. Savings of laws providing for acquisition of estates,etc. Notwithstanding anything contained in article 13, no law providing for-

(a) the acquisition by the State of any estate or of any rights therein or the extinguishment or modification of any such rights, or

(b) the taking over of the management of any property by the State for a limited period either in the public interest or in order to secure the proper management of the property, or

(c) the amalgamation of two or more corporations either in the public interest or in order to secure the proper management of any of the corporations, or

(d) the extinguishment or modification of any rights of managing agents, secretaries and treasurers, managing directors, directors or managers of corporations, or of any voting rights of shareholders thereof, or

(e) the extinguishment or modification of any rights accruing by virtue of any agreement, lease or licence for the purpose of searching for, or winning, any mineral or mineral oil, or the premature termination or cancellation of any such agreement, lease or licence, shall be deemed to be void on the ground that it is inconsistent with, or takes away or abridges any of the rights conferred by [article 14 or article 19]:

Provided that where such law is a law made by the Legislature of a State, the provisions of this article shall not apply thereto unless such law, having been reserved for the consideration of the President, has received his assent:] not be lawful for the State to acquire any portion of such land as is within the ceiling limit applicable to him under any law for the time being in force or any building or structure standing thereon or appurtenant thereto, unless the law relating to the acquisition of such land, building or structure, provides for payment of compensation at a rate which shall not be less than the market value thereof.] (2) In this article,-1

[(a) the expression "estate" shall, in relation to any local area, have the same meaning as that expression or its local equivalent has in the existing law relating to land tenures in force in that area and shall also include-

(i) any jagir, inam or muafi or other similar grant and in the States of [Tamil Nadu] and Kerala, any janmam right;

(ii) any land held under ryotwari settlement;

(iii) any land held or let for purposes of agriculture or for purposes ancillary thereto, including waste land, forest land, land for pasture or sites of buildings and other structures occupied by cultivators of land, agricultural labourers and village artisans;]

(b) the expression "rights", in relation to an estate, shall include any rights vesting in a proprietor, sub-proprietor, under-proprietor, tenure-holder, [raiyat, under-raiyat] or other intermediary and any rights or privileges in respect of land revenue.]

31B. Validation of certain Acts and Regulations: Without prejudice to the generality of the provisions contained in article 31A, none of the Acts and Regulations specified in the Ninth Schedule nor any of the provisions thereof shall be deemed to be void, or ever to have become void, on the ground that such Act, Regulation or provision is inconsistent with, or takes away or abridges any of the rights conferred by, any provisions of this Part, and notwithstanding any judgment, decree or order of any court or Tribunal to the contrary, each of the said Acts and Regulations shall, subject to the power of any competent Legislature to repeal or amend it, continue in force.]

31C. Saving of laws giving effect to certain directive principles: Notwithstanding anything contained in article 13, no law giving effect to the policy of the State towards securing [all or any of the principles laid down in Part IV] shall be deemed to be void on the ground that it is inconsistent with, or takes away or abridges any of the rights conferred by [article 14 or article 19]; and no law containing a declaration that it is for giving effect to such policy shall be called in question in any court on the ground that it does not give effect to such policy Provided that where such law is made by the Legislature of a State, the provisions of this article shall not apply thereto unless such law, having been reserved for the consideration of the President, has received his assent.]

31D. [Repealed.]: [Saving of laws in respect of anti-national Rep. by the Constitution (Forty-third Amendment) Act, 1977, s. 2 (w.e.f. 13-4-1978).

Right to constitutional remedies

Article 32. Remedies for enforcement of rights conferred by this Part:

(1) The right to move the Supreme Court by appropriate proceedings for the enforcement of the rights conferred by this Part is guaranteed.

(2) The Supreme Court shall have power to issue directions or orders or writs, including writs in the

nature of habeas corpus, mandamus, prohibition, quo warranto and certiorari, whichever may be appropriate, for the enforcement of any of the rights conferred by this Part.

(3) Without prejudice to the powers conferred on the Supreme Court by clauses (1) and (2), Parliament may by law empower any other court to exercise within the local limits of its jurisdiction all or any of the powers exercisable by the Supreme Court under clause (2).

(4) The right guaranteed by this article shall not be suspended except as otherwise provided for by this Constitution.

32A. [Repealed.]: [Constitutional validity of State laws not to be considered in proceedings under article 32.] Rep. by the Constitution (Forty-third Amendment) Act, 1977, s. 3 (w.e.f. 13-4-1978).

Article 33. Power of Parliament to modify the rights conferred by this Part in their application to Forces, etc.: Parliament may, by law, determine to what extent any of the rights conferred by this Part shall, in their application to,-

(a) the members of the Armed Forces; or

(b) the members of the Forces charged with the maintenance of public order; or

(c) persons employed in any bureau or other organisation established by the State for purposes of intelligence or counter intelligence; or

(d) persons employed in, or in connection with, the telecommunication systems set up for the purposes of any Force, bureau or organisation referred to in clauses (a) to (c), be restricted or abrogated so as to ensure the proper discharge of their duties and the maintenance of discipline among them.]

Article 34. Restriction on rights conferred by this Part while martial law is in force in any area: Notwithstanding anything in the foregoing provisions of this Part, Parliament may by law indemnify any person in the service of the Union or of a State or any other person in respect of any act done by him in connection with the maintenance or restoration of order in any area within the territory of India where martial law was in force or validate any sentence passed, punishment inflicted, forfeiture ordered or other act done under martial law in such area.

Article 35. Legislation to give effect to the provisions of this Part: Notwithstanding anything in this Constitution,-

(a) Parliament shall have, and the Legislature of a State shall not have, power to make laws-

  (i) with respect to any of the matters which under clause (3) of article 16, clause (3) of article 32, article 33 and article 34 may be provided for by law made by Parliament; and

  (ii) for prescribing punishment for those acts which are declared to be offences under this Part; and Parliament shall, as soon as may be after the commencement of this Constitution, make laws for prescribing punishment for the acts referred to in sub-clause (ii);

(b) any law in force immediately before the commencement of this Constitution in the territory of India with respect to any of the matters referred to in sub-clause (i) of clause (a) or providing for punishment for any act referred to in sub-clause (ii) of that clause shall, subject to the terms thereof and to any adaptations and modifications that may be made therein under article 372, continue in force until altered or repealed or amended by Parliament. Explanation.-In this article, the expression "law in force" has the same meaning as in article 372.

9

Protection of Human Rights

Human rights are not always interpreted similarly across societies, these norms nonetheless form a common human rights vocabulary in which the claims of various cultures can be articulated. The widespread ratification of international human rights agreements such as those listed above is taken as evidence that these are widely shared values. Having human rights norms in place imposes certain requirements on governments and legitimizes the complaints of individuals in those cases where fundamental rights and freedoms are not respected.

Such norms constitute a standard for the conduct of government and the administration of force. They can be used as "universal, non-discriminatory standards" for formulating or criticizing law and act as guidelines for proper conduct. Many conflicts are sparked by a failure to protect human rights, and the trauma that results from severe human rights violations often leads to new human rights violations. As conflict intensifies, hatred accumulates and makes restoration of peace more difficult. In order to stop this cycle of violence, states must institute policies aimed at human rights protection.

Many believe that the protection of human rights "is essential to the sustainable achievement of the three agreed global priorities of peace, development and democracy."

Respect for human rights has therefore become an integral part of international law and foreign policy. The specific goal of expanding such rights is to "increase safeguards for the dignity of the person." Despite what resembles a widespread consensus on the importance of human rights and the expansion of international treaties on such matters, the protection of human rights still often leaves much to be desired.

Although international organizations have been created or utilized to embody these values, there is little to enforce the commitments states have made to human rights. Military intervention is a rare occurrence. Sanctions have a spotty track record of effectiveness. Although not to be dismissed as insignificant, often the only consequence for failing to protect human rights is "naming and shaming."

To protect human rights is to ensure that people receive some degree of decent, humane treatment. Because political systems that protect human rights are thought to reduce the threat of world conflict, all nations have a stake in promoting worldwide respect for human rights. International human rights law, humanitarian intervention law and refugee law all protect the right to life and physical integrity and attempt to limit the unrestrained power of the state. These laws aim to preserve humanity and protect against anything that challenges people's health, economic well-being, social stability and political peace. Underlying such laws is the principle of nondiscrimination, the notion that rights apply universally.

Responsibility to protect human rights resides first and foremost with the states themselves. However, in many cases public authorities and government officials institute policies that violate basic human rights. Such abuses of power by political leaders and state authorities have devastating effects, including genocide, war crimes and crimes against humanity. What can be done to safeguard human rights when those in power are responsible for human rights violations? Can outside forces intervene in order to protect human rights?

In some cases, the perceived need to protect human rights and maintain peace has led to humanitarian intervention. There is evidence that internationally we are moving towards the notion that governments have not only a negative duty to respect human rights, but also a positive duty to safeguard these rights, preserve life and protect people from having their rights violated by others. Many believe that states' duties to intervene should not be determined by proximity, but rather by the severity of the crisis. There are two kinds of humanitarian intervention involving the military: unilateral interventions by a single state, and collective interventions by a group of states. Because relatively few states have sufficient force and capacity to intervene on their own, most modern interventions are collective. Some also argue that there is a normative consensus that multilateral intervention is the only acceptable form at present.

There is much disagreement about when and to what extent outside countries can engage in such interventions. More specifically, there is debate about the efficacy of using military force to protect the human rights of individuals in other nations. This sort of debate stems largely from a tension between state sovereignty and the rights of individuals.

Some defend the principles of state sovereignty and nonintervention, and argue that other states must be permitted to determine their own course. They point out that the principles of state sovereignty and the non-use of force are enshrined in the charter of the United Nations, which is regarded as an authoritative source on international legal order. This argument suggests that different states have different conceptions of justice, and international coexistence depends on a pluralist ethic whereby each state can uphold its own conception of the good. Among this group, there is "a profound skepticism about the possibilities of realizing notions of universal justice."

States that presume to judge what counts as a violation of human rights in another nation interfere with that nation's right to self-determination. Suspicions are further raised by the inconsistent respect for sovereignty (or human rights for that matter); namely, the Permanent Members of the UN Security Council have tremendous say over application of international principles. In addition, requiring some country to respect human rights is liable to cause friction and can lead to far-reaching disagreements. Thus, acts of intervention may disrupt interstate order and lead to further conflict. Even greater human suffering might thereby result if states set aside the norm of nonintervention.

Others point out that humanitarian intervention does not, in principle, threaten the territorial integrity and political independence of states. Rather than aiming to destabilize a target state and meddle in its affairs, humanitarian intervention aims to restore rule of law and promote humane treatment of individuals. Furthermore, people who advocate this approach maintain that "only the vigilant eye of the international community can ensure the proper observance of international standards, in the interest not of one state or another but of the individuals themselves." They maintain that massive violations of human rights, such as genocide and crimes against humanity, warrant intervention, even if it causes some tension or disagreement. Certain rights are inalienable and universal, and "taking basic rights seriously means taking responsibility for their protection everywhere."

If, through its atrocious actions, a state destroys the lives and rights of its citizens, it temporarily forfeits its claims to legitimacy and sovereignty. Outside governments then have a positive duty to take steps to protect human rights and preserve lives. In addition, it is thought that political systems that protect human rights reduce the threat of world conflict. Thus, intervention might also be justified on the ground of preserving international security, promoting justice and maintaining international order. Nevertheless, governments are often reluctant to commit military forces and resources to defend human rights in other states.

In addition, the use of violence to end human rights violations poses a moral dilemma insofar as such interventions may lead to further loss of innocent lives. Therefore, it is imperative that the least amount of force necessary to achieve humanitarian objectives be used, and that intervention not do more harm than good. Lastly, there is a need to ensure that intervention is legitimate, and motivated by genuine humanitarian concerns. The purposes of intervention must be apolitical and disinterested. However, if risks and costs of intervention are high, it is unlikely that states will intervene unless their own interests are involved. For this reason, some doubt whether interventions are ever driven by humanitarian concerns rather than self-interest.

Many note that in order to truly address human rights violations, we must strive to understand the underlying causes of these breaches. These causes have to do with underdevelopment, economic pressures, social problems and international conditions. Indeed, the roots of repression, discrimination and other denials of human rights stem from deeper and more complex political, social and economic problems. It is only by understanding and ameliorating these root causes and strengthening both democracy and civil society that we can truly protect human rights.

In the aftermath of conflict, violence and suspicion often persist. Government institutions and the judiciary, which bear the main responsibility for the observation of human rights, are often severely weakened by the conflict or complicit in it. Yet, a general improvement in the human rights situation is essential for rehabilitation of war-torn societies. Many argue that healing the psychological scars caused by atrocities and reconciliation at the community level cannot take place if the truth about past crimes is not revealed and if human rights are not protected. To preserve political stability, human rights implementation must be managed effectively.

Issues of mistrust and betrayal must be addressed, and the rule of law must be restored. In such an environment, the international community can often play an important supporting role in providing at least implicit guarantees that former opponents will not abandon the peace. Because all international norms are subject to cultural interpretation, external agents that assist in the restoration of human rights in post-conflict societies must be careful to find local terms with which to express human rights norms. While human rights are in theory universal, ideas about which basic needs should be guaranteed vary according to cultural, political, economic and religious circumstances.

Consequently, policies to promote and protect human rights must be culturally adapted to avoid distrust and perceptions of intrusion into internal affairs. To promote human rights standards in post-conflict societies, many psychological issues must be addressed. Societies must either introduce new social norms or reestablish old moral standards. They must design programs that will both address past injustice and prevent future human rights violations. Human rights must not become just another compartmentalized aspect of recovery, but must be infused throughout all peacebuilding and reconstruction activities.

Democratization implies the restoration of political and social rights. Government officials and members of security and police forces have to be trained to observe basic rights in the execution of their duties. Finally, being able to forgive past violations is central to society's reconciliation.

Methods for Protection of Rights

Various methods to advance and protect human rights are available:

— During violent conflict, safe havens to protect refugees and war victims from any surrounding violence in their communities can sometimes help to safeguard human lives.

— As violent conflict begins to subside, peacekeeping strategies to physically separate disputants and prevent further violence are crucial. These measures, together with violence prevention mechanisms, can help to safeguard human lives. Limiting the use of violence is crucial to ensuring groups' survival and creating the necessary conditions for a return to peace.

— Education about human rights must become part of general public education. Technical and financial assistance should be provided to increase knowledge about human rights. Members of the police and security forces have to be trained to ensure the observation of human rights standards for law enforcement. Research institutes and universities should be strengthened to train lawyers and judges. To uphold human rights standards in the long-term, their values must permeate all levels of society.

— Dialogue groups that assemble people from various ethnicities should be organized to overcome mistrust, fear and grief in society. Getting to know the feelings of ordinary people of each side might help to change the demonic image of the enemy group. Dialogue also helps parties at the grassroots level to discover the truth about what has happened, and may provide opportunities for apology and forgiveness.

— External specialists can offer legislative assistance and provide guidance in drafting press freedom laws, minority legislation and laws securing gender equality. They can also assist in drafting a constitution, which guarantees fundamental political and economic rights.

— Those who perpetrate human rights violations find it much easier to do so in cases where their activities can remain secret. International witnesses, observers and reporters can exert modest pressure to bring violations of human rights to public notice and discourage further violence. Monitors should not only expose violations, but also make the public aware of any progress made in the realization of human rights. In order to ensure that proper action is taken after the results of investigations have been made public, effective mechanisms to address injustice must be in place.

— Truth commissions are sometimes established after a political transition. To distinguish them from other institutions established to deal with a legacy of human rights abuses, truth commissions can be understood as "bodies set up to investigate a past history of violations of human rights in a particular country — which can include violations by the military or other government forces or armed opposition forces." They are officially sanctioned temporary bodies that investigate a pattern of abuse in the past. Their goal is to uncover details of past abuses as a symbol of acknowledgment of past wrongs. They typically do not have the powers of courts, nor should they, since they do not have the same standards of evidence and protections for defendants. As such, they usually do not "name names" of those responsible for human rights abuses, but rather point to institutional failings that facilitated the crimes. Finally, they conclude with a report that contains recommendations to prevent a recurrence of the crimes and to provide reparations to victims.

— International war crimes tribunals are established to hold individuals criminally responsible for violations of international human rights law in special courts. The international community rarely has the will to create them. As the experiences with the war tribunals for Rwanda and Yugoslavia indicate, even where they are created, they are imperfect. They cannot hold all perpetrators accountable and typically aim for the top leadership. However, it remains difficult to sentence the top-level decision-makers, who bear the ultimate responsibility for atrocities. They often enjoy political immunity as members of the post-conflict government. Incriminating a popular leader might lead to violent protests and sometimes even to relapse into conflict. Leaders may be necessary to negotiate and implement a peace agreement.

— Various democratization measures can help to restore political and social rights. For sustainability and long-term viability of human rights standards, strong local enforcement mechanisms have to be established. An independent judiciary that provides impartial means and protects individuals against politically influenced persecution must be restored. Election monitors who help to guarantee fair voting procedures can help to ensure stable and peaceful elections. And various social structural changes, including reallocations of resources, increased political participation, and the strengthening of civil society can help to ensure that people's basic needs are met.

— Humanitarian aid and development assistance seeks to ease the impact that violent conflict has on civilians. During conflict, the primary aim is to prevent human casualties and ensure access to basic survival needs. These basics include water, sanitation, food, shelter and health care. Aid can also assist those who have been displaced and support rehabilitation work. Once conflict has ended, development assistance helps to advance reconstruction programs that rebuild infrastructure, institutions and the economy. This assistance helps countries to undergo peaceful development rather than sliding back into conflict.

Protection of Rights in India

The Constitution of India is one of the most rights-based constitutions in the world. Drafted around the same time as the Universal Declaration of Human Rights, the Indian Constitution captures the essence of human rights in its Preamble, and the sections on Fundamental Rights and the Directive Principles of State Policy. The Constitution of India is based on the principles that guided India's struggle against a colonial regime that consistently violated the civil, political, social, economic and cultural rights of the people of India.

The freedom struggle itself was informed by the many movements for social reform, against oppressive social practices like sati (the practice of the wife following her dead husband onto the funeral pyre), child marriage, untouchability etc. Thus by the mid-1920s, the Indian National Congress had already adopted most of the civil and political rights in its agenda. The movement led by Dr B R Ambedkar (one of the founding fathers of the Constitution) against discrimination against the Dalits (the erstwhile outcasts or so-called untouchables who formed the lowest strata of the caste hierarchy and who currently number more than 170 million or 16.5% of the total population of India) also had an impact on the Indian Constitution.

In spite of the fact that most of the human rights found clear expression in the Constitution of India, the independent Indian State carried forward many colonial tendencies and power structures, including those embedded in the elite Indian Civil Service. Though the Indian State under Jawaharlal Nehru took many proactive steps and followed a welfare state model, the police and bureaucracy remained largely colonial in their approach and sought to exert control and power over citizens.

The casteist, feudal and communal characteristics of the Indian polity, coupled with a colonial bureaucracy, weighed against and dampened the spirit of freedom, rights and affirmative action enshrined in the Constitution. In the first 15 years of the Indian republic, such inherent contradictions within the Indian polity were glossed over by the euphoria of 'nation-building', an agenda generally endorsed by political parties, the middle class and elite civil society. However, when the contradictions within the Indian polity and State came into the open in the late-'60s, the oppressive character of the State began to be challenged by student movements and ultra-left formations like the Naxalite movement.

When the Indian State began to suppress such expressions of political dissent and mini-rebellions, the violation of human rights by the State began to command attention. Over a period of 30 years, the articulation and assertion of human rights within civil society has grown into a much richer, more diverse and relatively more powerful discourse at multiple levels. A brief historical sketch of the different trajectories of human rights discourse will help us locate human rights in the historical context.

There are four specific trajectories of human rights discourse in the Indian context — Civil and Political Rights, Rights of the Marginalised (such as women, dalits and adivasis), Economic, Social and Cultural Rights, and the Right to Transparent and Accountable Governance. Though each of these trajectories is interconnected, they were promoted by different sets of actors (often with varying ideological affiliations) at different points in time.

There has always been tension and lack of mutual appreciation between those who promoted civil liberties and the left-oriented groups who worked towards the structural transformation of socio-economic conditions and consequently of the State. As the concept of human rights was perceived as a western idea to gloss over inequalities and as a means of legitimising the capitalist and imperialist projects of the west (particularly the US) the left-oriented groups were clearly sceptical about human rights, particularly as expressed by the civil liberties groups. Though in some quarters such scepticism still exits, there has been a greater recognition of the need to promote and protect human rights, in spite of the misuse of the human rights discourse by the new imperialist forces.

Civil and Political Rights

The growing disenchantment with the Indian State that was expressed in various movements and political formations in the late-'60s and early-'70s was not tolerated by Indira Gandhi s regime. Organisations like the People's Union for Civil Liberties (PUCL) played a significant role in initiating and promoting a new discourse on civil liberties. However, many of the mainstream left parties, influenced by the socialist pretensions of Mrs Gandhi's regime, viewed the middle class movement for civil liberties as the agenda of the bourgeoisie and mistrusted the liberal voices of human rights groups as part of the American agenda.

As many liberal institutions that promoted civil and political rights received funding from international agencies, the pro-establishment conservative groups as well as the leftist groups began to mistrust any organisation that received foreign funds. The insecurity of Mrs Gandhi's regime resulted in the suppression of all dissent and the ultimate suspension of most Civil and Political Rights during the Emergency (1975-77). Almost all political opponents and activists were imprisoned and democratic rights suspended. The forced eviction of slumdwellers in Delhi and forced mass sterilisations created a sense of fear and insecurity among the people. It was during the Emergency, when every civil and political right was violated by the State, that the need to promote and fight for human rights was accepted across political classes. The civil liberties movement highlighted and challenged arbitrary detention, custodial violence and police atrocities.

In the last 20 years, the movement for civil and political rights has become much more coherent and widespread. It has grown beyond a set of urban middle class liberal intellectuals to a wide and diverse socio-political base. With the increase of insurgencies in the 1980s and the consequent State suppression of separatist movements in different parts of the country, various kinds of human rights organisations — some genuine and some fronts for underground groups — began to appear. The massacre of the Sikh community following the assassination of Mrs Gandhi in 1984 raised serious questions about the role of the State in protecting the fundamental rights of citizens.

The rise of right-wing Hindu 'nationalist' forces, the biased stand of the State machinery, and the consequent communal violence all over the country in the last 15 years have given rise to a different set of actors who stress on the civil and political rights of the minorities. The complicity of the State in abetting and supporting the planned violence against the Muslim community in Gujarat in 2002, where more than 1,500 people were killed and hundreds of homes and shops destroyed and looted, brought out the contradictions inherent in the Indian polity and State. But the rise of fanatical and right-wing forces and their anti-human rights postures have, in a way, helped to bring together human rights activists across the political spectrum, including leftist groups and minority rights groups.

Public Interest Litigation and the judicial activism of the Supreme Court initiated by Justices V R Krishna Iyer and P N Bhagwati has played a major role in expanding the scope of human rights and giving it a much-needed legitimacy through some very important verdicts (on prisoners' rights, rights of landless labourers, release of bonded labourers, etc). Justice Krishna Iyer, the law minister of the first elected communist government in Kerala in 1956, was instrumental in building a new discourse that brought together the left-oriented groups and the civil liberties groups as part of the larger human rights community in India. Most of his judgements reiterated the obligation of the State to protect rights and equally, the participation of people in securing their rights and giving them meaning. The establishment of the National Commission of Human Rights under the Human Rights Act of 1993 provided a new impetus to civil and political rights in India.

Rights of the marginalised

While civil and political rights focused largely on the rights of the individual, in the mid-'70s a new human rights discourse, based on group rights, collective rights and people's rights, began to be articulated within the framework of social and political empowerment. The emergence of the women's movement in the 1970s gave a new dimension to the rights discourse in India. In 1974, the Committee on the Status of Women in India submitted a report that highlighted the marginalisation of women in every sphere of life. The emergence of a number of women's groups such as Self Employed Women's Association (SEWA), Manushi, Joint Women's Forum etc raised a new consciousness and public debate on the issue of women's status, domestic violence, dowry, rape, custodial violence, trafficking and the invisible labour of women in the household.

The women's movement not only critiqued the Indian patriarchy, casteism and feudalism, it also promoted a new awareness of women's rights. Though it began as a largely urban movement, over a period of 30 years, the women's movement has emerged as one of the most articulate and widespread movements in India, with new campaigns for women's political participation and rights. It is partly because of the pressure from the women's movement that the 73rd and 74th Constitutional Amendments to introduce local self-government provided 33% reservation for women in local self-government institutions.

The women's movement has played a key role in ensuring the participation of women in the electoral process and governance. In the post-Emergency period a number of political and social activists and public-spirited professionals opted out of party/electoral politics and focussed on the micro-level process of social mobilisation amongst marginalised communities. These social action groups working at the micro level began to highlight the historic and structural marginalisation of the Dalits (the so-called outcasts), Adivasis (more than 80 million tribal people who form around 8.3% of the Indian population) and landless labourers. The empowerment of the marginalised has been the key mission of such social action groups. However, when it came to the demand for entitlement for these communities, most of these groups began to use the rights language, particularly because of the constitutional guarantees.

As many of these groups were sceptical of mainstream human rights discourse, they have used the term 'People's Rights' to emphasise the collective characteristics of rights and to focus on the political aspect of their rights. Thus from the mid-'80s there has been a consistent effort to define and re-articulate Dalit rights, the rights of Adivasis, people's rights over natural resources, etc. This became more pronounced following the large-scale displacement caused by large dams, development projects, forestry projects, mining companies, etc. Most of the displaced people were Adivasis and Dalits.

The Narmada Bachao Andolan (Save Narmada Movement), the Fishworkers Struggle and the Dalit Human Rights campaigns brought the issue of people's rights and rights of the marginalised communities into the mainstream political discourse of India. This trajectory of human rights discourse combined an integrated vision of human rights based on social justice, affirmative action, people's participation and economic justice. The adverse effects of neo-liberal globalisation helped to develop a pan-Indian discourse on people's rights and also helped to connect with similar movements in the global south.

Economic, Social and Cultural Rights

The explicit focus on Economic, Social and Cultural (ESC) Rights is relatively new compared to civil and political rights and group rights. The emergence of ESC rights in the mainstream development agenda is in consonance with the emergence of more institutionalised and funded initiatives for poverty eradication and social development. In the initial years, many such initiatives and institutions (commonly termed non-government organisations or NGOs) began with a welfarist approach, trying to supplement or substitute the welfare State. However, over a period of time there has been a widespread realisation of the limitations of micro-level development intervention and poverty eradication programmes that do not question the politics and policy frameworks that perpetuate deprivation.

Most of the welfare/development NGOs, with foreign funding support, became either subcontractors of the dominant development models or well-meaning do-gooders who addressed the symptoms of poverty and not the socio-political conditions and structural inequalities that perpetuate poverty. A number of grassroots action groups and mass movements working with women, Dalits, Adivasis and the landless poor began to draw from the fundamental rights and directive principles of the Indian Constitution to pressurise and persuade the State to meet its obligation to fulfil ESC rights.

An activist judiciary has also served to expand the scope of fundamental rights to incorporate economic and social rights as well. Progressive and creative judicial intervention expanded the scope of Article 21 of the Indian Constitution which guarantees the Right to Life. Justice Krishna Iyer and other activist judges, through a series of very significant judgements, drew extensively from human rights law, to conclude that the right to life means the right to live with dignity, and that the right to live with dignity includes the right to livelihood, right to education and right to health. These progressive judicial pronouncements were in many ways a response to the social action groups and movements that sought judicial intervention to persuade and pressurise the government to protect and fulfil the rights of the most marginalised.

Thus the emergence of ESC rights is the result of advocacy efforts by grassroots action groups and NGOs in India. The series of World Summits, starting with the

Vienna Summit on Human Rights in 1993, helped to bring ESC rights onto the agenda of many international development organisations. This in turn also resulted in many of the specialised groups taking up campaigns to promote specific rights. This includes the campaign for the fundamental right to education, which resulted in the 86th amendment to the Constitution, guaranteeing the fundamental right to education. There have been similar campaigns for the rights of self-employed women and unorganised workers, the right to universal healthcare and a number of other campaigns focussing on economic and social rights.

The emergence of the environmental and consumer movements in the1980s paved the way for a series of new legislations and policy interventions to protect the rights of consumers and people. The resurgence of the Adivasi (tribal) movement and the increased marginalisation of the minority communities by the right-wing Hindu nationalist government has brought cultural rights into public debate and policy discourse. While the 1970s can be termed the decade of the emergence of the civil liberties movement, the 1980s witnessed the emergence of group rights and people's rights over resources and livelihoods. It is in the 1990s that ESC rights came centrestage.

Various factors including rights-based reorientation by international development agencies and organisations, political compulsions on the ground and the increased visibility of the rights discourse provided the right conditions for advocating ESC rights. However, it is ESC rights that are most elusive. This is because the rhetoric of economic and social rights is not necessarily reflected in policies, programmes and budgetary allocations. As a result, the State pretends to promote economic and social rights, while systematically undermining these rights following the dictums of the IMF, World Bank and WTO. This situation leads to a growing sense of disillusionment.

and cynicism about the so-called rights-based approach. As a result the political content and policy feasibility of the rights-based approach is increasingly questioned, particularly because it is more often used as a development strategy than a means for political empowerment of the people and policy transformation.

Right to Transparent and Accountable Governance

The great expectations of India's welfare State began to recede after 20 years of hope and optimism. Over a period of time, the welfare State became too fat to be functional. The saturated State failed to either deliver welfare or protect and fulfil rights. The government apparatus and the government itself faced a credibility crisis. Political parties as the legitimising vehicle of parliamentary democracy suffered a lack of credibility due to the criminalisation of politics. The proliferation of career politicians and increasing instances of corruption in all aspects of governance brought the issues of accountability and transparency into the development discourse.

The saturation of the State, coupled with the debt crisis, forced the government to seek financial and policy assistance from the Brettonwood institutions to make the failed welfare State work. However, the accompanying neo-liberal policy prescriptions of these institutions in the form of structural adjustments, privatisation and liberalisation further alienated the poor from the Indian State. That is how two clear tendencies in governance became clear by the mid-'90s.

The first set of actors, led by the World Bank, advocated 'good governance' to address resource leakage, misappropriation and mismanagement of the loans taken from the Bank and to ensure that there would be relatively less risk in credit management and repayment. This was more for strategic reasons than any commitment to the democratic principles of public accountability and transparency. The second set of proponents of transparent governance have been grassroots action groups (like the Mazdoor Kisaan Shakti Sangathan in Rajasthan) and advocacy organisations who sought government accountability as part of the citizen's right to know and the right to participate in governance.

The Jan Sunwais (public hearings) and social audits initiated by MKSS in Rajasthan are a well-known example of a process of mobilisation that combines a rights-based approach with people's participation. The people's planning process in local self-governance in Kerala promoted by the Kerala Shastra Sahitya Parishad (KSSP) is another example of participatory practices with a rights-based perspective. The Community Learning Movement for accountable governance, promoted by the National Centre for Advocacy Studies (NCAS), is an example of a rights-based praxis, based on the principles and practice of participation. Thus the new movements and institutions are working to advance the right to accountable governance and ensure that the peoples' right to participate in governance and development are the basic premises for people-centred governance and development.

In spite of the relatively greater visibility and legitimacy of the human rights discourse, the meaning and utility of rights is still a highly contested arena. Though India has ratified five of the six covenants (ICCPR, ICESCR, CEDAW, ICCRC, and CERD) and conventions that constitute the legally-binding international human rights treaties, the implementation of these rights is rather poor. Although the new policy papers and the documents of the Planning Commission of India increasingly use the rights language, in terms of real programmes and implementation the performance of the Government of India is far from satisfactory.

Linking rights with participation

If human rights are to have real meaning, they must be linked to public participation. And participation must be preceded by empowerment of the people. A sense of empowerment requires a sense of dignity, self-worth and the ability to ask questions. The sense of empowerment along with a sense of legal entitlements and constitutional guarantees gives rise to a political consciousness based on rights. A process of political empowerment and a sense of rights empowers citizens to participate in the public sphere.

Most mass movements in modern India (the All India Democratic Women's Association, Ragpickers Union etc) have emphasised the process of empowerment while they also 'struggled' for rights. The notion of 'struggle' was implicit in claiming and promoting rights. Most social action groups and people's organisations started by challenging and changing oppressive power structures that perpetuate patriarchy, casteism and poverty. Thus at the core of many such organisations was political transformation through people's empowerment wherein people can assert their rights and voices and demand justice.

The process of social and political empowerment encompassed a sense of conscientisation based on dignity, rights and participation. That is why the slogans of the Shramajeevi Sanghatana, the union of erstwhile bonded labourers and Adivasis (tribals) in Thane district of Maharashtra assert that "We are not animals, but human beings", "We are not here to beg, but to demand justice". People-centred advocacy is a possible link between rights and participation. People-centred advocacy seeks to connect social development, human rights and governance. It is about creating enabling conditions for socio-political empowerment and enhancing the capability of the marginalised to advocate for themselves so that they can claim their rights, seek public accountability and participate in the process of governance.

People-centred advocacy seeks to go beyond changing public policies to changing people's attitudes, behaviour and unjust power relationships. The Community Learning Movement (CLM) promoted by the National Centre for Advocacy Studies (NCAS) is an effort to empower grassroots communities so that they can seek accountability from the institutions of governance, demand their rights and participate in the political process. CLM takes a cluster of 10-25 villages. Four volunteers from each village participate in an action-learning cycle of 18 months, in six phases of three months each. Once in three months, the volunteers meet for two to three days to share experiences, learn new topics and build strategic plans for addressing local issues.

The Learning Space or Open Notice Board maintained by the CLM local unit provides information (policy, budget, local government etc) that affects the villagers and the volunteers update the Board regularly. As a result of these initiatives, the CLM group in Karnataka has come up with its own community newspaper and wall magazine. Ordinary women, who have developed a sense of their rights and responsibility, have sought accountability from local government officials and exposed corrupt forest officials involved in illegal tree-felling and smuggling of timber from the forest.

People-centred advocacy can be an effective way to link rights and participation. However, the challenge is how to transform this linkage into an emancipatory politics that would help the poor emerge from the structural inequalities that perpetuate poverty. Human rights are legtimised claims and the State has an obligation to respect, protect and fulfil these rights. However, rights become real only when people begin to realise their full potential as human beings and assert their rights in the private and public sphere.

National Human Rights Commission of India

The National Human Rights Commission (NHRC) of India is an autonomous commission constituted by the Central Government to protect human rights in India under the Protection of Human Rights Act (PHRA) of 1993. Created largely in response to the firestorm of international controversy that arose over the actions of India's Border Security Forces (BSF), the NHRC has been derrogated as being merely a mechanism for deflecting criticism of India's human rights record, rather than an organ of genuine power and accountability. Chapter II of the PHRA mandates that "The Central Government shall constitute a body to be known as the National Human Rights Commission to exercise the powers conferred upon, and to perform the functions assigned to it, under this Act," namely protecting "the rights relating to life, liberty, equality and dignity of the individual guaranteed by the Constitution and enforceable by courts in India."

Under the PHRA, the National Human Rights Commission is to consist of:

— a chairperson who has been a Chief Justice of the Supreme Court;

— one Member who is or has been, a Judge of the Supreme Court;

— one Member who is, or has been, the Chief Justice of a High Court;

— two Members to be appointed from amongst persons having knowledge of, or practical experience in, matters relating to human rights; and

— the Chairpersons of the National Commission for Minorities, the National Commission for the

Scheduled Castes and Tribes, and the National Commission for Women, as ex-officio Members.

While the first three positions have been filled by former justices as called for under the PHRA, the Commission has been criticized for failing to appoint any human rights professionals to the governing board. Despite the PHRA's provision for two such members, the final slots have instead been filled with an ex-diplomat and, despite a great deal of protest and a Supreme Court challenge, the ex-chief of the Indian Central Bureau of Investigation, Mr. P.C. Sharma. Mr. Sharma's selection, in particular, has netted the condemnation of civil society in India and has tarnished the organisation's credibility with some members of the public who feel that the appointment of the former head of a body from which a substantial number of complaints to the Commission arise stretches the bounds of good faith.

As per Chapter III of the PHRA, the following functions shall be performed by the NHRC:

(a) inquire, suo motu or on a petition presented to it by a victim or any person on his behalf, into complaint

— violation of human rights or abetment thereof or

— negligence in the prevention of such violation by a public servant

(b) intervene in any proceeding involving any allegation of violation of human rights pending before a court with the approval of such court

(c) visit, under intimation to the State Government, any jail or any other institution under the control of the State Government, where persons are detained or lodged for purposes of treatment, reformation or protection to study the living conditions of the inmates and make recommendations thereon

(d) review the safeguards provided by or under the Constitution of India or any law for the time being in force for the protection of human rights and recommend measures for their effective implementation

(e) review the factors, including acts of terrorism that inhibit the enjoyment of human rights and recommend appropriate remedial measures

(f) study treaties and other international instruments on human rights and make recommendations for their effective implementation

(g) undertake and promote research in the field of human rights

(h) spread human rights literacy among various sections of society and promote awareness of the safeguards available for the protection of these rights through publications, the media, seminars and other available means

(i) encourage the efforts of non-governmental organisations and institutions working in the field of human rights

(j) such other functions as it may consider necessary for the protection of human rights in India

The Commission shall have power to require any person, subject to any privilege which may be claimed by that person under any law for the time being in force, to furnish information on such points or matters as, in the opinion of the Commission, may be useful for, or relevant to, the subject matter of the inquiry and any person so required shall be deemed to be legally bound to furnish such information within the meaning of section 176 and section 177 of the Indian Penal Code.

10

Human Rights Act 1993

An Act to provide for the constitution of a National Human Rights Commission. State Human Rights Commission in States and Human Rights Courts for better protection of Human Rights and for matters connected therewith or incidental thereto.

CHAPTER I

PRELIMINARY

1. *Short title, extent and commencement*

(1) This Act may be called the Protection of Human Rights Act, 1993.

(2) It extends to the whole of India. Provided that it shall apply to the State of Jammu and Kashmir only in so far as it pertains to the matters relatable to any of the entries enumerated in List I or List lll in the Seventh Schedule to the Constitution as applicable to that State.

(3) It shall be deemed to have come into force on the 28th day of September, 1993.

2. *Definitions*

(1) In this Act, unless the context otherwise requires-

(a) "armed forces" means the naval, military and air forces and includes any other armed forces of the Union;

(b) "Chairperson" means the Chairperson of the Commission or of the State Commission, as the case may be;

(c) "Commission" means the National Human Rights Commission under section 3;

(d) "human rights" means the rights relating to life, liberty, equality and dignity of the individual guaranteed by the Constitution or embodied in the International Covenants and enforceable by courts in India.

(e) "Human Rights Court" means the Human Rights Court specified under section 30;

(f) "International Covenants" means the International Covenant on Civil and Political Rights and the International Covenant on Economic, Social and Cultural Rights adopted by the General Assembly of the United Nations on the 16th December, 1966;

(g) "Member" means a Member of the Commission or of the State Commission, as the case may be, and includes the Chairperson;

(h) "National Commission for Minorities" means the National Commission for Minorities constituted under section 3 of the National Commission for Minorities Act, 1992;

(i) "National Commission for the Scheduled Castes and Scheduled Tribes" means the National Commission for the Scheduled Castes and Scheduled Tribes referred to in article 338 of the Constitution;

(j) "National Commission for Women" means the National Commission for Women constituted under section 3 of the National Commission for Women Act, 1990;

(k) "Notification" means a notification published in the official Gazette;

(l) "Prescribed" means prescribed by rules made under this Act;

(m) "Public servant" shall have the meaning assigned to it in section 21 of the Indian Penal Code;

(n) "State Commission" means a State Human Rights Commission constituted under section 21.

(2) Any reference in this Act to a law, which is not in force in the State of Jammu and Kashmir, shall, in relation to that State, be construed as a reference to a corresponding law, if any, in force in that State.

Chapter II

The National Human Rights Commision

3. *Constitution of a National Human Rights Commission*

(1) The Central Government shall constitute a body to be known as the National Human Rights Commission to exercise the powers conferred upon, and to perform the functions assigned to it, under this Act.

(2) The Commission shall consist of:

(a) a Chairperson who has been a Chief Justice of the Supreme Court;

(b) one Member who is or has been, a Judge of the Supreme Court;

(c) one Member who is, or has been, the Chief Justice of a High Court;

(d) two Members to be appointed from amongst persons having knowledge of, or practical experience in, matters relating to human rights.

(3) The Chairpersons of the National Commission for Minorities, the National Commission for the Scheduled Castes and Scheduled Tribes and the National Commission for Women shall be deemed to be Members of the Commission for the discharge of functions specified in clauses (b) to (j) of section 12.

(4) There shall be a Secretary-General who shall be the Chief Executive Officer of the Commission and shall exercise such powers and discharge such functions of the Commission as it may delegate to him.

(5) The headquarters of the Commission shall be at Delhi and the Commission may, with the previous approval of the Central Government, establish offices at other places in India.

4. *Appointment of Chairperson and other Members*

(1) The Chairperson and other Members shall be appointed by the President by warrant under his hand and seal. Provided that every appointment under this sub-section shall be made after obtaining the recommendations of a Committee consisting of

(a) The Prime Minister —Chairperson

(b) Speaker of the House of the People — Member

(c) Minister in-charge of the Ministry of Home Affairs in the Government of India — Member

(d) Leader of the Opposition in the House of the People — Member

(e) Leader of the Opposition in the Council of States — Member

(f) Deputy Chairman of the Council of States — Member

Provided further that no sitting Judge of the Supreme Court or sitting Chief Justice of a High Court shall be appointed except after consultation with the Chief Justice of India.

(2) No appointment of a Chairperson or a Member shall be invalid merely by reason of any vacancy in the Committee.

5. Removal of a Member of the Commission

(1) Subject to the provisions of sub-section (2), the Chairperson or any other Member of the Commission shall only be removed from his office by order of the President on the ground of proved misbehaviour or incapacity after the Supreme Court, on reference being made to it by the President, has, on inquiry held in accordance with the procedure prescribed in that behalf by the Supreme Court, reported that the Chairperson or such other Member, as the case may be, ought on any such ground to be removed.

(2) Notwithstanding anything in sub-section (1), the President may by order remove from office the Chairperson or any other Member if the Chairperson or such other Member, as the case may be

(a) is adjudged an insolvent; or

(b) engages during his term of office in any paid employment out side the duties of his office: or

(c) is unfit to continue in office by reason of infirmity of mind or body; or

(d) is of unsound mind and stands so declared by a competent court; or

(e) is convicted and sentenced to imprisonment for an offence which in the opinion of the President involves moral turpitude.

6. Term of Office of Members

(1) A person appointed as Chairperson shall hold office for a term of five years from the date on which he enters upon his office or until he attains the age of seventy years, whichever is earlier.

(2) A person appointed as a Member shall hold office for a term of five years from the date on which he enters upon his office and shall be eligible for re-appointment for another term of five years. Provided that no Member shall hold office after he has attained the age of seventy years.

(3) On ceasing to hold office, a Chairperson or a Member shall be ineligible for further employment under the Government of India or under the Government of any State.

7. Member to Act as Chairperson or to Discharge his Functions in Certain Circumstances

(1) In the event of the occurrence of any vacancy in the office of the Chairperson by reason of his death, resignation or otherwise, the President may, by notification, authorise one of the Members to act as the Chairperson until the appointment of a new Chairperson to fill such vacancy.

(2) When the Chairperson is unable to discharge his functions owing to absence on leave or otherwise, such one of the Members as the President may, by

notification, authorise in this behalf, shall discharge the functions of the Chairperson until the date on which the Chairperson resumes his duties.

8. *Terms and Conditions of Service of Members*

The salaries and allowances payable to, and other terms and conditions of service of, the Members shall be such as may be prescribed. Provided that neither the salary and allowances nor the other terms and conditions of service of a Member shall be varied to his disadvantage after his appointment.

9. *Vacancies, etc., not to Invalidate the Proceedings of the Commission.*

No act or proceedings of the Commission shall be questioned or shall be invalidated merely on the ground of existence of any vacancy or defect in the constitution of the Commission.

10. *Procedure to be Regulated by the Commission*

(1) The Commission shall meet at such time and place as the Chairperson may think fit.

(2) The Commission shall regulate its own procedure.

(3) All orders and decisions of the Commission shall be audited by the Secretary-General or any other officer of the Commission duly authorised by the Chairperson in this behalf.

11. *Officers and Other Staff of the Commission*

(1) The Central Government shall make available to the Commission :

(a) an officer of the rank of the Secretary to the Government of India who shall be the Secretary-General of the Commission; and

(b) such police and investigative staff under an officer not below the rank of a Director General of Police and such other officers and staff as may be necessary for the efficient performance of the functions of the Commission.

(2) Subject to such rules as may be made by the Central Government in this behalf, the Commission may appoint such other administrative, technical and scientific staff as it may consider necessary.

(3) The salaries, allowances and conditions of service of the officers and other staff appointed under sub-section (2) shall be such as may be prescribed.

CHAPTER III

FINCTIONS AND POWERS OF THE COMMISION

12. *Functions of the Commission*

The Commission shall perform all or any of the following functions, namely :

(a) inquire, suo motu or on a petition presented to it by a victim or any person on his behalf, into complaint of

(i) violation of human rights or abetment thereof or

(ii) negligence in the prevention of such violation, by a public servant;

(b) intervene in any proceeding involving any allegation of violation of human rights pending before a court with the approval of such court;

(c) visit, under intimation to the State Government, any jail or any other institution under the control of the State Government, where persons are detained or lodged for purposes of treatment, reformation or protection to study the living conditions of the inmates and make recommendations thereon;

(d) review the safeguards provided by or under the Constitution or any law for the time being in force for the protection of human rights and recommend measures for their effective implementation;

(e) review the factors, including acts of terrorism that inhibit the enjoyment of human rights and recommend appropriate remedial measures;

(f) study treaties and other international instruments on human rights and make recommendations for their effective implementation;

(g) undertake and promote research in the field of human rights;

(h) spread human rights literacy among various sections of society and promote awareness of the safeguards available for the protection of these rights through publications, the media, seminars and other available means;

(i) encourage the efforts of non-governmental organisations and institutions working in the field of human rights;

(j) such other functions as it may consider necessary for the protection of human rights.

13. *Powers Relating to Inquiries*

(1) The Commission shall, while inquiring into complaints under this Act, have all the powers of a civil court trying a suit under the Code of Civil Procedure, 1908,

and in particular in respect of the following matters, namely :

(a) summoning and enforcing the attendance of witnesses and examine them on oath;

(b) discovery and production of any document;

(c) receiving evidence on affidavits;

(d) requisitioning any public record or copy thereof from any court or office;

(e) issuing commissions for the examination of witnesses or documents;

(f) any other matter which may be prescribed.

(2) The Commission shall have power to require any person, subject to any privilege which may be claimed by that person under any law for the time being in force, to furnish information on such points or matters as, in the opinion of the Commission, may be useful for, or relevant to, the subject matter of the inquiry and any person so required shall be deemed to be legally bound to furnish such information within the meaning of section 176 and section 177 of the Indian Penal Code.

(3) The Commission or any other officer, not below the rank of a Gazetted Officer, specially authorised in this behalf by the Commission may enter any building or place where the Commission has reason to believe that any document relating to the subject matter of the inquiry may be found, and may seize any such document or take extracts or copies therefrom subject to the provisions of section 100 of the Code of Criminal Procedure, 1973, in so far as it may be applicable.

(4) The Commission shall be deemed to be a civil court and when any offence as is described in section 175,

section 178, section 179, section 180 or section 228 of the Indian Penal Code is committed in the view or presence of the Commission, the Commission may, after recording the facts constituting the offence and the statement of the accused as provided for in the Code of Criminal Procedure, 1973, forward the case to a Magistrate having jurisdiction to try the same and the Magistrate to whom any such case is forwarded shall proceed to hear the complaint against the accused as if the case has been forwarded to him under section 346 of the Code of Criminal Procedure, 1973.

(5) Every proceeding before the Commission shall be deemed to be a judicial proceeding within the meaning of sections 193 and 228, and for the purposes of section 196, of the Indian Penal Code, and the Commission shall be deemed to be a civil court for all the purposes of section 195 and Chapter XXVI of the Code of Criminal Procedure, 1973.

14. *Investigation*

(1) The Commission may, for the purpose of conducting any investigation pertaining to the inquiry, utilise the services of any officer or investigation agency of the Central Government or any State Government with the concurrence of the Central Government or the State Government, as the case may be.

(2) For the purpose of investigating into any matter pertaining to the inquiry, any officer or agency whose services are utilised under sub-section (1) may, subject to the direction and control of the Commission.

(a) summon and enforce the attendance of any person and examine him;

(b) require the discovery and production of any document; and

(c) requisition any public record or copy thereof from any office.

(3) The provisions of section 15 shall apply in relation to any statement made by a person before any officer or agency whose services are utilised under sub-section (1) as they apply in relation to any statement made by a person in the course of giving evidence before the Commission.

(4) The officer or agency whose services are utilised under sub-section (1) shall investigate into any matter pertaining to the inquiry and submit a report thereon to the Commission within such period as may be specified by the Commission in this behalf.

(5) The Commission shall satisfy itself about the correctness of the facts stated and the conclusion, if any, arrived at in the report subbed to it under sub-section (4) and for this purpose the Commission may make such inquiry (including the examination of the person or persons who conducted or assisted in the investigation) as it thinks fit.

15. Statement Made by Persons to the Commission

No statement made by a person in the course of giving evidence before the Commission shall subject him to, or be used against him in, any civil or criminal proceeding except a prosecution for giving false evidence by such statement: Provided that the statement —

(a) is made in reply to the question which he is required by the Commission to answer; or

(b) is relevant to the subject matter of the inquiry.

16. Persons Likely to be Prejudicially Affected to be Heard

If, at any stage of the inquiry, the Commission-

(a) considers it necessary to inquire into the conduct of any person; or

(b) is of the opinion that the reputation of any person is likely to be prejudicially affected by the inquiry;

it shall give to that person a reasonable opportunity of being heard in the inquiry and to produce evidence in his defence: Provided that nothing in this section shall apply where the credit of a witness is being impeached.

CHAPTER IV

PROCEDURE

17. Inquiry into complaints

The Commission while inquiring into the complaints of violations of human rights may-

(i) call for information or report from the Central Government or any State Government or any other authority or organisation subordinate thereto within such time as may be specified by it; Provided that-

   (a) if the information or report is not received within the time stipulated by the Commission, it may proceed to inquire into the complaint on its own;

   (b) if, on receipt of information or report, the Commission is satisfied either that no further inquiry is required or that the required action has been initiated or taken by the concerned Government or authority, it may not proceed with the complaint and inform the complainant accordingly;

(ii) without prejudice to anything contained in clause (i), if it considers necessary, having regard to the nature of the complaint, initiate an inquiry.

18. Steps after Inquiry

The Commission may take any of the following steps upon the completion of an inquiry held under this Act namely:

(1) where the inquiry discloses, the commission of violation of human rights or negligence in the prevention of violation of human rights by a public servant, it may recommend to the concerned Government or authority the initiation of proceedings for prosecution or such other action as the Commission may deem fit against the concerned person or persons;

(2) approach the Supreme Court or the High Court concerned for such directions, orders or writs as that Court may deem necessary;

(3) recommend to the concerned Government or authority for the grant of such immediate interim relief to the victim or the members of his family as the Commission may consider necessary;

(4) subject to the provisions of clause (5), provide a copy of the inquiry report to the petitioner or his representative;

(5) the Commission shall send a copy of its inquiry report together with its recommendations to the concerned Government or authority and the concerned Government or authority shall, within a period of one month, or such further time as the Commission may allow, forward its comments on the report, including the action taken or proposed to be taken thereon, to the Commission;

(6) the Commission shall publish its inquiry report together with the comments of the concerned Government or authority, if any, and the action taken or proposed to be taken by the concerned Government

or authority on the recommendations of the Commission.

19. Procedure with Respect to Armed Forces

(1) Notwithstanding anything contained in this Act, while dealing with complaints of violation of human rights by members of the armed forces, the Commission shall adopt the following procedure, namely :

(a) it may, either on its own motion or on receipt of a petition, seek a report from the Central Government;

(b) after the receipt of the report, it may, either not proceed with the complaint or, as the case may be, make its recommendations to that Government.

(2) The Central Government shall inform the Commission of the action taken on the recommendations within three months or such further time as the Commission may allow.

(3) The Commission shall publish its report together with its recommendations made to the Central Government and the action taken by that Government on such recommendations.

(4) The Commission shall provide a copy of the report published under sub-section (3) to the petitioner or his representative.

20. Annual and Special Reports of the Commission

(1) The Commission shall submit an annual report to the Central Government and to the State Government concerned and may at any time submit special reports on any matter which, in its opinion, is of such urgency or importance that it should not be deferred till submission of the annual report.

(2) The Central Government and the State Government, as the case may be, shall cause the annual and special reports of the Commission to be laid before each House of Parliament or the State Legislature respectively, as the case may be, along with a memorandum of action taken or proposed to be taken on the recommendations of the Commission and the reasons for non-acceptance of the recommendations, if any.

CHAPTER V

STATE HUMAN RIGHTS COMMISSIONS

21. Constitution of State Human Rights Commissions

(1) A State Government may constitute a body to be known as the...................... (name of the State) Human Rights Commission to exercise the powers conferred upon, and to perform the functions assigned to, a State Commission under this chapter.

(2) The State Commission shall consist of

(a) a Chairperson who has been a Chief Justice of a High Court;

(b) one Member who is, or has been, a Judge of a High Court;

(c) one Member who is, or has been, a district judge in that State;

(d) two Members to be appointed from amongst persons having knowledge of, or practical experience in, matters relating to human rights.

(3) There shall be a Secretary who shall be the Chief Executive Officer of the State Commission and shall exercise such powers and discharge such functions of the State Commission as it may delegate to him.

(4) The headquarters of the State Commission shall be at such place as the State Government may, by notification, specify.

(5) A State Commission may inquire into violation of human rights only in respect of matters relatable to any of the entries enumerated in List II and List lll in the Seventh Schedule to the Constitution:

Provided that if any such matter is already being inquired into by the Commission or any other Commission duly constituted under any law for the time being in force, the State Commission shall not inquire into the said matter: Provided further that in relation to the Jammu and Kashmir Human Rights Commission, this sub-section shall have effect as if for the words and figures "List ll and List lll in the Seventh Schedule to the Constitution", the words and figures "List lll in the Seventh Schedule to the Constitution as applicable to the State of Jammu and Kashmir and in respect of matters in relation to which the Legislature of that State has power to make laws" had been substituted.

22. Appointment of Chairperson and other Members of State Commission

(1) The Chairperson and other Members shall be appointed by the Governor by warrant under his hand and seal: Provided that every appointment under this sub-section shall be made after obtaining the recommendation of a Committee consisting of

(a) the Chief Minister — Chairperson

(b) Speaker of the Legislative Assembly — Member

(c) Minister in-charge of the Department of Home, in that State — Member

(d) Leader of the Opposition in the Legislative Assembly — Member

Provided further that where there is a Legislative Council in a State, the Chairman of that Council and the Leader of the Opposition in that Council shall also be members of the Committee. Provided also that no sitting Judge of a High Court or a sitting District Judge shall be appointed except after consultation with the Chief Justice of the High Court of the concerned State.

(2) No appointment of a Chairperson or a Member of the State Commission shall be invalid merely by reason of any vacancy in the Committee.

23. *Removal of a Member of the State Commission*

(1) Subject to the provisions of sub-section (2), the Chairperson or any other member of the State Commission shall only be removed from his office by order of the President on the ground of proved misbehaviour or incapacity after the Supreme Court, on a reference being made to it by the President, has, on inquiry held in accordance with the procedure prescribed in that behalf by the Supreme Court, reported that the Chairperson or such other Member, as the case may be, ought on any such ground to be removed.

(2) Notwithstanding anything in sub-section (1), the President may by order remove from office the Chairperson or any other Member if the Chairperson or such other Member, as the case may be –

(a) is adjudged an insolvent; OR

(b) engages during his term of office in any paid employment outside the duties of his office; OR

(c) is unfit to continue in office by reason of infirmity of mind or body; OR

(d) is of unsound mind and stands so declared by a competent court; OR

(e) is convicted and sentenced to imprisonment for an offence which in the opinion of the President involves moral turpitude.

24. *Term of Office of Members of the State Commission*

(1) A person appointed as Chairperson shall hold office for a term of five years from the date on which he enters upon his office or until he attains the age of seventy years, whichever is earlier;

(2) A person appointed as a Member shall hold office for a term of five years from the date on which he enters upon his office and shall be eligible for re-appointment for another term of five years; Provided that no Member shall hold office after he has attained the age of seventy years.

(3) On ceasing to hold office, a Chairperson or a Member shall be ineligible for further employment under the Government of a State or under the Government of India.

25. *Member to act as Chairperson or to Discharge his Functions in Certain Circumstances*

(1) In the event of the occurrence of any vacancy in the office of the Chairperson by reason of his death, resignation or otherwise, the Governor may, by notification, authorise one of the Members to act as the Chairperson until the appointment of a new Chairperson to fill such vacancy.

(2) When the Chairperson is unable to discharge his functions owing to absence on leave or otherwise, such one of the Members as the Governor may, by notification, authorise in this behalf, shall discharge the functions of the Chairperson until the date on which the Chairperson resumes his duties.

26. *Terms and Conditions of Service of Members of the State Commission*

The salaries and allowances payable to, and other terms and conditions of service of, the Members shall be such as may be prescribed by the State Government. Provided that neither the salary and allowances nor the other terms and conditions of service of a Member shall be varied to his disadvantage after his appointment.

27. *Officers and Other Staff of the State Commission*

(1) The State Government shall make available to the Commission

(a) an officer not below the rank of a Secretary to the State Government who shall be the Secretary of the State Commission; and

(b) such police and investigative staff under an officer not below the rank of an Inspector General of Police and such other officers and staff as may be necessary for the efficient performance of the functions of the State Commission.

(2) subject to such rules as may be made by the State Government in this behalf, the State Commission may appoint such other addministrative, technical and scientific staff as it may consider necessary.

(3) The salaries, allowances and conditions of service of the officers and other staff appointed under sub-section (2) shall be such as may be prescribed by the State Government.

28. *Annual and special reports of State Commission*

(1) The State Commission shall submit an annual report to the State Government and may at any time submit special reports on any matter which, in its opinion, is

of such urgency or importance that it should not be deferred till submission of the annual report.

(2) The State Government shall cause the annual and special reports of the State Commission to be laid before each House of State Legislature where it consists of two Houses, or where such Legislature consists of one House, before that House along with a memorandum of action taken or proposed to be taken on the recommendations of the State Commission and the reasons for non-acceptance of the rections, if any.

29. Application of Certain Provisions Relating to National Human Rights Commission to State Commissions

The provisions of sections 9, 10, 12, 13, 14, 15, 16, 17 and 18 shall apply to a State Commission and shall have effect, subject to the following modifications, namely :-

(a) references to "Commission" shall be construed as refer ences to "State Commission";

(b) in section 10, in sub-section (3), for the word "Secretary General", the word "Secretary" shall be substituted;

(c) in section 12, clause (f) shall be omitted;

(d) in section 17, in clause (i), the words "Central Government or any" shall be omitted;

Chapter VI

Human Rights Courts

30. For the Purpose of Providing Speedy Trial of Offences Arising out of Violation of Human Rights, the State

Government may, with the concurrence of the Chief Justice of the High Court, by notification, specify for each district a Court of Session to be a Human Rights Court to try the said offences. Provided that nothing in this section shall apply if

(a) a Court of Session is already specified as a special court; or

(b) a special court is already constituted, for such offences under any other law for the time being in force.

31. *Special Public Prosecutor*

For every Human Rights Court, the State Government shall, by notification, specify a Public Prosecutor or appoint an advocate who has been in practice as an advocate for not less than seven years, as a Special Public Prosecutor for the purpose of conducting cases in that Court.

Chapter VII

Finance, Accounts and Audit

32. *Grants by the Central Government*

(1) The Central Government shall after due appropriation made by Parliament by law in this behalf, pay to the Commission by way of grants such sums of money as the Central Government may think fit for being utilised for the purposes of this Act.

(2) The Commission may spend such sums as it thinks fit for performing the functions under this Act, and such sums shall be treated as expenditure payable out of the grants referred to in sub-section (1).

33. *Grants by the State Government*

(1) The State Government shall, after due appropriation

made by Legislature by law in this behalf, pay to the State Commission by way of grants such sums of money as the State Government may think fit for being utilised for the purposes of this Act.

(2) The State Commission may spend such sums as it thinks fit for performing the functions under Chapter V, and such sums shall be treated as expenditure payable out of the grants referred to in sub-section (1).

34. *Accounts and Audit*

(1) The Commission shall maintain proper accounts and other relevant records and prepare an annual statement of accounts in such form as may be prescribed by the Central Government in consultation with the Comptrollerand Auditor-General of India.

(2) The Accounts of the Commission shall be audited by the Comptroller and Auditor-General at such intervals as may be specified by him and any expenditure incurred in connection with such audit shall be payable by the Commission to the Comptroller and Auditor-General.

(3) The Comptroller and Auditor-General or any person appointed by him in connection with the audit of the accounts of the Commision under this Act shall have the same rights and privileges and the authority in connection with such audit as the Comptroller and Auditor-General generally has in connection with the audit of Government ac counts and, in particular, shall have the right to demand the production of books, accounts, connected vouchers and other documents and papers and to inspect any of the offices of the Commission.

(4) The accounts of the Commission as certified by the Comptroller and Auditor-General or any other person

appointed by him in this behalf, together with the audit report thereon shall be forwarded only to the Central Government by the Commission and the Central Government shall cause the audit report to be laid as soon as may be after it is received before each House of Parliament.

35. *Accounts and Audit of State Commission*

(1) The State Commission shall maintain proper accounts and other relevant records and prepare an annual statement of accounts in such form as may be prescribed by the State Government in consultation with the Comptroller and Auditor-General of India.

(2) The accounts of the State Commission shall be audited by the Comptroller and Auditor-General at such intervals as may be specified by him and any expenditure incurred in connection with such audit shall be payable by the State Commission to the Comptroller and Auditor-General.

(3) The Comptroller and Auditor-General or any person appointed by him in connection with the audit of the accounts of the State Commission under this Act shall have the same rights and privileges and the authority in connection with such audit as the Comptroller and Auditor-General generally has in connection with the audit of Government accounts and, in particular, shall have the right to demand the production of books, accounts, connected vouchers and other documents and papers and to inspect any of the offices of the State Commission.

(4) The accounts of the State Commission, as certified by the Comptroller and Auditor-General or any other person appointed by him in this behalf, together with the audit report thereon, shall be forwarded annually to the State Government by the State Commission and

the State Government shall cause the audit report to be laid, as soon as may be after it is received, before the State Legislature.

CHAPTER VIII

MISCELLANEOUS

36. Matters not Subject to Jurisdiction of the Commission

(1) The Commission shall not inquire into any matter which is pending before a State Commission or any other Commission duly constituted under any law for the time being in force.

(2) The Commission or the State Commission shall not inquire into any matter after the expiry of one year from the date on which the act constituting violation of human rights is alleged to have been commited.

37. Constitution of special investigation teams

Notwithstanding anything contained in any other law for the time being in force, where the Government considers it necessary so to do, it may constitute one or more special investigation teams, consisting of such police officers as it thinks necessary for purposes of investigation and prosecution of offences arising out of violations of human rights.

38. Protection of action taken in good faith

No suit or other legal proceeding shall lie against the Central Government, State Government, Commission, the State Commission or any Member thereof or any person acting under the direction either of the Central Government, State Government, Commission or the State Commission in respect of anything which is in good faith done or intended to be done in pursuance of this Act or of any rules or any order made thereunder or in respect of the publication by or under the authority of the Central Government, State Government, Commission or the State Commission of any report paper or proceedings.

39. Members and officers to be public servants

Every Member of the Commission, State Commission and every officer appointed or authorised by the Commission or the State Commission to exercise functions under this Act shall be deemed to be a public servant within the meaning of section 21 of the Indian Penal Code.

40. Power of Central Government to make rules

(1) The Central Government may, by notification, make rules to carry out the provisions of this Act.

(2) In particular and without prejudice to the generality of the foregoing power, such rules may provide for all or any of the following matters namely :

(a) the salaries and allowances and other terms and conditions of service of the Members under section 8;

(b) the conditions subject to which other administrative, technical and scientific staff may be appointed by the Commission and the salaries and allowances of officers and other staff under sub-section (3) of section 11;

(c) any other power of a civil court required to be prescribed under clause (f) of sub-section (1) of section 13;

(d) the form in which the annual statement of accounts is to be pre pared by the Commission under sub-section (1) of section 34; and

(e) any other matter which has to be, or may be, prescribed.

(3) Every rule made under this Act shall be laid, as soon as may be after it is made, before each House of Parliament, while it is in session, for a total period of thirty days which may be comprised in one session or in two or more successive sessions, and if, before the expiry of the session immediately following the session or the successive sessions aforesaid, both Houses agree in making any modification in the rule or both Houses agree that the rule should not be made, the rule shall thereafter have effect only in such modified form or be of no effect, as the case may be; so however, that any such modification or annulment shall be without prejudice to the validity of anything previously done under that rule.

41. Power of State Government to Make Rules

(1) The State Government may, by notification, make rules to carry out the provisions of this Act.

(2) In particular and without prejudice to the generality of the fore ing power, such rules may provide for all or any of the following matters, namely :

(a) the salaries and allowances and other terms and conditions of service of the members under section 26;

(b) the conditions subject to which other administrative, technical and scientific staff may be appointed by the State Commission and the salaries and allowances of officers and other staff under sub-section (3) of section 27;

(c) the form in which the annual statement of accounts is to be prepared under sub-section (1) of section 35.

(3) Every rule made by the State Government under this section shall be laid, as soon as may be after it is made, before each House of the State Legislature where it consists of two Houses, or where such Legislature consists of one House, before that House.

42. *Power to Remove Difficulties*

(1) If any difficulty arises in giving effect to the provisions of this Act, the Central Government, may by order published in the Official Gazette, make such provisions, not inconsistent with the provisions of this Act as appear to it to be necessary or expedient for removing the difficulty. Provided that no such order shall be made after the exry of the period of two years from the date of commencement of this Act.

(2) Every order made under this section shall, as soon as may be after it is made, be laid before each house of Parliament.

43. *Repeal and Savings*

(1) The Protection of Human Rights Ordinance, 1993 is hereby repealed.

(2) Notwithstanding such repeal, anything done or any action taken under the said Ordinance, shall be deemed to have been done or taken under the corresponding provisions of this Act.

Index